SHAKE

A SIX PACK

TITUS ANDRONICUS

RICHARD III

THE MERCHANT OF VENICE

MEASURE FOR MEASURE

OTHELLO

THE TEMPEST

BY

PAUL CLARK

New Generation Publishing

To my daughters Caroline, Dido and Rowena,
especially Rowena,
whose own studies inspired me to put pen to paper.

Contents

INTRODUCTION

In the following six essays I have aimed to obey the spirit, as far as possible, of Quintilian's advice: *Diligentur legendum est, ac paene ad scribendi sollicitudine.*

In his 'Essay on Criticism' (lines 233-234) Pope renders Quintilian's words as:

A perfect Judge will read each work of Wit
With the same spirit that its author writ.

The essays are for readers, playgoers and actors who are already familiar with the plays. They are offered as contributions for informal discussion. There's no editorial apparatus - no footnotes, for textual problems or critical evaluations, etc.

They focus on authentically 'Shakespearean' rather than 'contemporary' interpretations. However problematic, it's worthwhile to make an effort to re-enter the culture and mind-set of Shakespeare's original audience. More than four hundred years have passed since the plays were new, and we need, of course, to understand how this limits our ability to regard Shakespeare as 'our contemporary'. But the differences become increasingly important as the decades and centuries tick by. We now have to make a conscious decision to set aside interpretations reflecting our own values and concerns and look instead for older meanings waiting to be discovered anew.

In addition the depth of the specifically Christian culture needs to be recognised. It amounts to more than 'references'. It's often a matter of overall context. The six plays discussed here illustrate this point especially strongly.

The texts and line-references I use are from the latest Arden editions, i.e.

Titus Andronicus, ed. Jonathan Bate, 1995
Richard the Third, ed. James S. Siemon, 2009
The Merchant of Venice, ed. John Drakakis, 2010
Measure for Measure, ed. J.W. Lever, 1965
Othello, ed. E.A.J. Honigmann, 1997
The Tempest, ed. Virginia M. and Alden T. Vaughan, 1999

Paul Clark

2015

TITUS ANDRONICUS

The first scene (635 lines, no less!) is a humdinger. It stages impressive ceremonial moments, unfolds a swift and intricately plotted succession of events, and gives vivid delineations of all the main characters, except Aaron. We're gripped from the start.

The scene is ancient Rome. The action opens with the troubled election campaign between Saturninus and Bassianus for succession to the vacant Roman throne. Armed 'factions' (1.1.18) roam the streets and civil disorder threatens. Tribune Marcus Andronicus appears on a building high above the crowd (the upper stage) to propose a third candidate, his brother Titus, returning to Rome in triumph after the 'weary wars against the barbarous Goths'. (1.1.28) Marcus speaks with authority, claiming to have both popular and patrician backing, and his proposal goes down well. The two rivals disband their supporters, who go off to join the crowds gathering for the victory parade.

And here the conquering hero comes! - parading his battle-worn army through the streets of Rome, with the Andronici war-dead (including his own eldest son, whose name we never learn) piled on carts and a column of Gothic captives shuffling along in chains at the rear.

The electioneering speeches of the rival candidates have a lofty 'statesmanlike' ring, invoking the political and military might of Rome and bristling with words like 'noble', 'justice', 'imperial', 'honour', 'right', 'royal', 'virtue', 'consecrate' and 'freedom'. By contrast, when Titus speaks (1.1.73-98) he strikes a much more sombre note. He 'resalutes his country with his tears.' (1.1.78)

3

This ceremony isn't just an opportunity for the people to cheer their heroes and celebrate victory; the war has cost Rome dear in terms of life and treasure and it's also a funeral procession. There's grief as well as gratitude.

Titus calls on Jupiter, the patron of Rome, to 'stand gracious to the rites that we intend.' (1.1.81) The burial of the Andronicus heir is one of these 'rites', but not the only one. When the Andronici tomb is opened and the grieving Titus exclaims:

How many sons of mine hast thou in store
That thou will never render to me more! (1.1.98)

there's a mood shift. Lucius, now Titus's heir, points towards the captive Goths and demands that Alarbus, the eldest son of the Goth queen Tamora, be offered up as a sacrifice to the gods. This is the other 'rite' that's intended. 'Give us the proudest prisoner of the Goths,' he demands,

That we may hew his limbs and on a pile
Ad manes fratrum sacrifice his flesh…
So that the shadows *(i.e. of the slain Andronici brothers)* be not unappeased. (1.1.99-103)

Titus has no qualms about it. He's lost his own eldest son, and Roman religious law now requires that the defeated queen lose hers. It's quits. 'I give him you', he tells Lucius -

……… the noblest that survives,
The eldest son of this distressed queen. (1.1.105-106)

Tamora falls on her knees.

Stay, Roman brethren, gracious conqueror,
Victorious Titus, rue the tears I shed,

4

A mother's tears in passion for her son!
And if thy sons were ever dear to thee,
O, think my son to be as dear to me.
Sufficeth not that we are brought to Rome
To beautify thy triumphs, and return
Captive to thee and to thy Roman yoke?
But must my sons be slaughtered in the streets
For valiant doings in their country's cause?
O, if to fight for king and commonweal
Were piety in thine, it is in these.
Andronicus, stain not thy tomb with blood.
Wilt thou draw near the nature of the gods?
Draw near them then in being merciful.
Sweet mercy is nobility's true badge:
Thrice noble Titus, spare my first-born son. (1.1.107-123)

Titus brushes her plea aside. 'Patient yourself, madam, and
pardon me.'(1.1.124) He understands her distress. He's not
inhuman and he knows what it is to lose a son – he's lost
over twenty himself! - but rules are rules. He explains that

....for their brethren slain
Religiously they ask a sacrifice.' (1.1.127)

For Titus 'nobility's true badge' is Roman religious
correctness, not 'sweet mercy'.

Early on (1.1.23) his brother Marcus mentioned that Titus
is 'surnamed Pius'. It's an important clue to his character.
He's dutiful to a fault and a dyed-in-the-wool stoic. He
doesn't exactly deny his feelings, but he knows that they
count for nothing in the face of Necessity. The examples
that the gods provide for men to copy (see 1.1.120-121)
are not of mercy but of justice. It's a tough world and
Tamora will just have to face up to it. His 'pardon me' is

5

sincere. He hopes that she'll understand that he's only doing his duty and not bear a grudge.

But of course when the despairing Tamora screams, 'O cruel, irreligious piety!' (1.1.133) we're emotionally and morally entirely on **her** side. The Andronici have finally got their enemies where they want them and they're in no mood to start splitting hairs about the point at which strict justice ends and emotionally-gratifying retribution begins. At the best of times it's always a pretty subtle distinction, whichever end of it you're on. Naturally, Tamora and her sons will see the execution of Alarbus as the revenge of the Andronici and they'll be out to get even with them. But Titus doesn't care if they do; and if they do what can they do about it? He has no second thoughts. He's gotta do what a Roman's gotta do. Alarbus must die.

So the first atrocity in this play of atrocities is perpetrated by 'civilised' Romans on their 'barbarian' prisoners of war. There's no 'public' room for pity. The massive stone of Roman imperialism has been prised up and we've had a glimpse of what lies beneath. We see that when ugly things happen and feelings run high ruthless things will be done which are distinguishable from crimes only by the fact that they have the authority of the state behind them. We see Titus implicitly placing his faith in Roman justice and it's this faith that's now about to be tested to destruction.

Titus's military success has, for the moment at least, given him huge political prestige and his brother Marcus sees that the imperial crown is his for the taking. He invites him formally to accept this once-in-a-lifetime opportunity.

Titus Andronicus, the people of Rome,
Whose friend in justice thou hast ever been,

Send thee by me, their tribune and their trust,
This palliament of white and spotless hue,
And name thee in election for the empire
With these our late-deceased emperor's sons.
Be *candidatus* then and put it on,
And help to set a head on headless Rome. (1.1 182-189)

Titus has his answer ready, though. He has no such
ambition – and he's too old.

Give me a staff of honour for my age,
But not a sceptre to control the world. (1.1.201-202)

He sees himself as a superannuated (and balding?)
Cincinnatus wishing only to retire from public life, his
duty done. But it isn't quite done yet. He finds himself in
the position of a kingmaker and he feels obliged to
arbitrate in the Saturninus-Bassianus succession issue.
Personally - for what that's worth - he'd prefer the throne
to go to Bassianus, Saturninus's younger brother and his
own prospective son-in-law, but he believes that the
constitutional rule to be applied is primogeniture. He
decides in favour of Saturninus, the previous emperor's
eldest son. It's a no-brainer - principle before personal
preference - and such is Titus's authority that Bassianus,
Marcus and the people of Rome unhesitatingly follow him
in offering their loyalty and submission to the new
emperor - even though he's got trouble written all over
him.

The text of the play is in English, masquerading as Latin,
of course, and with a fair helping of literary quotations in
actual Latin. Although Tamora and her sons are Goths we
never hear a single word of Gothic spoken. Unwilling
immigrants they may be, but they assimilate remarkably

quickly and adopt the language of the Roman host community. Their high rank in Gothic society entitles them to positions in the top echelon of Roman political life where the Darwinian principle of the survival of the fittest prevails. It's soon clear that in this new environment Tamora will prove to be exceptionally 'fit'. She has all the qualities needed to survive and flourish – high IQ, self-confidence, ruthlessness (she's thoroughly assimilated her lesson about mercy!), a gift for duplicity and, last but by no means least, a powerful sexuality which in no time at all has Saturninus (not to mention Aaron) wrapped round her little finger.

The speed with which Tamora becomes the emperor's bedmate, and political brains, is another indication that Roman 'civilisation' and Gothic 'barbarism' are less antithetical than we might have supposed. Tamora has no problem with cultural adaptation. She slides easily into her new role. 'I am incorporate in Rome,' she soon informs Titus, her former captor, 'a Roman now adopted happily.' (1.1.467-468) In fact, she now outranks him, holds the levers of power in her hands and will soon be engineering 'settlements' between the emperor and him which, with her lover Aaron's help, bring about his downfall.

Tamora hasn't just managed to pick up the language remarkably well; she's acquired more than a smattering of literary culture, too! On the morning of the hunt (Act 2, Scene 2) we find her out in the forest where Aaron and her sons have set up the murder of Bassianus and the rape and mutilation of Lavinia. At the moment, though, it's love that's on her mind. She eagerly awaits her date with her 'lovely Moor', in the beauty-spot where later, at nightfall, when all the grisly business of the day is done, she'll conceive his 'blackamore' child (or so the text at 4.2.91-92 seems to suggest).

Finding Aaron alone she breaks into pastoral verse.

The birds chant melody on every bush,
The snake lies rolled in the cheerful sun,
The green leaves quiver with the cooling wind,
And make a chequer'd shadow on the ground.
Under their sweet shade …….. (2.2.12-16)

This is high-quality imitation Ovid, but there's also a hint of the Garden of Eden with that snake.

Tamora's expressing her delight in the natural world where in forests, the poets tell us, primitive desires can be freely enacted in seclusion without unwanted others seeing, disapproving and spoiling the fun. In a spot as wild as this erotic and blood-thirsty impulses - this is a hunt, remember: we've come here to kill things! - can be given free rein!

But the Gothic queen's literary tastes don't stop with pastoral verse. She knows her epic poetry as well. Her assignation with Aaron in the forest puts her in mind of a similar scene, in Book IV of Virgil's 'Aeneid', lines 160-172, where Aeneas and Dido mingle erotic thrills with the thrills of the chase; venison **and** venery, so to say. 'Let us sit down,' she tells Aaron,

And after conflict such as was supposed
The wandering prince *(i.e. Aeneas)* and Dido once enjoyed,
When with a happy storm they were surprised
And curtained with a counsel-keeping cave,
We may, each wreathed in the other's arms,
Our pastimes done, possess a golden slumber. (2.2.21-26)

We find ourselves in a complex network of associations and our response to it will fall short if we aren't prepared to toy with 'maybe' readings. The overall mood, obviously, is languorous sensuousness: as 'sit down', 'enjoyed', 'curtained', 'wreathed in each others arms', 'possess a golden slumber' all testify. But it's not all that straightforward. In 'happy storm' we find contentment mixed with an element of disturbance; and when Aeneas and Dido find shelter and secrecy in the cave the initial sexual tension between them is a 'conflict' which they later come to 'enjoy'. Consider the situation as well as the words that Tamora uses. She's found Aaron 'sad', (2.2.10) i.e. still wrapped up in villainous thoughts, and what she says is meant to draw him into the pale of her own amorous desires. The phrase 'our pastimes done' seems to suggest, in an anticipatory way, that the present mood-difference between them will prove to be no more than fore-play preceding their love-making, with the post-coital 'golden slumber' to follow.

Tamora blurs the line between cultural sophistication and erotic appetite. 'Gothic' in desire and 'Roman' in culture, she'd like to rub the line out completely if she could.

It's like mother like sons.

Her son Demetrius also knows his Latin poetry. In Act 1, Scene 1 he tried to comfort his mother for the death of Alarbus with these words:

.....madam, stand resolved, but hope withal
The self-same gods that armed the queen of Troy
With opportunity of sharp revenge
Upon the Thracian tyrant in his tent
May favour Tamora, the queen of Goths......,
To quit the bloody wrongs upon her foes. (1.1.136-144)

He's reminding her of the tale of Hecuba, Queen of Troy, as told by Ovid in Book XIII of 'Metamorphoses'. After the fall of Troy, Hecuba has lost almost everything – father, husband, children, and her throne. Her last remaining hope is that her youngest son, Polydorus - who's been evacuated from the war-zone and entrusted to the care of Polymestor, the king of Thrace - might escape the fate of the rest of the family. Her hope's in vain. Polymestor kills Polydorus and tosses his body into the sea. Hecuba finds it washed up on the shore and goes to seek out 'the Thracian tyrant' with bloody revenge in her heart. Though old and weaponless she's lent strength by those 'self-same gods' and she kills him with her bare hands.

............digitos in perfida lumina condit
expellitque genis oculos (facit ira potentem)
inmergitque manus foedatusque sanguine sonti
non lumen (neque enim superest), loca luminis haurit.
(Ovid, Metamorphoses, Book XIII, lines 560-563)

(She sank her fingers into his perfidious eyes and prised them clean out. Her anger gave her the strength. Then, covered with the criminal's blood, she plunged her hands in again and dragged out the sockets, the eyes being no longer there.)

This reference to Hecuba helps to set the violent tone of the play but it's merely incidental compared to the pivotal importance of the story of Tereus's rape of Philomela from Book VI of the same poem. The atrocities that Chiron and Demetrius commit against Lavinia ape and exceed those of Tereus. Not that Ovid soft-pedals on the gruesome details. Describing how Tereus, having violated Philomela, cuts her tongue out so that she can't incriminate him he adds this:

ille indignantem et nomen patris usque vocantem
luctantemque loqui conprensam forcipe linguam
abstulit ense fero. radix micat ultima linguae
ipsa iacet terraeque tremens immurmurat atrae,
utque salire solet mutilatae cauda colubrae,
palpitet et moriens dominae vestigia quaerit. (555-560)

Arthur Golding, whose 1567 translation of 'Metamorphoses' Shakespeare is known to have used, though he knew the original too, renders this as:

But as she yirnde and called aye upon her father's name,
And strived to have spoken still, the cruel tyrant came,
And with a pair of pinsons fast did catch hir by the tung
And with his sword did cut it off. The stumpe wheron it hung
Did patter still. The tip fell downe, and quivering on the ground
As though that it had murmured it made a certain sound,
And as an Adders tayle cut off doth skip a while: even so
The tip of Philomelas tongue did wriggle to and fro,
And nearer to hir mistressward in dying still did go.
(Golding 707-715)

In the end Tereus is caught and punished by being made to eat his own son in a pie – yes, another unmistakable connection between Ovid and the play. He makes the mistake of leaving Philomela her hands, which she uses to stitch his name into an embroidery. Tamora's more astute and ruthless boys see where he slipped up and they cut off Lavinia's hands, too. But why not just kill her, we wonder, and have done? It's what Lavinia, like Philomela, would have preferred. But no, that won't do. Apart from 'having a laugh' they see themselves as doing their family duty - getting revenge for Alarbus in a way that makes Lavinia and all the Andronici suffer as much as possible.

This is very nasty stuff and it leaves some people with no stomach for the play at all. But the atrocities aren't simply 'showbiz sensationalism', cynically aiming to pull in the more bloodthirsty and least discriminating members of the Elizabethan theatre-going public, as is sometimes alleged. This isn't only a violent play but a **learned** one. Shakespeare may be catering for cruel tastes but he's also got a serious message for members of his audience who, like him, have been trained in classical languages and literature and who value that learning as part and parcel of their own cultural heritage. He wants to remind them that classical poetry is the source of the horrific spectacle that they're watching, and ask some challenging questions about the values of classical civilisation vis-a-vis his own, Christian, era.

We notice a tendency to exaggerate the violence he finds in his sources, which simultaneously maximises its dramatic and emotional impact and intensifies the revulsion we feel. For example, he replaces one Tereus with two Gothic sadists, and increases two outrageous cruelties – the rape of Philomena and the cutting-off of her tongue – to three, by having them lop off of her hands as well. What's Shakespeare's game? It's almost as if the itch of the disconcertingly well-read Chiron and Demetrius to 'outdo' the story that they're following reflects something in his attitude towards his classical sources. It may – I put it tentatively – put us in mind of what he does in another early play, 'The Comedy of Errors', where he himself 'outdoes' Plautus's ingenious plotting in 'Menaechmi' by adding a second pair of identical twins to the pair in the original. It may also make us think of his satirical rejection of Homeric epic values in 'Troilus and Cressida' and his distaste for Roman 'virtue' in 'Coriolanus'. His anything-you-can-do-I-can-do-better attitude is that of a man who sees himself both as an artistic rival and as a moral opponent of the classical poetry and culture that he first got to know as a pupil at Stratford Grammar School. As a rival we see him adding new extremities of event and experience to his sources. As a moral opponent, in this particular play at least, he chooses to focus as much on the sufferings of the victims as on the cruelty of the perpetrators, and to suggest in a variety of ways that he and his audience, are bringing 'eyes not yet created' (Sonnet 81) - Christian eyes - to bear on these ancient events.

Shakespeare shows us three of the main characters – Titus, Tamora and Aaron - in their role as parents. They all have strong 'natural' bonds with their offspring and they all feel what any parent would feel when their children die or suffer or are threatened. At the same time, these children all have great political significance for them.

Obviously, sons matter enormously to Titus, both emotionally and politically. He's had about twenty-five of them at the latest count, although he's lost quite a few of them in the wars, consoling himself with the belief that they've not died without serving the empire and bringing honour to the name of the Andronici. His sole daughter Lavinia is not as replaceable as his sons and when she comes to grief he can find no such consolation. But she, too, has a political price-tag. When the distinctly unpleasant new emperor Saturninus asks for Lavinia's hand in marriage Titus might well be thinking that he's done enough for him already by putting him on the throne, without having to hand over 'the cordial of mine age' (1.1.69) to him as well. He's aware, of course, that as empress Lavinia would add further lustre to the Andronicus family name, but it's out of duty rather than ambition that he agrees to let Saturninus, rather than

Bassianus, have her. Lavinia's own feelings aren't recorded, although perhaps they can be guessed. But that's beside the point. You do whatever the emperor asks.

Tamora, the second parent under scrutiny, has spoilt her sons rotten. We never hear of the boys' father (any more than we hear of the Andronici mother(s), for that matter) but if there ever was one he's clearly failed to have a positive influence on them. The boys have turned out to be absolute monsters, although Tamora likes them the way they are and is fiercely protective of them. She failed to save her eldest, Alarbus, and this trauma now shapes her political career in Rome. In the midst of brokering a treacherous peace between Saturninus and Titus she makes this aside:

I'll find a day to massacre them all *(i.e. the Andronici)*,
And raze their faction and their family,
The cruel father and his traitorous sons
To whom I sued for my dear son's life,
And make them know what tis to let a queen
Kneel in the streets and beg for grace in vain. (1.1.455-460)

The note of political grudge comes through clearer than the note of maternal grief, doesn't it? And we hear no note of maternal love at all when she gives birth to Aaron's blackamoor baby. She sends it in the midwife's arms straight to Aaron and bids him to 'christen it with his dagger's point'. (4.2.72)

The third parent is Aaron himself. Our out-and-out, hard-bitten villain suddenly goes all coochie-coo over his baby, which is regarded with disgust and embarrassment by the white characters. 'Sweet blowze,' he murmurs, 'you are a beauteous blossom, sure.' (4.2.74)

Aaron's boy is just as 'political' as all the other children in the play. If the spectacularly cuckolded emperor discovers his existence Tamora's position as empress and imperial consort will become impossible. But the baby that she wants dead brings out a defiant protectiveness in Aaron. Apart from the charm of his blackness he represents a precarious dynastic prospect that his low-born father sets great store by. Up to his neck in all sorts of trouble and scoring very low on the life-expectancy charts Aaron uses all his resources of courage and guile not to save himself but the boy, and at the end, against all the odds, it looks as if he pulls it off. (Or maybe not. We'll look at this again later.)

When his iron code of conduct calls for it Titus is an unflinching killer, dealing death in battle to the enemy in the ordinary way of business, but also to the captive Alarbus (no Geneva Convention in those days!) and to his own son, Mucius, when he dares to defy him. On the other hand, as injustices begin to fall on his own head he remains remarkably passive (until, finally..........).

It's like father like daughter.

Consider Lavinia's self-restraint when Saturninus, mere moments after plighting his troth to her, starts eyeing up Tamora and declaring to all within earshot that he wouldn't at all mind having that sexy Gothic queen for his bride, if he could 'choose anew'. (1.1.266) He gives Tamora every assurance of future favour, virtually promising to make her empress of Rome, the honour which until a moment ago was promised to Lavinia. It's a hugely uncalled-for slap in the face, but she keeps her cool. The right way to behave, learned from her father, is to bow to authority and not make a fuss, whatever one's personal feelings. Saturninus concludes his public flirtation with Tamora by impudently asking his betrothed: 'You are not displeased with this?' (1.1.274) and she replies:

Not I, my lord, sith that true nobility
Warrants these words in princely courtesy. (1.1.275-276)

This implied rebuke (which Saturninus doesn't seem to register) is administered without any loss of self-control and dignity. She's a credit to her dad.

Lavinia has no choice but to behave with restraint. It's for her menfolk to take up her cause - or not. Titus smarts under the emperor's insult but he **doesn't** take up her cause. If Lavinia is ousted by Tamora in the emperor's favours, there's nothing he can do about it. Duty forbids. The emperor is the emperor, even if it was Titus who gave him the job. But this isn't the view taken by Bassianus, the emperor's younger brother, who wants Lavinia for himself – and why shouldn't he have her? He was engaged to her first and the emperor evidently now prefers Tamora. With the support of Lucius and the younger Andronici brothers he kidnaps Lavinia from the court. Titus, intervening on behalf of the emperor, kills his own son Mucius in the kerfuffle that ensues. By his lights, anyone who resists the will of the emperor (and any son who presumes to get between him and his duty) is a traitor. And it's only with the greatest difficulty that Marcus can persuade him to allow Mucius to be buried in the family tomb.

If Titus tells his daughter to marry the repellent Saturninus, be his empress and live unhappily ever after, that's what she will do. But spared that fate by the emperor's fickleness she quickly settles, as Titus himself does, for Plan B - marriage to her first-betrothed, Bassianus, the emperor's younger brother. Lavinia is a political pawn, as high-born Roman ladies have to be, but as we saw in her rebuke to the emperor there's a true patrician spark in her. When, with her new husband Bassianus, she comes upon Tamora alone in the forest – Aaron just slinking away - they mockingly compare her to Diana (goddess of chastity!) who was surprised when bathing (see Book 3 of 'Metamorphoses') by the hunter Actaeon. Just as annoyed as, but less easily embarrassed than, the goddess, Tamora keeps her wits – if little else – about her and comes up with a ready reply. She twists the Ovid story by imagining Bassianus, like Actaeon, being 'planted presently with horns', (2.2.62-63), that is to say, cuckolded. It's a smart bit of repartee but it also reveals the nasty way her mind works. She knows that her boys will soon be on hand to kill Bassianus, have their way with Lavinia, cuckolding him *post mortem,* as it were. Unaware of the danger, Lavinia continues to hold her own in the vein of ribald literary innuendo, adding a further horn=cuckold=hunt comment:

Under your patience, gentle empress,
'Tis thought you have a goodly gift in horning,
And to be doubted that your Moor and you
Are singled forth to try experiments.
Jove shield your husband from his hounds today;
(Diana had Actaeon's hounds tear him to pieces, if you remember)
'Tis pity they should take him for a stag. (2.2.66-71)

She's got spirit and wit, this Lavinia, but we tremble for her. The suffering and humiliation that are coming her way leave us with an indelible impression of her as a pitiful ruin of a woman, pure victim. But the spirit we see in her here is never quite broken. With admiration as well as pity we watch her desperate efforts to expose Chiron and Demetrius as her violators. Father and daughter both lose hands, but they both overcome their handicap in their common pursuit of revenge. One-handed, Titus bleeds her wrongers to death while she, with no hands, holds the bowl with her stumps to catch the blood. And it's a fair guess that she shows no surprise – though everybody else, including the audience, is shocked - when Titus suddenly stabs her to death at the final banquet. It's as if there's a death pact between them. His last words to his beloved daughter are:

…………..with thy shame thy father's sorrow die*(s)*. (5.3.46)

A single knife-stroke ends both.

But to return to Titus. As we've noted, what strikes us most about him at first is his patience in the face of misfortune and tyranny. The only time he flares up is when he has to listen to the ungrateful Saturninus's lock-stock-and-barrel rejection of him, Lavinia and the whole Andronicus family:

No, Titus, no, the emperor needs her not,
Nor her, nor thee, nor any of thy stock.
…………………….Full well, Andronicus,
Agree these *(i.e. your)* deeds with that proud brag of thine
That said I begged the empire at thy hands. (1.1. 304-306; 310-312)

Titus, usually so deferential, can't stop himself from coming back at him with:

O monstrous! What reproachful words are these? (1.1.313)

But this is still only 'hurt', not 'angry'. He still doesn't seem to **do** anger. A moment later, when he speaks of his 'wounded heart' (1.1.319) it's a plea for comfort, not a protest. And sure enough when the emperor, with Tamora whispering in his ear, makes a transparently insincere and ungracious offer of forgiveness (although **he's** the one who ought to be begging for forgiveness) Titus gratefully accepts it. 'I thank your majesty,' he says,

.... and her *(i.e. Tamora)*, my lord:
These words, these looks, infuse new life in me. (1.1.465)

Tamora knows an abject creep when she sees one and she doesn't miss her chance to rub in the humiliation. In her role of 'peace-maker', she calls on the whole Andronici family to get down on their knees and apologise to the emperor. Titus complies, and makes his seething sons and daughter do the same. Likewise he swallows, and makes his children swallow, the emperor's totally unjust jibe to Lavinia - 'you left me like a churl.' (1.1.490)

Tamora's got Titus's number. He wants peace at any price – the weakest of all political attitudes to adopt. When Saturninus invites him and his family to celebrate a double wedding – Tamora's to him and Lavinia's to Bassianus - he again accepts, and to mark the new spirit of reconciliation he invites the whole court to go out hunting in the forest with him on the following day!

The shaky *rapprochement* with Saturninus and Tamora lasts less than halfway through the day of the hunt. In Act 2, Scene 2 Aaron enters alone, carrying a bag of gold. He teases the audience by explaining that it's a sprat to catch Andronicus mackerels. If we want to know more – and of course we do - he assures us that he has 'a very excellent piece of villainy' (2.2.7) afoot. Watch this space. Tamora comes in to keep her assignation with him. *Al fresco* sex is item No 1 on her short-term agenda, but on Aaron's it's only item No 2. He rebuffs her 'come-on' signals with -

Madam, though Venus govern your desires
Saturn is dominator over mine. (2.2 30-31) -

and briefs her on his plans. Her boys will be here soon, all set up to kill Bassianus and rape Lavinia. He gives her a letter to pass on to Saturninus which, as we'll see in due course, will deflect suspicion from the true criminals and incriminate Titus's sons Quintus and Martius in the murder.

Aaron slips away and here, bang on cue, come the unsuspecting victims, closely followed, also bang on cue, by Demetrius and Chiron.

Tamora now carries out two 'Ovidian' transformations before our fascinated eyes.

In the first she transforms **herself**. Somewhat improbably (though there's an uncomfortable humour in it), she becomes a damsel in distress, complaining to her boys that she's fallen the victim of persecution and wrong. 'These two have 'ticed me hither to this place,' (2.2.92) she sobs, pointing at Bassianus and Lavinia, 'and if you two boys hadn't come along when you did they would have tied me to a yew-tree and left me to die, with their foul insults still ringing in my ears.'

Her second transformation is of '**this place**'. A little while ago it was the lovely sun-dappled bower where she waited impatiently for her lover Aaron. Now, suddenly, it's become 'a barren, detested vale.' (2.2.93) Her description casts a dismal spell over it that has her boys – and us – seeing it her way and entering into her dark mood.

The trees, though summer, yet forlorn and lean,
O'ercome with moss and baleful mistletoe;
Here never shines the sun, here nothing breeds
Unless the nightly owl or fatal raven.
And when they showed me this abhorred pit,
They told me here at dead time of the night
A thousand fiends, a thousand hissing snakes,
Ten thousand swelling toads, as many urchins (*goblins*),
Would make such fearful and confused cries
As any mortal body hearing it
Should straight fall mad, or else die suddenly. (2.2. 94-104)

This is powerful stuff, hardly calling for the services of the lighting engineer.

When Tamora calls for vengeance, her boys don't mess about. Bassianus 'gets his' in a trice, and Tamora – 'give me the poniard' (2.2.120) – acts as if she's going to see Lavinia off, too. But it's just a feint. There's another fate, worse than death, awaiting the Andronicus girl.

Tamora has caught the note of nightmare. 'The snake lying rolled in the cheerful sun' (2.2.13) in her previous description of the scene has become 'a 'thousand hissing snakes' in the scene she creates for us now. She also gives us the first mention of the 'abhorred pit' which will be the *idée fixe* in what is about to unfold. As Aaron brings Titus's sons Quintus and Martius to the pit into which Bassianus's body has been tipped the verse, moving more rapidly than before and in shorter periods, animates the scene before our eyes with images fusing sex and violence.

That fused 'sex-and-violence' imagery was there in Chiron's suggestion that he and Demetrius should

Drag hence her husband to some secret hole
And make his dead trunk pillow to our lust. (2.2.129-130)

It's there again as Lavinia begs Tamora to save her from her boys' 'worse-than-killing lust' (2.2 175) and in her plea to be 'tumbled' (2.2.176) – a word suggestive of male sexual aggression –

..............into some loathsome pit
Where never man's eye may behold my body. (2.2.176-177)

As Aaron steers the Andronici 'fall guys' towards the pit – it's a trap-door representing, ostensibly at least, an animal trap set by the hunters - he uses exactly the same words – 'loathsome pit' - that Lavinia has just used to describe the pit that she imagined herself being tumbled into. Aaron's 'loathsome pit', though, is 'where I espied the panther fast asleep.' (2.2.193-194)

The pit, in various guises, becomes an object of obsessive fear and loathing.

When Martius tumbles into the pit Quintus crawls cautiously closer to the edge in the hope of pulling him out. 'What subtle hole is this,' he wonders,

Whose mouth is covered with rude-growing briers
Upon whose leaves are drops of new-shed blood? (2.2.198-200)

That blood, of course, is the 'fused' blood of the murdered Bassanius and the raped and mutilated Lavinia.

Martius, his voice coming from within, describes the pit first as 'this unhallowed and bloodstained hole' (2.2.210) and later as 'this detested, dark, blood-drinking pit'. (2.2.224) We now learn that it's a **grave**, too, with a corpse in it! Bassianus! As his eyes grow more accustomed to the dark Martius notices that an eerie light coming from Bassianus's ring,

Like a taper in some monument
Doth shine upon the dead man's earthy cheeks
And shows the ragged entrails of this pit. (2.2.228-230)

This vein of imagery still isn't exhausted. A few lines further on Martius begs his brother to haul him out of

…….. this fell devouring receptacle,
As hateful as Cocytus misty mouth. (2.2.235-236)

Trapdoor/ animal trap, pit, hole, grave, ragged entrails, receptacle. And now 'devouring' adds a new frisson: it's also a **mouth** that eats people.

Quintus reaches down to try to haul Martius out, fearing – with good reason – that he

………may be plucked into the swallowing womb
Of this deep pit, poor Bassianus' grave. (2.2.239-240)

- and there are no prizes for guessing what happens next.

So finally we add **'womb'** to the list. You don't have to be Freud, do you?

Saturninus and Aaron, followed shortly by Tamora, Titus and his son Lucius, now gather around the pit. Tamora hands Saturninus the forged letter, purportedly from Titus to Martius, which convinces the emperor that it's the trapped Andronici brothers who must be the murderers of Bassianus, and Aaron clinches the matter when he unearths the bag of gold which is supposed to be the motivation for their crime. Saturninus orders them to be dragged back to Rome for execution. Aaron's stitch-up has worked a treat. Their father will fight to save them if he can but Quintus and Martius are dead meat.

This is classy plotting: by the villains – and by Shakespeare. All this has paved the way perfectly to what comes next.

Tamora gives Titus grounds for hope by undertaking to intercede with the emperor on behalf of his imprisoned sons. It's a smart move. Her purpose is to draw him further into the web of intrigue. It encourages him, in the next Act, to grovel to the judges and senators of Rome for his sons' lives – a futile public humiliation that gives her great satisfaction. A similar deceitful hope induces Titus to chop off his own hand. Aaron has told him that this sacrifice will earn the emperor's clemency. He even assists in the amputation and takes the hand to the emperor – laughing all the way:

Let fools do good and fair men call for grace,
Aaron will have his soul black like his face. (3.1.205-206)

'Calling for grace' is exactly what Titus does as he binds up his bleeding stump and waits for the return of his sons. He turns to the gods, falling on his knees with Lavinia, saying:

................heaven shall hear our prayers,
Or with our sighs we'll breathe the welkin dim. (3.1.211-212)

Even if the gods who rule over the natural world are deaf to paltry human cries surely they'll notice a great commotion in the elements! In language that his brother, Marcus, understandably considers border-line psychotic but which we, thinking in more literary terms, would describe as hyperbolic and 'conceited', Titus prays:

When heaven doth weep, doth not the earth o'erflow?
If the winds rage, doth not the sea wax mad,
Threatening the welkin with his big-swollen face?
And wilt thou have a reason for this coil *(disturbance)*?
I am the sea. Hark how her sighs doth blow.
She is the weeping welkin, I the earth.
Then must my sea be moved with her sighs,
Then must my earth with her continual tears
Become a deluge overflowed and drowned,
For why my bowels cannot hide their woes,
But like a drunkard must I vomit them.
Then give me leave, for losers will have leave
To ease their stomachs with their bitter tongues. (3.1.222-234)

And here, bang on cue again, comes the answer to his prayer. A messenger, not from the gods but from the emperor, brings in the severed heads of Quintus and Martius, and – to add insult to injury – Titus's own severed hand!

These gods! Are they totally deaf? Don't they care at all? Or do they actually find amusement in human suffering? In any case, they don't seem to bother themselves with justice on earth. It's the wicked - Aaron, Saturninus, Tamora and her vicious sons – whom they favour. They make them their god-deputies and put the world in their power. No wronged man, however pious, should hope to get 'grace' from them. He's just a 'loser', and his patience is a mug's game.

Back to Act 2, Scene 3. The day of the hunt. Shouts and laughter. Demetrius and Chiron emerge from the trees in high spirits, pushing and dragging the barely recognisable figure of Lavinia. They've raped her, cut out her tongue and chopped off her hands. She'll never speak again or 'play the scribe' (2.3.4) to write down any accusation. Hooting with delight, they abandon her in the dismal forest.

Long pause, as we look, and try not to look, at the sight before us.

The winding of horns tells us that the hunting party isn't far off. Enter Marcus, through the trees. As Lavinia tries to scuttle away he sees her from a distance and only from behind. At first he's not sure it's her. 'Who is this, he asks, 'my niece that flies away so fast?' (2.3.11)

No answer.

What's she doing here alone? Is something wrong? 'Where is your husband?' (2.3.12)

Then she turns to face him.

Think about it. Imagine that you're Shakespeare and you've got to write this scene. What on earth would you have them say or do next?

Uncle and niece **both** stand speechless – forever, it seems. But sooner or later one of them has to say something and it can only be Marcus:

If I do dream would all my wealth would wake me:
If I do wake, some planet strike me down
That I may slumber in eternal sleep. (2.3.13-15)

The sentence has three first person nominatives (I), two first person accusatives (me), and one first person possessive pronoun (my). Marcus is talking about himself: but he's not sure if he's waking, sleeping, dreaming or dying. Human experience is ordinarily a pretty seamless unity combining external reality and the perceiving mind, but from the way that Marcus is talking now object and subject seem to have taken leave of each other and gone their separate ways. He talks about his shock, but not what's caused it. Lavinia, the 'second person' in both the grammatical and the emotional sense, goes without her personal noun or any pronouns. Physically she's there, but verbally she's yet to arrive.

Again, a long pause.

'Speak, gentle niece,' (2.3.16) Marcus begs. She doesn't, so he has to speak again:

....................................What stern ungentle hands
Hath lopped and hewed and made thy body bare
Of her two branches. (2.3.16-18)

Lavinia's 'there' now, in two possessive pronouns, 'thy' and 'her'.

Marcus's reference to hands shows how curiously words can behave in extreme situations. He has to mention them because somehow they can't **not** be mentioned, but when he does so he finds himself speaking of the criminals' 'stern ungentle' hands, not the hands that Lavinia no longer has. His words manage to be both a reference and a flinch. Shakespeare's subconscious mind, on loan as it were to Marcus, starts throwing up images which are both highly relevant and emotionally inadmissible. 'Body bare' gives us a split-second visualisation, 'denied' by its syntactical relation to 'hewed' and 'branches', of Lavinia being stripped for sexual violation. 'Lopped and hewed' gives us a flashback to the sacrificial 'hewing' (1.1.132) and 'lopping' (1.1.146) of Alarbus's limbs in the first scene, with its suggestion that the two outrages are somehow one. And 'branches' gives Lavinia a subliminal 'inhuman' affinity with the 'lean and forlorn' (2.2.94) forest where the crime has taken place.

While Lavinia is doomed to tree-like silence Marcus is doomed to the agony of having to say something when he can only muster excruciatingly 'unfit' words to say it. Those 'branches' - Lavinia's hands - now become

………………………..those sweet ornaments
Whose circling shadows kings have sought to sleep in
And might not gain so great a happiness
As half thy love. (2.3.18-21)

Here's a horrified uncle staring at his mutilated niece and all he can do is babble on about 'sweet ornaments', 'circling shadows', 'kings', 'happiness', 'love' – off-the-wall metaphors and airy references to things that haven't happened and never will. Such verse 'fits not with the hour'.

Allow me to digress for the next seven paragraphs. No skipping, though. As you'll see, it all has a bearing on this Lavinia-Marcus encounter.

Opening his section on tragedy in 'The Art of Poetrie' (1595), Sir Philip Sidney remembers the story of Alexander Pheroeus, an 'abhominable Tyrant….from whose eyes a Tragedy well made, and represented, drewe abundance of teares: who without pittie, had murthered infinite numbers, and some of his owne blood. So as he, that was not ashamed to make matters for Tragedies *(i.e. cause them in real life)*, yet could not resist the **sweet violence** of a Tragedie *(i.e. on the stage)*'.

'Sweet violence' compactly expresses the antithesis between poetic charm and the ugly deeds and events of tragedy, and it's precisely this antithesis that Shakespeare's exploring – and finding a way to exploit – in this scene.

When 'Titus' was first staged, probably in 1594, Shakespeare was at the beginning of his career as a playwright. But he was already famous as a poet. In the previous three years, while H&S anti-plague regs had shut the theatres for much of the time, he'd written two narrative poems: 'Venus and Adonis', published in 1593, which went down very well, and striking while the iron was hot, 'The Rape of Lucrece' in the following year. (Incidentally, Shakespeare seems to have had rape on his mind at this time, doesn't he?) These poems were not casual efforts. Of 1194 and 1855 lines respectively they were substantial and learned works which, together with the Sonnets circulating in manuscript, gained him discerning and, as in the case of the Earl of Southampton, wealthy supporters. They also **defined** his reputation. He became 'sweet' Shakespeare.

'Sweet', 'sugard', 'honie-tong'd', 'mellifluous' – these were the critical laurels usually hung round his neck by his contemporaries. They weren't empty rave-words like 'great' or 'fabulous' with pop-fans today. 'Sweet', 'sugard', etc, were accepted terms in the criticism of poetry and rhetoric. If a song or a speech hit the button in all or most of the following ways – if it engaged your eager interest in its line of thought, if it was felicitously expressed, if it contained arresting imagery and telling examples, if it had a sense of 'flow', if the details and the overall structure harmonised and if, whatever it was about, the handling of the words gave you aesthetic pleasure – 'sweet' (or one of its equivalents) was the word you'd use, and people would know what you meant.

Before the plague years Thomas Kyd's 'The Spanish Tragedy' (1587), a strong-meat revenge play, had been the greatest theatrical sensation of its day. It was a model for the young (29) Shakespeare, keen to make his own mark on the stage, to emulate and outdo. Whatever its other merits, Kyd's play (which we'll look at more closely later on) wasn't noted for its 'sweet' verse: rough and ready did the job there. But what could people expect of a play by 'sweet' Shakespeare, with enough rapes, mutilations, murders and revenges to make the Spanish play seem like a vicar's tea-party? Obviously, the term 'sweet' described a quality of language rather than the deeds and events that the language was used to describe. Both the narrative poems had ended in violent death, but the verse – even that of 'The Rape of Lucrece' which carried a heavy freight of fear and despair - had only added to Shakespeare's reputation for 'sweetness'.

Putting 'page' poetry to 'stage' use wasn't a new idea. In Elizabethan times there was often a continuity as well as a contrast between them. Jumping ahead a year or two, Shakespeare would have the clever idea of writing the lovers' speeches in 'Romeo and Juliet' (1595) in the form of 'sugard sonnets'. And in this play we've already seen him doing something comparable, in Tamora's glowingly ornate description of the grove where she has her assignation with Aaron. She speaks Ovidian 'page' poetry but it works perfectly in stage terms, setting the scene and the mood, and a little later it provides Shakespeare with the opportunity to demonstrate how poetic words can transform the world. Tamora can make the grove glowingly ornate in one description and then metamorphose it into a scene of dismal menace in another. Things change, and it's words that change them.

However, Marcus's encounter with the mutilated Lavinia looks like a special case. Here the relation isn't between ornate poetry and 'scenery', but between ornate poetry and extreme human suffering. The question becomes: how you can do 'speechless with horror' on the stage, in verse or any other sort of language for that matter? The modern inclination, perhaps, would be to abandon all the 'sweet' artifices of verse as inappropriate and tasteless and to search for a more 'fitting' vein of expression. But that's exactly what Shakespeare doesn't do. He stands his ground as the 'sweet' poet who can add poetic surplus value to any situation. He has Marcus pull out all the stops in a supreme effort to make poetry equal to the exquisitely atrocious appearance of Lavinia, and it makes its effect by falling short. Marcus's inadequate emotional response and ludicrous failure of expression are as near as we're going to get to his (and our) identification with Lavinia's ruin. Dramatically, the scene works, and works in a very original way, both through and against his words.

Digression over. So back to Act 2, Scene 3.

Single-voiced eloquence has failed. We need two voices. Marcus tries to open a dialogue with his niece, to try to get answers to the questions that will move his mind from the intolerable 'what happened?' to the more tolerable 'who did it?'

'Why dost not speak to me? (2.3.21) he asks.

Lavinia answers in the only way she can. She opens her mouth and blood, not words, comes out.

The dark, tongueless, bloody hole of Lavinia's mouth is the vision that Marcus's living nightmare has been unconsciously edging towards. The image is of the destruction of the powers of human communication. If no words will ever come from Lavinia's lips again what words can come from his? But they do come, somehow, and they're still the 'sweet' words drawn from the 'somewhere else', or 'someone else', of poetic diction. But they're dead-and-alive words, twitching helplessly on the ground like Philomela's tongue.

Alas, a crimson river of warm blood,
Like to a bubbling fountain stirred with wind,
Doth rise and fall between thy rosed lips,
Coming and going with thy honey breath. (2.3.22-25)

Should we laugh or cry? This is the question that we ask ourselves repeatedly in this play.

Marcus's next line brings him, at last, from the 'what?' to the 'who?' question.

But sure some Tereus hath deflowered thee
And, lest thou shouldst detect him, cut thy tongue. (2.3.26-27)

Tereus. Philomena. Ovid's 'Metamorphoses'. Of course! So **that**'s the story! Is that an obscure relief he feels? Lavinia's story in the ready-made form of an ancient myth puts it at certain distance. It lessens the immediate shock and suggests that it's already been drawn into the compass of human intelligibility and brought under emotional control. Not by him perhaps, not yet, but by previous men and women. The phrase '**some** Tereus' suggests not just a single precedent but an archetype, a pattern repeated through the ages. Might this atrocity yet prove to be less of an overwhelming personal trauma and more an act of recognition?

Well, that's as maybe, but it can offer precious little comfort to Lavinia, who's **not** a remote mythical figure. She's the outraged woman standing before him, blushing at the word 'deflowered'. Ah, blushes! They're a much-dwelt-on topos in the kind of verse that Marcus finds himself ventriloquised by. Helplessly, he mouths further ineptitudes. 'Ah, now thou turn'st away thy face for shame,' he says,

And notwithstanding all this loss of blood,
As from a conduit with three issuing spouts,
Yet do thy cheeks look red as Titan's *(the sun's)* face,
Blushing to be encountered with a cloud. (2.3.28-32)

It's excruciating. 'Notwithstanding all this loss of blood' sounds like doctor-talk, and 'a conduit with three issuing spouts' sounds like plumber-talk! And the comparison of Lavinia's red cheeks glowing like 'Titan's face' and in need of a cloud to cover them is.... well, I can't think of exactly the right word, so please feel free to choose your own. Marcus's language, without ceasing to be 'poetic', has become as abject and humiliated as the woman he's talking to.

He checks that her story is Philomela's story. 'Shall I say 'tis so?' (2.3.33) he asks, and she nods.

That's the unbearable 'what happened' question out of the way then. Now he can move on to the less painful 'who did it?' question.

O that I knew thy heart, and knew the beast,
That I might rail at him to ease my mind!
Sorrow concealed, like an oven stopped,
Doth burn the heart to cinders where it is. (2.3.34-37)

Why do I say 'less painful'? Well, if we do a count of the nouns and personal prepositions in lines 34 and 35 – it's two-and-a-half 'I's and one 'my' against one 'thy' referring to Lavinia – we see that he's become the subject of his own sentences again. That helps.

Marcus assumes that Lavinia has been raped by one man ('Tereus') - not two. He wants to catch the man and 'rail at' him, to ease the pain of being a helpless grieving uncle and become a purposeful avenger. If you can't curse and avenge yourself on those who do terrible things to you and those you love your heart will burn to ashes inside you. The 'oven stopped' isn't the sort of image we've had before: it's thuddingly realistic, and anything but 'sweet'. Marcus's 'oven' is 'stopped' by not knowing who the criminal is. But if we apply the image to Lavinia, which seems to be the obvious thing to do, its power is greatly magnified. Her 'sorrow' is 'concealed' forever in permanent silence. She'll never be able to 'ease her mind' by railing at anybody.

Or will she?

Comparisons between Titus and Job have been made, but they don't take us very far. God's ways might be inexplicable to Job but He was certainly **there** for him, at the other end of his prayers. He was a father figure who meant His children well – however gratuitously punitive He seemed to be at times. Patience under sufferings sent (or at least not alleviated) by God, although not easy, made some sense. Not so with Titus. He's tried that with his gods and it didn't work. He's come to the point where he has no more trust in them and no more forbearance towards those who've done him wrong. 'I have not another tear to shed', (3.1.267) he says – not another tear for himself, let alone his enemies. The one thing to live for now is justice. He's going to get it by hook or by crook and it won't be his fault if it isn't **divine** justice! What a fool he's been, ever seeing things otherwise, but the penny's dropped at last!

Ha, ha, ha! (3.1.265)

Marcus remarks nervously that Titus's guffaw 'fits not with the hour', (3.1.266) He wonders if his brother's going off his rocker – which seems quite likely, considering what he's been going through. But we know better. Titus has reached the end of the road of patience, and is starting out on another – in the opposite direction - the road of revenge. The first road brought no joy, only a bitterness that couldn't even own up to itself. But the second road holds out the promise of some sort of satisfaction. There's hope, of a kind, in that guffaw.

Voices start telling Titus what he's got to do.

For these two heads *(i.e. his sons')* do seem to speak to me
And threat me that I shall never come to bliss
Till all these mischiefs be returned again
Even in their throats that hath committed them. (3.1.271-275)

Yes, things **are** looking up, in an odd way. 'I shall never come to bliss' is an unmistakably Christian phrase, associated with the idea of salvation through mercy, and a sharp reminder to the audience that they must have Christian misgivings about Titus's 'conversion' to revenge. For them, and us, 'come to bliss' doesn't sit easily in a sentence otherwise full of guilt and resentment. It's a sign that his doom is sealed. On the other hand, it's also a sign that he's not going to go quietly. What happens next should be pretty sensational - and, let's face it, that's why we're here. But 'bliss' – forget it. This can only end one way.

Titus isn't just hearing voices. He's thinking 'symbolically'. And it's in classical literature, Virgil, Ovid and others, that he finds the symbols.

In Act 4, Scene 2 Titus puts his grandson, the boy Lucius, at hair-raising risk by sending him on an errand to his enemies Aaron, Chiron and Demetrius. His job is to present them with a bundle of weapons wrapped in a scroll inscribed with the first two lines of Horace's Ode XXII:

Integer vitae, scelerisque purus,
Non eget Mauri iaculis, nec arcu.

(The man untainted by crime has no need of Moorish spears or bows.)

Chiron places the quotation at once -

O, 'tis a verse in Horace, I know it well.
I read it in the grammar long ago. (4.2.22-23)

- but he doesn't 'get the point'. Aaron does, although he doesn't bother to explain it to the boys, whom he regards as academic idiots. In an aside he says,

Now what a thing it is to be an ass.
Here's no sound jest! The old man *(Titus)* has found their guilt,

37

And sends them weapons wrapped around with lines
That wound beyond their feelings to the quick. (4.2.25-28)

This incident anticipates the even more over-the-top
'words-and-weapons' symbolism of the following scene,
Act 4, Scene 3. One of the classical precedents here is an
incident, recorded by Plutarch, in the war against the
Persians in 467 BC. What happened, in a nutshell, is that
at the siege of Phaselis some of Cimon's followers 'shot
arrows over the walls with papers attached to them telling
the people inside what they were doing.' (See 'The Rise
and Fall of Athens' by Plutarch, Penguin Classics,
translated by Ian Scott-Kilvert, p154.)

Quite an idea! Worth bearing in mind.

'Terras Astraea reliquit,' (4.3.4) Titus announces, quoting
yet again from Ovid's 'Metamorphoses' - the book that he
and Lavinia have on the stage with them as they try to
track down Chiron and Demetrius. The goddess of justice
has gone awol. 'She's gone, she's fled.' (4.3.5). But he has
need of her, so he sends his followers to go and find her.

You, cousins, shall go sound the ocean
And cast your nets:
Happily you may catch her in the sea;
No, Publius and Sempronius, you must do it,
'Tis you must dig with mattock and with spade,
And pierce the inmost centre of the earth.
Then, when you come to Pluto's region,
I pray you deliver him this petition.
Tell him it is for justice and for aid,
And that it comes from old Andronicus,
Shaken with sorrows in ungrateful Rome……….
Go, get you gone, and pray be careful all,
And leave you not a man-of-war unsearched:

The wicked emperor may have shipped her hence,
And, kinsmen, then we may go pipe for justice. (4.3.6-17,
21-24)

There's a foreshadowing of Prospero sending Ariel on an
errand here, isn't there? - except that Ariel does what he's
told and Titus's followers don't. They pretend to go, to
humour him, but soon return to report that she's not to be
found anywhere. The search must be extended, then –
upwards, into the heavens where the gods live. But how to
reach them? Arrow-post! He'll copy Cimons' missile-
missive technology. He scribbles letters to Jupiter, Apollo,
Mars, Mercury, Pallas, (though not Saturn – that name
bodes ill!) asking if they have any information about
Astraea's whereabouts, and he fastens them to arrows. It's
a very long shot, but it makes a kind of symbolic sense.

Marcus plays along with his brother's *jeu d'esprit*, but he's
thinking politics rather than prayers. He adapts Titus's idea
a little. What goes up must come down – somewhere. So
why don't we shoot at a slant so that the arrows fall into
the emperor's palace? Titus accepts the suggestion. With
luck someone might get hurt. And he won't mind at all if
Saturninus and Tamora get to open the mail addressed to
the gods. Again, it makes a kind of sense.

His mind fills with thoughts of the mayhem this barrage
will cause. It's a woman, Lavinia, being avenged and it's
women she's being avenged on. He gleefully sees (or
imagines – the distinction doesn't apply) an arrow whizz
into 'Virgo's lap'. (4.3.65) (Virgo is the constellation of
Astraea, that being the fancy name often given by
flattering courtiers to Elizabeth, 'the virgin queen'.) Good
shot! He urges the boy Lucius to 'give it Pallas' (4.3.65) -
another virginal figure - in the same way. And all the time
of course he's aware that it's Tamora's **un**virginal lap

that's the real target. The sick-joke symbolism spirals out of control in an obscene and politically transgressive conflation of images. They're beside themselves with cruel joy. I don't think it would be taking things too far to have Titus stick an arrow between his legs, flight-feathers outward, miming the agony of the stricken women. Apply the unconscious mind!

As in 'Hamlet' Shakespeare uses madness to cast light into dangerous sexual and political corners. Two points of affinity between Titus and Hamlet stand out. The first is that the 'revenge' language in both plays has more than a tinge of madness in itself. Anguish, logical inconsequentiality, hyperbole, oblique symbolism, far-flung associations and emotional exaggeration are the very stuff of it. Of course there's a range of registers from the matter-of-fact to the wildly outlandish, but what makes the strongest dramatic mark on us, obviously, comes from the outlandish end to which the demented heroes repeatedly veer. The second point is that although we're not always sure whether they're outright mad, or hovering on the edge of madness, or just pretending to be mad, we don't doubt that the protagonists' underlying purpose of revenge remains intact, and that though they lose **some** of their wits they keep enough for them to pursue that purpose.

In contrast, Aaron is a model of lucidity. The best thing he has to say about his fellow men is that their idiotic impulses to do good make life easier than it would otherwise be for villains like him. He's no erring sinner wandering on and off the path of grace and virtue. He doesn't swerve. When he's captured and confesses his crimes Lucius asks him: 'Art thou not sorry for these heinous deeds?' (5.1.123) and he replies:

Ay, that I had not done a thousand more.
Even now I curse the day – and yet I think
Few come within the compass of my curse –
Wherein I did not some notorious ill. (5.1.124-127)

Here Shakespeare's taking a leaf out of Marlowe's 'The
Jew of Malta', in which Barabas represented 'state of the
art' stage villainy. The threat of plague kept the London
theatres shut for most of the next three years since 'The
Jew' was staged in 1591 but when they re-opened in 1594
Marlowe was dead and Shakespeare had every intention of
having his black villain picking up where the evil Jew had
left off - and out-doing him, of course. Aaron's boasts
could easily be Barabas's:

As for myself, I walk abroad at nights,
And kill sick people groaning under walls:
Sometimes I go about and poison wells, etc. (Jew of Malta,
Act 2)

Marlowe had set the mark. The best (i.e. worst) villains
had to be totally shamelessness and self-glorifying.
Dramatists knew their public and recruited their villains
from suspect social groups. Jews and Moors especially –
and **this** Moor is a self-declared atheist! – were notorious
for the tin ear that they turned towards God's offer of
forgiveness and redemption. Their refusal to repent was
worse than their actual crimes, however heinous. The
audience got a powerful whiff of the ultimate evil -
blasphemy – in their reckless moral defiance.

But Shakespeare gives it an unexpected twist. The atheist
Aaron insists that, in return for spilling the beans about the
crimes of the imperial couple and their circle, including
himself, Lucius must swear a **religious** oath to guarantee
his baby son's life. It's almost as if we've been fast-

forwarded out of ancient Rome into the Christian era. 'I know thou art religious,' he tells Lucius,

And hast a thing with thee called conscience
With twenty popish tricks and ceremonies
Which I have seen thee careful to observe. (5.1.74-77)

An ordinary promise won't do. He scorns Lucius as 'an idiot (who) believes his bauble for a god' (5.1.79); nevertheless, as a realist, he knows that the oath of a man who calls on God to be his witness ought to be more reliable than that of a disbeliever. 'Popish' is a strikingly anachronistic word for him to use, and it would have made the 'reformed' Christians in the audience prick up their ears. Hang on a minute, they'd think, isn't Aaron throwing the 'conscience' baby out with the 'tricks and ceremonies' bathwater? There might even be a hint that a 'popish' conscience, just because it's supposed to be more superstitious than a reformed one, might be more trustworthy.

Now we've started tallying up Christian references let's see what else we can find.

The Goth soldier who brings the Moor and his baby son to Lucius describes how he captured them. Infant squalling drew him towards a 'ruinous monastery' (5.1.21) where he found father and son taking shelter amongst the fallen stones. Monastery? Another glaring Christian anachronism! But let's not get too excited. Anachronisms weren't necessarily as significant for the Elizabethans as they are for us. Shakespeare may have inserted it in a casual, why-not spirit, as when he has Aaron calling Tamora's sons 'ye painted alehouse signs'. (4.2.100) But it's not **quite** the same, is it? Alehouse signs are 'profane' things, but ruinous monasteries still had 'sacred'

42

connotations in Reformation England. It was still only 60-odd years since the Dissolution and the embers of the religious conflicts of that time were still glowing hot under the ashes. But my own feeling, for what it's worth, is that we don't need to strip-search this monastery for hidden politico-religious messages. Shakespeare could have made more of it if he'd wanted to, but it seems he decided not to. It's too thought-provoking to be merely a picturesque 'scenic' touch, though. The Goth's speech (5.1.20-39) gives us the picture of Aaron, the incarnation of atheistical wickedness, lurking in the ruins of a pre-Reformation, i.e. Catholic, monastery. It 'makes us think', but heaven knows **what** we're supposed to think. Let's just add it to our tally of Christian references and wait to see what, overall, they seem to be telling us about the play.

The Clown in Act 4 is clearly another Christian reference. Like other Shakespearean clowns, fools, porters and grave-diggers etc. he appears only briefly and is inessential to the main plot. But **un**like many of the others he's not clever. He's more your holy fool. With him again we get that fast-forward feeling. He's a Christian. No question. He's never even heard of Jupiter! He 'never drank with him in all my (*his*) life.' (4.3.84-85) It seems unfeeling to classify him as 'comic relief', considering the cruel end he comes to, but that's what he is - although, like Lear's Fool, he becomes a very poignant strand in the emotional fabric of the play.

As he wanders on to the stage we recognise a simple English peasant 'up from the country', looking rather lost and vulnerable in the big-city surroundings. He's carrying a wicker basket with two pigeons in it. No big deal, we think, but when Titus sees him he gets very excited:

News, news, from heaven! (4.3.77)

43

Those arrows that he had his followers shoot into the heavens to fall to earth in the imperial court are being answered by return of post! And the Clown is the postman! Grabbing him, Titus asks:

Sirrah, what tidings? Have you any letters?
Shall I have justice? What says Jupiter? (4.3.77-79)

The Clown looks blank and his mouth starts working. Who's this Jubiter? Or Jewbiter? Or is it Gibberer? etc. The actor can entertain the audience with a series of increasingly ridiculous variants of his own devising before coming up with the 'gibbet-maker' that appears in the text. Of course! Gibbet-maker! That must be it. He says: 'he (the gibbet-maker) hath taken them down again for the man must not be hanged till the next week.'(4.3.80-82)

It's an obscure remark for us, but it wasn't in 1594. A big talking point in London a few months before had been the fate of two Puritans sentenced to death for religious offences. They were reprieved at the last moment, and the gibbet at Tyburn taken down; but their sentences were re-imposed a week later and they were hanged as soon as the gibbet could be rebuilt. In his ignorance, the Clown assumes that the chap Titus is talking about is the fellow responsible for cruel and farcical public executions.

Titus, for his part, is sure that this man with doves has come from heaven with a reply to his letters. The Clown explains that he's merely a carrier of humble pigeons going about his humble private business, not a divine messenger. But for Titus symbols speak louder than facts. Pigeons, doves – what's the difference? They both have feathers - as arrows do! – and they are used to carry messages from low to high and high to low, between heaven and earth. Prayers and messages – that sort of thing. And this general idea is picked up by the Clown who declares that he's come to town to on a mission of reconciliation – though only between his uncle and 'one of the emperal's men' (there's a Bristol pronunciation, surely) and that the pigeons are to be his peace offering. Doves and pigeons are symbols of reconciliation for all of us. We release them at the opening of Olympic Games as a sign of international good will. In Genesis 8:11 the dove that returns with an olive leaf to Noah's Ark is delivering a message of reconciliation. And there are others. In Leviticus 12 the mother of a new-born child is told to take two turtledoves or young pigeons to a priest, one for a burnt offering and the other to be sacrificed for atonement and purification. In Luke 2:22-35 Jesus's parents bring their son to the temple to offer a similar sacrifice of two turtle doves or young pigeons, where they meet Simeon who recognises Jesus as the coming Saviour. In all these instances (except the anachronistic Olympic Games, of course) there are promises of reconciliation which Shakespeare's audience would hardly have missed.

In Act 4, Scene 2 sending the boy Lucius into the criminal camp with weapons wrapped in scraps of poetry was the first 'Daniel-in-the-lions' episode in the play. Now, in the following scene, there's another one. Marcus sees a use for the Clown and his pigeons. You're quite right, Titus, he says, in effect. The Clown **is** the postman. So let's send him, pigeons and all, to emperor Saturninus, with a dagger sheathed in a letter, as a *(faux)* peace offering.

Young Lucius came back alive. The poor Clown isn't so lucky.

Arriving at court, he greets the Emperor and Empress in true Christian style:

God and St Stephen give you good e'en.
I have brought you a letter and a couple of pigeons here.
(4.4.42-43)

Saturninus, not in the most equable of moods after the shower of arrows, reads the letter (the contents of which we never learn, but can imagine), finds the dagger and explodes in rage:

Go take him away and hang him presently. (4.4.44)

Blessed are the peacemakers? Nowadays, perhaps, or perhaps not, but certainly not then. Nobody gives peace a chance in Rome. The only successful 'peace-maker' here is the devious Tamora. The poor Clown seems to come from, and point in the direction of, a world where there may be room for forgiveness and peace, but in Rome he just looks ridiculous - and imperilled. He's the only innocent man in a city where everyone else is as guilty as hell. He hasn't got a chance. He must die, and Marcus and Titus are as much to blame for his death as Saturninus and Tamora.

While we're at it, let's keep tallying up the religious references scattered throughout the play.

Titus struggles to communicate with Lavinia, who struggles to communicate with him. 'Speechless complainer,' he says,

I will learn thy thought.
In thy dumb action I'll be as perfect
As begging hermits in their holy prayers. (3.2.39-41)

All other means of communication being blocked he'll learn her sign language. But how can he overcome the communication blockage vis-à-vis his own gods? He often prays, or tries to pray, but it's not working. Now suddenly he takes an example from the prayers of what can only be Christian hermits in an age he'll never live to see. Now how did **that** idea find its way into his tortured pagan soul?

But as a reminder to myself not to read too much into anachronisms, I'll add one further example. Titus uses the word 'martyred' of Lavinia (3.1.108) and, even more surprisingly, 'martyr' (as a verb) as he gets ready to butcher Tamora's sons. (5.2.180) In these cases, the religious resonances of the word are not heard; it simply refers in a general sense to 'cruelty'.

Nevertheless, let me risk a few 'religious' speculations about the play. You can take them or leave them. Suit yourself.

The first is this. Could the black baby whose father is an 'incarnate devil' (5.1.40) and whose mother is the 'devil's dam' (4.2.67) be the Antichrist, the harbinger of an alternative and entirely evil future for mankind? He certainly has the right pedigree. As the play draws towards its end, after Lucius and his Goth allies have made their revolutionary coup, the question is: who takes over now? It's the question which the play started with, when Titus made a bad call by putting Saturninus on the imperial throne. Now his son Lucius is the *candidatus*, but he's come to Rome not leading a column of Goth prisoners as his father had, but as a 'liberator' aided by Gothic backers. Will the Roman people accept him? When Marcus begins his speech recommending Lucius he draws the attention of the populace to Aaron's baby, declaring: 'Behold the child.' (5.3.118) The question that for a moment we think he's going to pose is: Would they prefer **this** inheritor, the offspring of Aaron and Tamora, to Lucius, Titus's son and heir? But in the event he doesn't go down that route at all. Marcus simply reminds them of the wrongs that Titus endured and argues that his revenge was justified. But it's not certain that the boy's still alive. Yes, Lucius made this promise to Aaron:

Say on, and if it please me which thou speak'st,
Thy child shall live and I will see it nourished (5.1.59-60)

- but note the condition. Lucius might have sworn his religious oath, sure in his heart that nothing in Aaron's confession could possibly **please** him, if he judged it in terms of moral acceptability rather than factual accuracy or political usefulness. If so, he tricked Aaron without breaking his oath. So when Marcus points at the baby saying 'Behold the child', we might be looking at its corpse. There's a directorial choice here. On the practical level you can hardly use a live baby, and a doll, even in swaddling clothes, will tend to appear to be dead. Either way, though, the possibility that the baby might be, or might have been, the Antichrist lingers. There's a tempting symmetry between the dangers that Aaron's so determined to protect his son from and the dangers that the child Jesus is protected from by his Father at the time of the Massacre of the Innocents.

My second speculation is this. In Matthew 5: 21-26 Jesus, explaining that he's 'completing', not abolishing, the Law of the prophets, roundly condemns revenge and anger. Shakespeare must have known those words. What's more, Jesus goes on (in verse 30) to say: 'And if your right hand should cause you to sin, cut it off and throw it away; for it will do you less harm to lose one part of you than to have your whole body go to hell.' Shakespeare would have known these words, too, and associated them with Titus's severed hand. And please don't say 'tosh' until you've checked the passage for yourself.

And here's my third speculation. Remember Timon? Yes, Timon of Athens. Like Titus, he's a worm that turns very slowly but when he does turn he turns completely. It's generosity-to-misanthropy in Timon's case and patience-to-revenge in Titus's - not too dissimilar – but where they click most neatly is in their laying on of special banquets to 'serve their enemies right'. There's nothing in the text to suggest a comparison between those feasts and the Last Supper, but it's bound to occur to some people, and if it does it'll be a **moral** comparison. Vengeful pagan banquets – no! Redemptive Last Supper – yes!

Francis Bacon's remark that 'revenge is a kind of wild justice' is neat and memorable, but neither incontrovertible nor original. The 'wild justice' idea had a long history, but whether or not Shakespeare knew and was remembering Aeschylean or Senecan plays when he wrote 'Titus Andronicus' it's clear that he had Thomas Kyd's 'The Spanish Tragedy' (1587) very much in mind. The only question was what to copy and what to out-do in the play that many in his audience would undoubtedly be comparing his own play with.

Heironymo, the Titus-equivalent in Kyd's play, loses his son in a treacherous murder and seeks to bring the criminals to book. But he can't find out who they are. In vain he calls on the 'sacred heavens':

…………………… If this unhallowed deed…..
Shall unrevealed and unrevenged pass,

49

How should we term your dealings to be just? (ST: 3.2.5
and 3.2.9-10).

The rulers and heirs of Spain and Portugal, to whom
responsibility for justice has been delegated by the gods,
are themselves implicated in the crime and have no interest
in dark deeds coming to light.

This is very much the sort of situation that we find in
'Titus Andronicus' (and, up to a point, in 'Hamlet'). The
hero can't leave the matter to the gods, or the worldly
authorities; he has to investigate and take justice into his
own hands. (It's still a very popular topic: think of all
those maverick cop films where the hero, unable to nail the
villains by legitimate means, goes for 'wild' justice
instead.)

The two plays also have very particular imagery, as well as
a general situation, in common. Tongues, speech, writing
and weapons figure in both.

When Heironymo eventually finds out who his son's
killers are he stages a play-in-a-play at court. (Yes,
Shakespeare used Kyd in 'Hamlet', too.) Pretend stabbings
turn out to be real ones. The king's guilty son and heir dies
under his father's eyes! Ah! revenge is sweet, etc. But
when the king realises what's happened he arrests
Heironymo and threatens him with torture to make him
reveal his secrets - although (to me at least) it's not clear
what secrets he's still concealing. It's an odd situation
(which was eliminated in the 1602 revised version of the
play), but in the original version Heironymo defies the
king with:

……... never shalt thou force me to reveal
The thing which I have vowed inviolate:

And therefore in despite of all thy threats…
First take my tongue, and afterwards my heart. (ST: 4.4.189-192)

Upon which he bites out his own tongue!

Can't speak, won't speak!

The King's brother, the Duke of Castile, who has also just lost his criminal son in the play-within-a-play, points out that there are other ways to extract the information:

Yet can he write. (ST: 4.4.196)

So a pen and paper are brought, and when Heironymo mutely indicates that he needs 'a knife to mend his pen' (4.4.200) he's handed just the tool he needs to finish the job. He sticks it into the Duke.

All these images recur in 'Titus' but they're used differently.

In Act 4, Scene 1 we find Lavinia frantically ruffling with her stumps through a copy of Ovid's 'Metamorphoses', looking for the passage that tells **her** story – Philomena's rape and mutilation by Tereus. When Titus sees it he cottons on quickly. 'Lavinia', he says,

     …..wert thou thus surprised, sweet girl,
Ravished and wronged as Philomena was,
Forced in the ruthless, vast and gloomy woods? (4.1.51-53)

She nods - just as she nodded when her uncle Marcus opened up this line of enquiry in Act 2.

Ovid tells him what's happened but not who did it. But he can see possibilities. Lavinia isn't deaf and she can give signs to say yes or no (or don't know) to any proposition that he puts to her. It would be possible to follow a painstaking process of elimination - did you know the man before? - was he a Roman? - or a Goth? - patrician or prole? etc, etc, and it might get him there in the end. (If Tamora's boys had played more parlour games of this kind at home as well as studying criminal literature in school they might have realised that their ruthless precautions weren't as copper-bottomed as they thought.) But Titus's mind, like Lavinia's, doesn't work like that. He's not into the progressive elimination of suspects; he looks for answers in the field of classical learning. Like Chiron and Demetrius he believes that history, poetry and myth have precedents for everything that happens. Just find the right precedent and you have the answer. But the Philomena story isn't coming up with any clues to the identity of the culprits, so Titus tries history. 'Give signs, sweet girl', he says, 'what Roman lord (two false assumptions there, note) it was that durst do the deed.' (4.1.61-62)

He recalls the story of Lucrece, raped by the emperor Tarquinius. (Yes, the same story that Shakespeare had recently told in his long narrative poem). If that story provides the precedent he's looking for it would point the finger at the current emperor, Saturnine, his enemy. 'Slunk not Saturnine,' he asks,

> ……… as Tarquin erst,
> That left the camp to sin in Lucrece's bed? (4.1.63-64)

Lavinia shakes her head. Nice try, but he's barking up the wrong tree.

Nil desperandum. There must be another way. But what? Then Marcus has a brain-wave. She can write it down. Yes, she **can**. Like this. He demonstrates by writing his name in the sand, holding one end of his staff in his mouth and steering the other end with his foot. If he can do it with his feet Lavinia can do it with her stumps. Not easy, but it'll work. Now where on earth did he get that idea from? Native ingenuity, or mythological precedent? The answer, believe it or not, is mythological precedent. And it's Ovid's 'Metamorphoses' again.

littera pro verbis, quam pes in pulvere duxit,
corporis indicium mutate triste peregit. (Book 1, lines 649-650)

(With her foot/hoof she scratched in the dust letters, in lieu of spoken words, giving the sad account of her bodily transformation.)

It's the story of Zeus – yes, him again! – who's raped Io and tried to conceal his crime by transforming her into a heifer. She can only make lowing sounds, but not speak, so she writes down what's happened for her father to read. Lavinia, please copy. She does, and it works. Titus reads:

Stuprum (rape) *– Chiron – Demetrius.* (4.1.78)

Only connect. People do a lot of connecting in this play, more than in most. And speaking of connecting, some people, possibly even Shakespeare, might be reminded of Jesus writing with his finger in the dust, rather than saying out loud, the sins of bystanders eager to condemn the woman taken in adultery. (John: 8)

As Titus's moment of revenge draws near he may be off the rails but as host at the banquet he can still put on a display of patrician courtesy and deference towards his guests.

Welcome, my gracious lord; welcome, dread queen;
Welcome, ye warlike Goths; welcome, Lucius;
And welcome, all. Although the cheer be poor,
'Twill fill your stomachs. Please you, eat of it. (5.3.26-29)

We shudder, but his guests don't. They're hungry!

As genial host he gets the conversation under way, too. Asking the emperor for his advice on a matter of family ethics he cites the case of a man called Virginius who slew his daughter because she'd been 'enforced, stained, and defloured'. (5.3.38) Had he done the right thing? Saturninus says he did,

'……..because the girl should not survive her shame.' (5.3.40)

The highest moral and legal authority in Rome, the emperor, - don't laugh! - recommends it as a 'pattern, precedent and lively warrant.' (5.3.43). It was an honour killing. So Titus unhesitatingly follows Virginius's example. He unveils the shrouded female figure standing at his side and plunges his knife into her, crying:

Die, die, Lavinia, and thy shame with thee;
And with thy shame thy father's sorrow die. (5.3.45-46)

'What hast thou done, unnatural and unkind?' (5.3.47) Saturninus asks, and Titus's answers: 'Killed her for whom my tears have made me blind.' (5.3.48) It was the right thing to do, so please don't let it upset you or put you off your supper.

Will't please you eat? Will't please your highness feed? (5.3.53)

Tamora, less fastidious and tucking into her meat pie, looks up and asks, 'Why hast thou slain thy only daughter thus?' and Titus has his reply ready. It was your beloved boys, Chiron and Demetrius who did it.

What?

They ravished her and cut away her tongue,
And they, twas they, who did her all this wrong. (5.3.56-57)

Tongue/wrong. From here on we need to look out for rhymes. They clinch things, and there are a lot of things being clinched now.

When Saturninus calls for the boys to be brought in for questioning Titus helps him to locate them without delay.

Why, there they are both, baked in that pie
Whereof their mother daintily hath fed,
Eating the flesh that she herself hath bred. (5.3.59-61)

Here there needs to be a longish silence, perhaps punctuated with incredulous laughter.

But this isn't just a 'sensation'; it's a moment of truth - logic even. Things now start happening very quickly, like a runaway machine in pell-mell self-repetition. In as many seconds three characters fall gasping or shrieking onto the floor, near Lavinia's body lying in a still-spreading pool of blood. Titus stabs Tamora and (in my imagination at least) stands over her for a moment with the pie-knife in his hand, watching her die. Then, in his rage and grief

Saturninus rushes at Titus and stabs him. Upon which Titus's son Lucius kills the emperor, saying,

Can the son's eye behold the father bleed?
There's meed for meed, and death for deadly deed -
(5.3.64-65)

Were you watching out for rhymes while this was happening? There was unkind/blind (47-48), tongue/wrong (56-57), fed/bred (60-61) and now bleed/deed (64-65). Rhyme – an ornament of verse, and so 'fitting' on occasions like this, don't you think?

Then, the stage direction tells us, there's 'uproar'. We don't know how Shakespeare's players would have done 'uproar' but we can probably assume that they didn't underplay it. This is a highly dramatic moment when the camera previously focussed on individuals pans out to encompass a new political landscape forming before our eyes. An emperor and an empress have been assassinated, a political revolution has broken out and there's a contingent of the Goth army on hand to quell resistance. 'Uproar' calls for more than a few shouts and a bit of running around on and off the stage with swords drawn. The director needs to build a substantial scene without words, using the whole stage, to make it clear what's happening and to give it full dramatic impact.

When some measure of order eventually returns the play's essentially over. Marcus and Lucius take charge and address the people from a gallery above the stage. This is a new start for Rome but, we have to ask ourselves, what's really new? The older generation is dead, but the youngsters are taking over pretty much where they left off. The revenge mind-set - an eye for an eye and a tooth for a tooth - is still alive and well. Lucius, whom we first saw suggesting that Alarbus should be dismembered and burnt, is now the top dog, and **still** condemning people to cruel deaths; Aaron is to be buried up to his neck in the ground until he starves. And he passes a *post mortem* sentence on Tamora, too. 'That heinous tiger,' he says,

No funeral rite, nor man in mournful weeds,
No mournful bell shall ring her burial;
But throw her forth to beasts and birds of prey.
Her life was beast-like and devoid of pity,
And, being dead, let birds on her take pity. (5.3.194-199)

Pity/pity – the perfect rhyme, a simple repetition. Nothing changes.

RICHARD THE THIRD

As every schoolchild should know, Richard the Third was slain at the Battle of Bosworth in 1485. For over a hundred years after that stories about his villainous reign circulated by word of mouth and in historical narratives such as Hall's 'The Union of the Two Noble and Illustrate Famelies of Lancastre and York' (1548). Hall's book incorporates Thomas More's famous account of Richard's life and character, which Shakespeare used as a major source. By the time the play appeared in 1594 Richard was already well-established as the nation's most celebrated monster monarch.

Many of the original audience would have turned up looking forward to a play about spectacularly dirty work at the political crossroads and wondering what it would tell them about Richard that they didn't know already.

And there he is, the man himself. *Solus*. Soliloquising. Nowhere else does Shakespeare open a play by showing the central character talking to himself, but it works very well here. It gives us immediate access to his scheming, sardonic mind.

Richard describes the current political situation and some of the events that led up to it. This is what it boils down to, if we add a few dates and details to link it with 'history'. The 'Wars of the Roses' have been over for a decade or more. In 1471, at the battle of Tewkesbury, the House of York, of which Richard himself is a leading member, finally overcame the rivalry of the House of Lancaster, and Edward IV (b.1442), the eldest son of the old Duke of York (1412-1460), became king. Since then there's been a period of exhaustion and bitter memories – 'the blessings of peace', as the current regime might describe them – in which the nation has had a chance to lick its wounds.

Richard's two opening lines –

Now is the winter of our discontent
Made glorious summer by this son of York (1.1.1/2) –

seem to strike a positive note. Dismal winter has turned into bright summer! In other words, things have got better since the war ended. But it's not **quite** that simple. Richard is reciting official Yorkist propaganda with his tongue in his cheek. He's not in a summery mood at all! The 'son of York' he's talking about is his elder brother, the current king, but he's by no means the only 'son of York' on the scene. The old Duke of York had two other sons - Clarence (b. 1449) and Richard himself (b. 1452), and since then no less than three more 'sons of York' have come to swell the scene – the king's sons, Edward Prince of Wales and the current Duke of York (the 'Princes in the Tower'), not to mention Clarence's young son. From Richard's point of view, of course, the fewer sons of York around the better. They have set him back from second to fifth in line to the throne.

'Son' is the word we see in the text, but in the context of Richard's 'seasonal' metaphor we can hear it as 'sun'. It's a pun on King Edward's royal symbol, the sun. Puns, of course, suggest a playful and ambiguous attitude to words and meanings, and for Shakespeare to put one into Richard's mouth in the second line of the play can be taken, without too much of a stretch, as a stroke of early characterisation. We've got a witty one here, it suggests. Witty and tricky. Later, Richard will sign up to that characterisation of himself when he identifies himself as the Vice Iniquity who, typically, 'moralises two meanings in one word'. (3.1.83)

What's a 'Vice'? you may ask. The answer is that he's a figure borrowed from the kind of old-fashioned Morality plays that used to tour the country from mediaeval times until they were banned under Elizabeth for being too closely associated with Catholic popular culture. (Young Will Shakespeare probably saw them staged in Stratford.) The Vice was originally a personification of a particular sin, e.g. Avarice, but later he came to represent evil in general. He was good box office, figuring simultaneously as MC/showman, star actor and up-to-no-good intriguer whose wicked machinations drove the plot forward. He often caused uncertainty as to whether he was simply an amusing theatrical entertainer or had to be taken rather more seriously than that. He was a virtuoso of cruel hypocrisy, feigning human sympathy to suit his purposes, but refusing to feign anything like shame. He was much given to soliloquy, not so much of the introspective as of the scheming kind, and always eager to take the audience into his confidence. He also set himself up as a dark moral commentator, putting his own unscrupulous but entertaining gloss on his own wicked deeds.

Vice is the stage name of the devil, of course. In the play Richard is referred to as a Vice only once, but repeatedly as a devil. (Too often for me to be bothered to count, but please feel free to count them yourself, if you're interested, and send me the answer on a postcard.)

Many in the audience will remember Richard as a younger (non-central) character in the Henry VI trilogy which had been staged a few years earlier. There he boasted that he could 'set the murtherous Machevil ('make-evil' –

geddit?) to school'. (3H6:3.2.193) The present play, which is essentially a sequel to that trilogy, brings us up to date on Richard's later career but it doesn't really give us a different take on his character. He takes his place in a line of spectacular theatrical villains which included Marlowe's Tamburlaine (1587-88) and Barabas in 'The Jew of Malta' (1590?), not to mention Aaron in Shakespeare's own 'Titus Andronicus' (1591–1594: there's disagreement about the precise date). The common stamp of these characters is godlessness, ambition, misanthropy and disdain for conventional ethics. Richard has all those attributes in full measure. He's as full of wintry discontent as his embattled old dad had been, and he identifies himself closely with him, sharing his Christian name and facial features (see 3.7.12-14) and regarding himself as the heir to the throne that the old Duke almost had within his grasp. He takes the view that ruthless warfare and political duplicity have much to be said for them: they are much more interesting than the insipid pursuits of 'this weak piping time of peace'. (1.1.24)

By his own account Richard is

Deformed, unfinished, sent before my time
Into this breathing world scarce half made up. (1.1.20-21)

His deformity, he says, rules him out for amorous and other trivial courtly pursuits, although it's no handicap in soldiering and political 'bustling'. If his misshapenness has cast him as a villain he's more than happy to play the part. He acknowledges a connection between outward deformity and inner aggression.

It's worth reflecting how physical deformity was often regarded in those pre-PC times. In 1612, the year that his cousin and political enemy Sir Robert Cecil died, Francis Bacon published an essay on Deformity. He doesn't actually name Cecil but everyone knew who it was that he had in his sights. Sir Robert, severely crippled from birth, had earned a fearsome reputation for cunning and cruelty in public life.

'Deformed persons,' Bacon wrote, 'are commonly even with Nature: for as Nature has done ill to them, so do they by nature; being for the most part (as the Scripture saith) void of natural affection; and so they have their Revenge of Nature....Whosoever hath anything fixed in his person that doth induce contempt, hath also a perpetual spur in himself to rescue and deliver himself from scorn. Therefore all deformed persons are extreme bold: first, as in their own defence, as being exposed to scorn; but as in process of time, by a general habit. Also, it stirreth in them Industry, and especially of this kind, to watch and observe the Weakness of Others, that they may have somewhat to repay....In a great Wit, deformity is an Advantage to Rising.'

Richard probably wouldn't have quarrelled with Bacon's analysis, although as a matter of fact he doesn't make much of his deformity or offer it as an excuse for what he does. Its chief relevance is to the attitude of others at the time towards deformed persons, who questioned whether a Creator who didn't even bother to fashion them properly was withholding the blessing He usually put on the rest of His human creation. They suspected that physical deformity was a sign of a generally deformed nature and a mark of divine displeasure.

'Watch me,' Richard tells us as the play opens. 'I'm going to stage an extravaganza of criminal duplicity which will make the world sit up. I'll deceive others, but not myself -

and not you. You'll have a ringside view of my villainous machinations as I devise them. They'll be clever and wicked and great fun, and I promise I won't spoil things for you by getting heavy about the ethics.'

Obviously these are dangerous waters that Richard's drawing us into, but he has a charisma which, at this stage anyway, is hard to resist. We're far more attracted to his high spirits than repelled by his physical ugliness or concerned about any harm that he intends to do to others.

Soliloquy over, Richard plunges straight into his agenda.

For what it's worth we can put a historical date on the beginning of the play. It's 1478, the year of his brother Clarence's death. Clarence stands ahead of Richard in the queue for the throne, so he's got to go, hasn't he? Richard doesn't beat about the bush. He reveals with startling candour how he has done the necessary preliminary work by pouring 'drunken prophecies, libels, and dreams' (1.1.33) into the king's ear in order to turn him against him. And here, right on cue, Clarence enters, under arrest on the king's orders and being escorted to the Tower. He hasn't the foggiest idea what's going on. As he approaches we see Richard transform himself, chameleon-like, from wicked plotter into loving brother. 'Dive, thoughts, down to my soul,' (1.1.41) he tells himself, switching on the breathtaking hypocrisy that this chance meeting calls for. With superb aplomb, he offers Clarence his sympathy and support, and gives him to understand that it's King Edward's wife, Queen Elizabeth, who's been plotting against him.

'Simple plain Clarence' is completely taken in. Later on, one step short of his doom, he will fondly remember how Richard

.... bewept my fortune,
And hugg'd me in his arms. (1.4.243-244)

We feel for Clarence as he describes his horrific *timor mortis* dream (1.4.2-75) but that was probably offset by our admiration for Richard's brilliant ability to 'moralise two meanings', telling Clarence that his plight 'touches me dearer than you can imagine' (1.1.112) and promising that 'I will deliver you or lie for you'. (1.1.115)

As Clarence is led trustingly off to the slaughter Richard immediately turns his attention to his next victim – Hastings - warning him that

.....they that were your enemies are his
And have prevailed as much on him as you. (1.1.130/131)

He's just getting the murderous ball rolling!

In 'Richard III' we shouldn't concern ourselves overmuch with 'historical' tie-ins. If we do we're liable to get very confused. The next scene, for example, is wildly anachronistic. As we noticed, Clarence died in 1478 but now, unaccountably, we're back in 1471, when Richard intercepted Lady Anne taking the body of Henry VI, her father-in-law, to Chertsey for burial.

When Richard halts the procession she turns on him in fury, berating him both for the murder of the king and of her husband, Edward, Prince of Wales. Richard's quite unfazed. He comments on her fury rather than on the charges that she's laying against him. Is it right, he asks, for Christians to allow themselves to get into such an incandescent rage? Aren't we taught to turn the other cheek?

Lady, you know no rules of charity,
Which renders good for bad, blessings for curses.
(1.2.68/69)

Somehow he's got onto the moral high ground and he's telling **her** off!

Richard's more-in-sorrow-than-in-anger reproach seems to slip unnoticed into the turbulent stream of Lady Anne's invective, but it doesn't sink entirely out of sight and mind. For the moment she rants on, further infuriated by his impudence. But he stands his ground as an innocent man would, and eventually his words find their target. Inside that storm of wrath there's a Christian woman in whose heart words like 'charity' and 'blessings' command respect, even if she suspects that they are being spoken by 'a devil telling the truth.' Richard has slipped a verbal wedge between the violence of her feelings and her sense of virtue and is forcing her to accept that he may just possibly have something to say that she ought to listen to. He's no longer **simply** a hate-object to be wildly assailed; now she must think about what she's saying to him and have answers to what he says to her. It takes some of the wind out of her sails. Her flow of vituperation is disrupted and their exchanges assume a new pattern - a dialogue, a 'keen encounter of wits'. (1.2.118) Richard has created room for manoeuvre in which he can reply to each of Lady Anne's outbursts in ways that may be more cheeky than convincing but which allows him to pose as the more dignified and reasonable of the two.

When she accuses Richard of killing King Henry VI, whose bier rests on the ground nearby, he remains unruffled and doesn't immediately deny it. (Historically speaking, it was probably his brother King Edward IV who was to blame, but that's beside the point here.) But when she goes on to assert that the sainted King Henry is 'in heaven, where thou shalt never come' (1.2.108) he does own up, though in chillingly cynical terms:

Let him thank me that holp him thither;
For he was fitter for that place than earth. (1.2.109/110)

This pious-perverse remark, coming as it does in the course of what has become a quick-fire exchange, finds Lady Anne short of a ready reply. She knows that it wasn't only Richard who thought that Henry had been too religious and unworldly to cut the mustard as a king. It was the view of a large section of public opinion, shared even by those who nevertheless set their faces firmly against rebellion and usurpation. It may even have been her own view. So Richard's reference, linked on one side with Richard's confession of the murder and on the other side with the pious sentiment about heavenly reward, has Lady Anne flummoxed. (This may be the point where the actress playing her shows the first signs of faltering in her attack.) Richard realises that now **he** has the initiative. To recover lost ground, Lady Anne needs either a fresh outburst of fury – although she's beginning to realise that fury is like water off a duck's back with Richard – or a smart riposte of her own - though she can't for the life of her think of one at the moment.

We may recall that Richard has already used the 'heavenly reward' sentiment in the previous scene. Of his brother, 'simple, plain Clarence' being taken under guard to the Tower he said,

..... I do love thee so
That I will shortly send thy soul to heaven,
If heaven will take the present at our hands. (1.1.118/120)

In other words: saints belong in heaven, leaving **this** world to people like me – which makes everybody happy. But the remark about Clarence was in a monologue; no-one else was expected to think up a reply. But that's just what Lady Anne has to do now – and she fails.

At another point, when she urges Richard to hang himself, he gives her another 'pious' reply. He reminds her of the Christian ban on suicide and protests that 'by such despair I should accuse myself.' (1.2.85) The question of suicide comes up again later in the same scene, although in a different connection. As Richard transmutes into lover mode he reminds her that suicide **is** often considered an option for the rejected suitor, if that is what he is to be. If Lady Anne rejects him he will kill himself – or, craftily shifting the responsibility, he'll get **her** to kill **him**. He puts on a stagey display of submission by placing his sword in her hands and inviting her to plunge it into his breast. She can't bring herself to do it (women don't take up these offers as often as they should, do they?) – and this gives him the nerve to push his luck a bit further. If you're too squeamish to do it yourself, he tells her, 'then bid myself to kill myself, and I will do it.' (1.2.189) But Lady Anne, having given full vent to rage for several minutes, finds that her resources of negative emotional energy have waned, and when it comes to it, her hunger for revenge has its limits. 'Though I wish thy death,' she says, 'I will not be thy executioner.' (1.2.187-188)

Accept me then, says Richard, or 'bid me to kill myself'. She replies, 'I have already' - as indeed she has - but he can see how to sidestep that now. 'That was in thy rage,' he says, (1.2.190) implying that her rage is now spent, and she makes no attempt to contradict him on this point. Richard pushes his luck again. If she still wants him to kill himself, he says, she has only to 'speak it again',

…………….. and even with the word,
This hand, which for thy love did kill thy love,
Shall for thy love kill a far truer love;
To both their deaths thou shalt be accessory. (1.2.191-194)

Even as lovers' pleas go - 'I killed your husband to win your love so my love is truer than his ever was' and 'if you reject my plea you'll be responsible for two deaths' - these are pretty absurd. Lady Anne must see that. Nevertheless, she can't bring herself to 'speak it again'. She can't revive, or pretend to revive, her rage. As other women will realise later in the play rage is often no more than an escape-valve for the feelings of impotent victims. It isn't revenge, which is what they're really after; it's **instead of** revenge.

If Richard's getting the upper hand it can hardly be because of his superior powers of logic. Although his arguments about suicide are feeble Lady Anne never even tries to dent them. Once her rage is spent she's reduced to a series of six short, stichomythic quibbles, protests and concessions. (1.2.195,197,199,201,203,205). How has she managed to lose a contest that she thought she couldn't possibly lose, justice being so overwhelmingly on her side? We've been watching closely but even we may not be quite sure exactly how it all went wrong.

It would be surprising if Richard didn't have flattery in his repertoire of wicked arts and yes, it's flattery that's the key here. He sees where her hope and security lie. She's been deeply shaken by the loss of her powerful patrons – her husband the Prince of Wales and her father-in-law King Henry VI - and now stands in need of male protection – which is what, if he chooses, he can offer. If only he were sincere that would be too good to be true for Lady Anne! But is he sincere? On the evidence so far, certainly not; but maybe he can still convince her. He puts his finger on her key weakness. Her rage spent, she has a better nature to be appealed to. She's not like Queen Margaret, never forgiving or forgetting. With her *ira,* like *vita,* is *brevis.* Short term she can do ranting virago in fine style but long-term she's a Christian woman for whom pious words would tend to have an effect, however untrustworthy coming from tricky Dicky, and still hold a serious and hopeful meaning for her.

At the end of the encounter Richard asks her to let him have the body of King Henry, the king he (allegedly) killed, so that as chief mourner he can take it to Chertsey for burial and 'wet his grave with his repentant tears.' (1.2.218) Oh, how Lady Anne **wants** to believe him! So she does, or pretends to herself that she does. It comforts her, as a Christian, to be able to regard Richard as a sinner whom she has brought to repentance. 'With all my heart,' she says as she hands over the bier,

…………………………………..and much it joys me too
To see you are become so penitent. (1.2.222-223)

That was **moral** flattery, but Richard can do **romantic** flattery, too.

'Love' is a word to conjure with. He works 'love' four times into two lines of the love plea quoted above. (1.2.191-194) After all that she's been through it's a word that brings balm to her tortured soul – even, if there's no-one else to say it, on Richard's lips. 'Divine perfection of a woman' (1.2.75), 'fairer than tongue can name thee' (1.2.81), 'fair creature' (1.2.135), 'sweet lady' (1.2.152) – these cast their devilish spell. If this were a pantomime – which up to a point it is – we'd shout: 'Don't listen to him!' although we know that she will. And when Richard makes the startling claim that it was her beauty that drove him to murder her menfolk (which, as we've noted, puts **her** in the wrong) he offers it as the ultimate proof of his devotion. What's a poor girl supposed to make of a compliment like that? She can hardly believe that her beauty **really** drove him to do such things, and if it did it shouldn't have, of course. But it might have been a factor, and she doesn't feel in a position to reject love out of hand, whoever's offering it. After all, Richard wouldn't be the first man to come under the spell of her beauty. Men are like that. And oh, how much she would like to feel that she had some – any! – hold on this terrifying man! And what kind of hold could it possibly be except sexual attraction? How different her prospects might be if, in spite of everything he's done, he **had** fallen for her! True, he's ugly, but that's not the main thing. He's certainly not a nonentity. He's a confident and capable man who knows how to look after himself in a dangerous world. How reassuring to believe that he'd really turned over a new leaf and wanted to take her under his wing!

The matter's far from settled, though. He's set her thoughts running along this new track but her original thoughts remain, which may now include self-disgust. She spits at him and wants to flee this 'diffused infection of a man' (1.2.78) who makes her feel so muddled and weary. He's won all the tricks, and even robbed her of what she could hardly imagine losing – her moral advantage. As she stumbles off stage leaving King Henry's bier in Richard's care, one thing is clear, though. Richard has taken her response to be a yes. Whatever her feelings, she has nothing left to say that will make him take no for an answer.

Shakespeare doesn't allow us to share any illusions that Anne may have in her moment of surrender. When she's gone we're back with the soliloquising Richard as he makes his feelings – or lack of them – clear:

I'll have her, but I will not keep her long. (1.2.232)

Richard's well-known methods of duplicity and intimidation have given him a negative political image. So far he's been able to live with it, and he certainly isn't plagued from within by conscience. But as he draws nearer to the throne a 'public relations' problem crops up which demands a different approach. He's short of political support in London. Hitherto we've watched his brilliant **solo** performances, but now he decides that the best way to tackle this problem is to go into a double act, with Buckingham as his stooge.

In Act 3, Scene 5 Richard and Bolingbroke go to the robing-room to select costumes for the parts they're going to play. They emerge in outfits described in the stage directions as 'rotten armour, marvellous ill-favoured', i.e. homely to the point of humble.

Richard talks his stooge into his part.

Come, cousin, canst thou quake and change thy colour,
Murder thy breath in middle of a word,
And then again begin, and stop again,
As if thou were distraught and mad with terror? (3.5.1-4)

No problem, says Buckingham. (You're not the only actor round here, you know.)

Tut, I can counterfeit the deep tragedian,
Speak, and look back, and pry on every side,
Tremble and start at wagging of a straw,

Intending deep suspicion. Ghastly looks
Are at my service like enforced smiles,
And both are ready in their offices
At any time to grace my stratagems. (3.5.5-11)

When the Lord Mayor of London enters the play-within-
the-play begins. They put him off balance by conjuring up
an atmosphere of (non-existent) civil disturbance, shouting
'look to the drawbridge', (3.5.15) 'o'erlook the walls'
(3.5.17) and 'here are enemies'. (3.5.19) As the Mayor
looks around anxiously for the attackers they hasten to
assure him that there's nothing to worry about after all. It's
only Lovell and Ratcliffe - friends. Phew! That's a relief,
he thinks, but what's that they're carrying? Lovell explains
that it's Hastings's freshly severed head!

In no more than nine swiftly spoken lines (3.5.14-23)
Richard and Buckingham have the Lord Mayor in just the
state of do-dah that they want him in.

Richard comes up with a perfectly judged 'more-in-
sorrow-than-in anger' speech - 'So dear I loved the man
that I must weep', etc. (3.5.24-32) - depicting himself as
the unsuspecting victim of a treacherous Hastings whose
plot to murder him he's discovered just in time. Even now
he can't rid himself of a sad, disillusioned love for the man
whose head his friends are waving about over there.
Buckingham chimes in, solemnly attributing the
unmasking of Hastings to Divine Providence. It's by that
'great preservation' that he and Richard are still around to
tell the story. 'The subtle traitor,' Buckingham explains,

This day had plotted in the council house
To murder me and my good lord of Gloucester *(i.e.
Richard)*. (3.5.37-39)

As the Lord Mayor tries to absorb this sensational news he senses Richard and Buckingham easing him into a political half-Nelson. Do you accept our story or do you think we are 'Turks or infidels' (3.5.41) capable of committing barbarous crimes in pursuit of tyrannical power? Can you imagine that anything other than dire peril to ourselves and our country would have induced us to act so drastically? The summary execution of Hastings is itself proof of the imminent danger that he posed for us all. It was him or us. Whose side are you on?

The Lord Mayor may or may not be persuaded. (The actor playing him needs to be given time to show us to what extent he's conned or cowed, or both.) As he dithers Buckingham admits that things haven't worked out exactly as he and Richard would have wished. They intended to haul Hastings up before him so that he could hear his confession from his own lips; unfortunately, though, Lovell and Ratcliffe, in their pardonable eagerness to see justice done and the interests of the state defended, have gone right ahead and chopped his head off. You saw them yourself just now, running in and waving it about. No, not a pretty sight! They meant well, of course, but they should have observed the due process of law. Their hot-headedness might tempt those of a critical or hostile disposition to 'misconster us' (3.5.61) and expose us to 'the censures of the carping world'. (3.5.68)

By now the Lord Mayor's anxious to assure them of his support, and he rushes off to a press conference at the Guildhall to make an official statement. And then, striking while the iron's hot, Richard starts briefing Buckingham on the follow-up story: that young Edward, Prince of Wales, the king's eldest son, is illegitimate and not entitled to succeed to the throne. Listen carefully, Buckingham, he says, this is what you tell them: first, that the king has always been a notorious libertine and the boy they call the Prince of Wales is just one of his many wild oats; and second, for good measure, that the king **himself** is illegitimate.

What!

Yes, listen! Edward may be my brother - in a way - but there's a dirty little secret about him which it's now time to make public.

Tell them, when that my mother was with child
Of that insatiate Edward, noble York
My princely father then had wars in France,
And by true computation of the time
Found that the issue was not his begot,
Which well appeared in his lineaments,
Being nothing like the noble duke, my father –
Yet touch this sparingly, as 'twere far off;
Because, my lord, you know my mother lives. (3.5.86-94)

This is news management of a high order, even by present-day standards, isn't it? It gets things moving in the right direction but it'll take more than this to win the hearts and minds of the Londoners who are still reluctant to join the cry of 'God save Richard, England's royal king!' (3.7.22) which Richard's stooges are raising in the streets. He needs a complete image-makeover, to bring him across to the public as a religious recluse, say, a man of God with a clear moral edge over all the worldly rascals who've sat on the throne before, particularly his own loose-living brother Edward. Interestingly, the model he selects for the purpose is Henry VI, whom he despised for his failure to assert his kingly authority but who, now he's murdered him (according to the play, anyway), has come to figure in the public mind as something of a royal saint and martyr. It's a deliciously perverse idea, but it might just do the trick. So that's how Richard now stages himself, flanked by two clergymen and clutching a prayer-book, protesting that the crown is the last thing he's interested in. All he craves is a bit of peace and quiet to pursue his pious studies. 'Alas', he says,

…why would you heap this care on me?
I am unfit for state and majesty.
I do beseech you to take it not amiss.
I can not nor I will not yield to you. (3.7.203-206)

Buckingham and Catesby keep up their pleas for him to think again, feigning exasperation with his backwardness-in-coming-forward. It's only when they pretend to run out of patience and seem to accept that when he says no he means no that Richard judges that the public will be convinced of his sincerity and he'll be safe to accept the crown, while still protesting, of course, 'how far I am from the desire of this'. (3.7.235)

It works. Enough of the people have been fooled enough of the time.

'Richard the Third' is a star-vehicle *par excellence*. Everything either focuses on or revolves around the career of Numero Uno. But it's anything but a one-man play. The list of *dramatis personae* is exceptionally long, including no less than thirty-five named characters and (about) twenty-four unnamed ones, not counting various 'extras' - halberdiers, gentlemen, lords, citizens, attendants, soldiers, etc. But this huge supporting cast doesn't generate anything worth describing as a sub-plot. Most of the characters figure in isolated episodes in Richard's career and then play no further part: examples are Clarence's two murderers (Act 1, Scenes 3 and 4), the three citizens (Act 2, Scene 3), the Lord Mayor of London (Act 3, Scenes 5 and 7), the Scrivener (Act 3, Scene 6) and Sir James Tyrell (Act 4, Scenes 2 and 3). But there are others, Richard's victims, who only get to strut the stage (though 'strut' is hardly the *mot juste* here) for as long as it takes Richard to dispose of them, and who put in brief reappearances as ghosts at the end. Overall, they contribute to the varied panorama of English life at the time – which is important in a history play – but as individuals they have only an *ad hoc* interest for us. We might even be tempted to classify Richmond, who goes largely unmentioned for most of the play and who only appears in the final act, as one of these transient figures, but the temptation has to be resisted because he personifies the better future that the play has been working towards. He's much more than just another come-and-go figure; he's the come-and-**stay** one.

Although Richmond is necessary for the dramatic outcome, he can't provide an adequate emotional or moral counter-balance to Richard as the play unfolds. That's provided by another group of characters who make more-than-occasional appearances and engage our emotional interest in an ongoing and incremental way. They help us to detach ourselves from our amused connivance in the villain's wickedness. They create more attention-space for the historical and personal memories of the victims, which 'bustling' Richard may not be interested in but which are essential features of the structure and eventual emotional direction of 'his' play. For much of the time things race along in their whacky-wicked way at Richard's pace but at other times they need to pause, reflect on suffering, articulate more consensual moral values than Richard's and 'wait' – patiently or impatiently – for the restoration of justice when Richard's appalling career has finally run its course. They complicate the structure of the play with variations of mood and tempo, making it much more than a series of interactions between the fascinating star character and his transient victims.

Yes, I mean the **women** characters.

There are four of them: 'old Queen Margaret'; the Duchess of York, widow of the 'grand old Duke', a leading campaigner in the civil war; Lady Anne, whose wooing by Richard we've already looked at; and Queen Elizabeth, the wife and now the widow of Edward IV and the mother of the Princes in the Tower.

Richard calls them 'these tell tale women' (4.4.150), as if they're a gaggle of gossips and there's an element of cartoon-style truth in this. From time to time they meet in a sort of committee to exchange somewhat competitive sob-stories and - up to a point, but only up to a point – to unite in their common misery. But they have their individual tales to tell, as well as a collective voice, and each gets her own opportunity to pronounce her own personal doom on him.

The first tell-tale woman is 'old Queen Margaret'. She was exiled to France in 1478 and died there about a year before Richard made it to the throne in 1483, so historically speaking she couldn't have been present in any of the scenes in which Shakespeare includes her. But that's neither here nor there. An anachronism? A poisonous political forget-me-not? A ghost? A prophetic fury? She's all of those not-quite-substantial things, but on stage also an powerful immediate presence. If Richard is a general-purpose Vice in a Morality play, Margaret figures as the Vice of Revenge. A French-born queen and widow of Henry VI, she bears an outsize grudge that the Lancastrians lost the war and that she lost her throne. She clamours for retribution but she's anything but an innocent bystander. She'd been a ruthless political and military leader in her own right, the perpetrator as well as the victim of a long tally of war crimes, although the only crimes she remembers now are the ones she was on the receiving end of. She wishes everyone ill but it's Richard that's she's now got especially in her sights.

Margaret's appearances have something hallucinatory, even hellish, about them. She frightens the audience (well, she frightens me) as well as the other characters. She doesn't hesitate to tell God where His duty lies. He must destroy Richard, no questions asked and without further ado, and considering her passion and eloquence we wouldn't be surprised if God decided that it would be wise to do exactly what she tells Him. Of course He doesn't (or not immediately) but her vituperation certainly leaves its mark on our expectations. Even when Richard's riding high she persuades us (as Shakespeare's prophets and soothsayers always do) that it's only a matter of time before he'll get his comeuppance.

In Act 1, Scene 3 they clash head-on. Margaret has been lurking in the shadows, making bitter asides as the courtiers - 'wrangling pirates' (1.3.157) as she calls them - argue amongst themselves. Now as she steps forward they recoil as if confronted by an apparition and 'quake like rebels' (1.3.161) - or at least that's how she sees it - as she demands that they pay her allegiance as their true queen. For her nothing has changed. In her all the old arrogance and resentment are preserved intact. But Richard's not impressed. The 'wrinkled witch' (1.3.163) is 'history'. He's got better (i.e. worse) things to do than listen to her. As he makes to go she calls him back with

Ah, gentle villain, do not turn away. (1.3.162)

He stops, and reminds her that she was banished on pain of death. Not that she's bothered by that! - ghosts don't fear death, do they? – and she launches into a tirade against them all. Richard counters by reminding her of her own crimes and insults against his own family and this rallies the pirates behind him - the killing of young Rutland, in particular, is indelibly recorded in the annals of national atrocity. But where is all this getting anybody? It's time to draw a line and move on, as the politicians like to say, but Margaret doesn't see it that way at all. She's not come to make friends and influence people, and she proceeds to denounce each and every one of them, cursing Queen Elizabeth, Rivers, Dorset and Hastings to their faces. Richard makes another move towards the door. But Margaret isn't going to let him go. The others were just practice shots to get her eye in. Richard's her main target. She hauls him back with:

Stay, dog, for thou shalt hear me. (1.3.215)

In the course of the colourful abuse that follows she calls him 'the troubler of the world's peace'.(1.3.220) It's a phrase that suggests that she thinks she's speaking on behalf of all Richard's poor, peace-loving victims, including herself, and how can he possibly gainsay her accusations? But the scene doesn't follow the expected route and develops in a quite unexpected way. As she heaps insults upon his head -

Thou elvish-marked, abortive, rooting hog,
Thou that was sealed in thy nativity
The slave of nature and the son of hell;
Thou slander of thy heavy mother's womb,
Thou loathed issue of thy father's loins,
Thou rag of honour, thou detested -- (1.3.227-232)

Richard suddenly interrupts her with 'Margaret!'

In other words, that's enough about **me**. Let's talk about **you.**

But she won't have it. 'Richard!' she screams back at him, it's **'thou'** I'm talking about!

Ha? says Richard, disconcertingly, as if asking, 'Are you addressing **me**?'

Margaret hesitates. Those six 'thous' stacked up on top of each other are addressing him all right, as he's well aware, so why's he talking as if she'd just called for his attention? 'I call thee not,' she replies.

Richard has arrested Margaret's apparently unstoppable rant at the word 'detested' (1.3.232) and the next four speeches – 'Margaret!', 'Richard!' 'Ha?' and 'I call thee not' – are all packed into the next line, 1.3.233. It's a remarkable example of the use of rhythmic variety for dramatic effect. It suddenly collapses Margaret's sustained diatribe into a dialogue of cross purposes, as follows:

Richard: I cry thee mercy then, for I did think
That thou hadst called me all those bitter names.
Margaret: Why so I did, but look'd for no reply.
O, let me make the period to my curse.
Richard: Tis done by me *(i.e. making the reply and finishing the curse)* and ends in 'Margaret'. (1.3.234-238)

Queen Elizabeth, a moment ago herself on the wrong end of Margaret's tongue, steps in as referee: 'Thus have you *(Margaret)* breath'd your curse against yourself.' (1.3.239)

The play abounds in curses. (If you counted up 'devils' before perhaps you'd like to tot up the curses now, and send me the answer on another postcard?) They include several examples of the boomerang, biter/bit kind - of which this is one - another being Lady Anne's curse on any woman 'mad' enough to marry Richard (4.1.74-76) - just before she does that very thing.

In one sense, the purely predictive, Margaret seems to have everything going for her. But in another sense, the moral, she's not going anywhere. Her words explode like bomb-blasts, sending deadly splinters out at 360 degrees. They're meant to be definitive **last** words, but they fall short of that. Ghost-like, she's obsessed with old unsettled scores, while the longer-term agenda of the play is to bring us beyond all that, to a place where they are settled and a new phase can begin. The God that Margaret believes in is Revenge. He's only there to mete out the sort of retribution that she, as a loser, isn't able to mete out herself. Like Richard, she's guilty of monstrous spiritual arrogance, although in her it takes a rather different form. He merely ignores the will of God because it isn't his own will; she takes it upon herself to tell God, in no uncertain terms, whom He must punish. They both strike us as wicked, completely ego-driven, power-mad individuals. Neither of them has any inkling of a more merciful Providence which it's the play's underlying purpose to reveal.

Shakespeare might well have given Margaret just that one grand-standing scene in Act 1, Scene 3 where she has that hair-raising set-to with Richard, and left it at that. But no, that was just for starters. He brings her back in Act 4, where she tells us of the direction that she now sees events beginning to take:

So now prosperity begins to mellow
And drop into the rotten mouth of death.
Here in these confines slily have I lurked
To watch the waning of mine enemies.
A dire induction am I witness to,
And will to France, hoping the consequence
Will prove as bitter, black and tragical. (4.4.1-7)

She's not off to France just yet, though. She lurks around
in the shadows a little longer, making bitter asides, before
emerging once again onto centre-stage, leading the other
women (although they are still her enemies and rivals!) in
a series of 'choral' laments. 'I had an Edward', *(i.e. the*
Prince of Wales, died 1471, son of Henry VI and the
previous husband of Lady Anne) she grieves,

     ..... till a Richard kill'd him;
I had a husband, *(i.e. Henry VI)* till a Richard kill'd him:
Thou (*Queen Elizabeth*) hadst an Edward, *(i.e. the younger*
of the princes in the Tower) till a Richard kill'd him.
(4.4.40-42)

To which the Duchess of York's rejoinder, coming from
the opposite side in the war, is:

I had a Richard *(i.e. the old Duke of York)* too, and thou
didst kill him;
I had a Rutland too; thou holp'st to kill him. (4.4.44-45)

The individual grievances still fester, but the tit-for-tat,
measure-for-measure rhythm of these - and other similar -
verses seems to summon up a collective curse-incantation
against the one man that they **all** have a grudge against –
Richard.

The second tell-tale woman is the Duchess of York. Widowed since 1460 she bore the 'grand old Duke' four sons: Edward IV; her beloved boy Rutland, captured in battle and killed by the Lancastrians 20-plus years ago; Clarence, recently murdered – as we've seen - by Richard, and Richard himself, the baby of the family. Blood may be thicker than water but she seems never to have had any motherly feelings for her last-born. He was always a wrong'un – a terrifying infant, born with teeth (see 2.4.28) who got nastier and nastier as he grew up, returning her lack of affection in spades. This is how he greets her in Act 2, Scene 2.

Richard: Madam my mother, I do cry you mercy:
I did not see your grace. Humbly on my knee
I crave your blessing.
Duchess: God bless thee and put meekness in thy breast;
Love, charity, obedience and true duty.
Richard: Amen; (rising; aside) and make me die a good old man.
That is the butt-end of a mother's blessing;
I marvel that her grace did leave it out. (2.2.104-11)

In Act 4, Scene 4, just after Margaret has made her last exit, the Duchess and her daughter-in-law Queen Elizabeth hear Richard approaching, 'marching with drums and trumpets.' Queen Elizabeth is rather dreading seeing Richard again, but the Duchess can't wait to go and give him a bit of her mind. 'Go with me,' she says,

And in the breath of bitter words let's smother
My damned son, that thy two sweet sons smother'd.
(4.4.133-134)

'Smother/smother'd' in the mouth of a mother! Am I stretching it to suggest that there's something subliminal going on here? Two (or two and a half) child murders haunt her imagination. The first is the death of her grandsons, the Princes in the Tower - has gossip reached her, or is she just imagining, that they died by suffocation? The second is the half-murder that she **didn't** commit on her own son, but wishes she had. She could have smothered him with blankets when he was a baby – an undetectable cot death. Now it's too late. 'Smothering' him with bitter words is a belated substitute.

The Duchess is set to add her own 'last-straw' maternal curse to the heap of curses that Richard has already brought down on himself. These are her last words to her son as he braces himself for the battle to save his life and secure his crown:

My prayers on the adverse party fight,
And there the little souls of Edward's children
Whisper the spirits of thine enemies
And promise them success and victory.
Bloody thou art; bloody will be thy end.
Shame serves thy life and doth thy death attend. (4.4.191-
196)

Spirit-shaking words! But if Richard himself feels shaken he certainly doesn't show it. But he wouldn't, would he?

The third tell-tale woman is Lady Anne. Since we last saw her in Act 1 she's become Richard's wife, and by Act 4, when he's finally clambered to the top of the greasy pole, she's about to become the new queen of England. Success story? Hardly. Her married life has been sheer hell. She's lived with the belief that he murdered her previous husband and her father-in-law Henry VI. She sorely regrets that she ever let her 'woman's heart...grossly grow captive to his honey words' (4.1.78-79) and recalls the boomerang curse she placed on him at the time.

> .... 'Be thou,' quoth I, 'accurs'd
> For making me, so young, so old a widow;
> And when thou wed'st, let sorrow haunt thy bed;
> And be thy wife, if any be so mad,
> More miserable by the life of thee
> Than thou has made me by my dear lord's death.' (4.1. 71-76)

She should have been more careful about what she wished for!

Stanley enters to tell her that Richard requires her presence immediately. She's to be crowned queen. Her reaction is: 'Despiteful tidings! O displeasing news!' (4.1.36)

After her unimpressive showing in Act 1, Scene 2 we might be tempted to share Richard's dim view of Lady Anne. The Christian woman who 'forgave' him has hated him virulently ever since, and now she's willing to share a private-life secret with the other tell-tale women, confident that it'll go straight from them into the tabloids:

> ......never yet one hour in his bed
> Did I enjoy the golden dew of sleep,
> But with his timorous dreams was still awaked. (4.1.82-84)

'Timorous dreams!' So Richard isn't all Nietzschian Will to Power; he's also prey to unconscious terrors. He has a psychological Achilles heel.

The fourth tell-tale woman is Queen Elizabeth. At the beginning of the play she figured as the wife of the ailing Edward IV, opposing Richard's attacks on her family.

Now, since Edward's death in 1483 she figures as his beleaguered widow and the anguished mother of the Princes in the Tower. Richard despises her and her family because they are *arrivistes;* not the stuff of genuine royalty. In Act 4 she learns to her dismay that Richard has vetoed her from visiting her captive sons and she has to face the fact - although there's been a news blackout – that they've probably been done away with. She has ceased to be Queen of England, which is the least of her cares, except that it leaves her and her family fully exposed to Richard's malice. And he's got his eye on her. When she decides (with Stanley's complicity) to send her son Dorset to safety with the exiled Richmond in Brittany she aligns herself with the opposition party plotting invasion and regime change. She has one good card left to play - her young daughter.

Rumours have been circulating that Lady Anne hasn't been enjoying the best of health and now – surprise, surprise – her death is announced. Natural causes or murder? Few details have emerged but Richard seems neither shifty nor grief-stricken. But he wouldn't, would he? He simply starts looking for a new bride-queen to strengthen his political position. For a man with such a reputation as a devious intriguer he goes about things in a remarkably straightforward way. He sets off as a 'jolly thriving wooer' (4.3.43) to see Queen Elizabeth and persuade her to let him marry her daughter. Naturally, she'll offer resistance but he's confident of overcoming it, just as he overcame Lady Anne's.

The 'tell-tale women' (i.e. Margaret, Queen Elizabeth and the Duchess of York) have been having one of their get-togethers. Queen Elizabeth, aware that Richard is coming to find her, has asked Margaret for a bit of pre-match morale-boosting and coaching in the rhetoric of denunciation. She's going to need it. Margaret's advice is for her to psyche herself into maximum rage and include all the lies and exaggerations she can think of:

Margaret: Forbear to sleep the nights, and fast the day;
Compare dead happiness with living woe;
Think that thy babes were sweeter than they were,
And he that slew them fouler than he is.
Bettering thy loss makes the bad-causer worse.
Revolving this will teach thee how to curse.
Elizabeth: My words are dull. O quicken them with thine.
Margaret: Thy woes will make them sharp and pierce like mine. (4.4.118-125)

This is the last we hear of Margaret. She goes off, leaving her quaking *protégée* to cope on her own. She doesn't reappear as one of the ghosts on the night before Bosworth. She manages to get to get back to France and die (1482) in time, so she has the necessary death certificate, but Richard wasn't actually her 'cause of death' and in any case Shakespeare couldn't see her conforming to the formula he uses in Act 5, i.e. giving short speeches to each ghost first damning Richard and then praising Richmond, before evaporating back into the next world. Margaret would over-run on the damning and never get round to the praising because she just doesn't **do** praise, or hope. She's not really interested in the future, except in seeing vengeance done; she just wants the clock turned back to her own heyday.

With Margaret on her way back to Anjou and Lady Anne dead, the women's committee is now down to two. But as Richard arrives on stage with a fanfare of drums and trumpets they are both 'up for it'. Margaret's final pep-talk still rings in their ears. The Duchess says: 'The trumpet sounds; be copious in exclaims' (4.4.135) and 'copious' they certainly are. Richard walks straight into an ambush of accusation and denunciation. When he asks, 'Who intercepts me in my expedition?' (4.4.136) his mother tells him, amongst other things, that she wishes she could have 'intercepted' him by 'strangling him in her accursed womb'. (4.4.138) – aborted him! Then Queen Elizabeth joins the attack. 'Tell me, thou villain-slave, where are my children?' (4.4.144)

Oh dear, Richard thinks. The tell-tale women have been working themselves up into a state again. Dead children! Dead children! Don't they ever think about anything else?

He orders the soldiers to drown out the women's voices with their trumpets and drums - which they do, for a while. But when silence returns and they can hear themselves think again the Duchess is still speaking (*sotto voce?*), reciting her final curse on him. (4.4.191-196, as quoted above) Then she, too, is gone, forever.

When Richard confronted Lady Anne she had a small escort of soldiers with her – not that they were much use. Now he has Queen Elizabeth, all on her own. Is this going to be a re-run of the Lady Anne *débâcle*? She hasn't got Lady Anne's incandescent, though unsustainable, rage and has needed that last-minute motivational coaching from Margaret. On the other hand she may have more of the right stuff in her. Richard himself has given her a kind of testimonial when he described her son Prince Edward as

    …………a perilous boy,
Bold, quick, ingenious, forward, capable.
He is all the mother's, from the top to toe. (3.1.153-155)

She makes a rather diffident start.

Though far more cause *(i.e. than the Duchess),* yet much less spirit to curse
Abides in me. (4.4.197-198)

Good, thinks Richard. Cursing's a waste of time at the best of times. If she'll just pipe down for a minute I should be able to convince her that my proposal to marry her daughter is good news for all concerned.

Elizabeth's reply might sound more pleading than defiant were it not for its bitter irony -

I have no more sons of the royal blood
For thee to slaughter. For my daughters, Richard,
They shall be praying nuns, not weeping queens,
And therefore level not to hit their lives. (4.4.200-203)

It occurs to her to take a leaf out of Richard's book. In his spin-campaign to convince the public that the Princes in the Tower were not in true royal line for the throne, he'd put it about that their father, King Edward, was illegitimate, casting his - and his own - mother, the Duchess of York, in the role of an adulteress. What if she were now to put it about that her own daughter is illegitimate and herself an adulteress? Might it persuade him to reconsider his marriage plans?

Richard sees this as his chance to take a moral step up. (We remember how smoothly he did this with Lady Anne.) If she's prepared to resort to the same dark arts of public relations as he's used himself it rather undermines her claim of moral superiority, doesn't it? He doesn't actually say 'you wicked woman, to be talking like that' but the implication is there in his reproachful:

Wrong not her birth. She is a royal princess. (4.4.212)

All right, then. Nobody's perfect. So he judges that this might be as a good moment as any to own up that, yes, he was 'indirectly' (4.4.226) involved in the murder of her sons, although he hadn't done the killing personally, of course. What he did was bad but, to be fair, not **that** bad.

Our heart goes out to her, to have to listen to **that**. She ought to be murdering him in revenge for her sons, not arguing with him. Words are no substitutes for deeds. Vengeance is not what you say, it's what you do.

But that still use of grief makes wild grief tame,
My tongue should to thy ears not name my boys
Till that my nails were anchored in thine eyes,
And I in such a desperate bay of death,
Like a poor bark of sails and tackling reft,
Rush all to pieces on thy rocky bosom. (4.4.230-235)

It's worth teasing out the thought-sequence here. i) My angry words only diffuse my rage, which needs to be enacted; ii) I should be clawing your eyes out with my nails (we may recall Hecuba blinding Polymestor in Ovid's 'Metamorphoses') without having to explain why I'm doing it; and iii) but if I do attempt violence I'll be like a doomed and helpless ship beating itself to pieces on the rocky shore of your merciless heart. We notice how 'anchored' links an image of violence (nails gouging out Richard's eyes) to an image of victimhood (shipwreck casualty). Violence and victimhood, fury and failure – yes, it does rather look like the Lady Anne story all over again.

But Lady Anne **did** eventually take a sort of revenge on Richard. She told the world about his 'timorous dreams', his Achilles heel. But she had her own Achilles heel, too, which was that, as a Christian, she was over-eager to be taken in by Richard posing as a sinner willing to repent and make reparation. Richard saw that behind her self-stoking rage stood another Lady Anne longing to forgive him. He knew how to exploit the situation: just tell her what you know she's dying to hear. It worked a treat with her, so let's give it a go with Elizabeth. Love and making amends have a lot of pull with women, he's found.

'Rocky bosom'? he protests. **Me?** Oh, no. Where did you get **that** idea?

I intend more good to you and yours
Than ever you or yours by me were harmed. (4.4 238-239)

He means it - i.e. it's in his interests to have her believe it. He needs her help. Just tell your daughter that I love her 'from my soul' (4.4.256) and that if she marries me I'll make her the Queen of England. It's an offer you can't refuse.

Pull the other one, she thinks. How, after all the harm he's done to her and her children, could he **dare** to talk of making amends?

Elizabeth took a wrong step when she promised, albeit sardonically, to bastardise her daughter. Now Richard takes a wrong step in using the phrase 'from my soul'. It catches Elizabeth on the raw. She snaps back: 'So from thy love's soul didst thou love her brothers.' (4.46.260) He realises, too late, that he's failed to tread the faint and wobbly line between sincerity and protesting too much. The score's level again.

We've had our misgivings about Elizabeth, as she seems to have had herself, but her next remark makes us see that she's a woman to be reckoned with. That's as maybe, she says, but 'who dost thou mean shall be her king? (4.4.265)

To hint that the king in question might turn out to be Richmond is high treason. But Richard stays calm. He doesn't need telling that it could be Richmond, but he's not going to admit that. What on earth is she talking about? he asks. Who can the king be other than 'even he that makes her queen. Who else should be?' (4.4.266) In other words, who else could 'who else' be, but himself? He has no heir (yet), and he's not aware of any rivals.

We know all too well that Richard plays clever games with people, but now we see that Elizabeth can match him at it. She masks the riskiness of suggesting that there might be another king in the offing by the quiet and accommodating manner in which she agrees to advise him on how to woo her daughter. But that's another feint. Since you ask, she says, the best way to woo the girl might be to take her through a tick-list of the seven members of her family that you've bumped off over the years.

Richard pretends to be naively hurt by her sarcasm.

You mock me madam. This is not the way
To win your daughter. (4.4.283-284)

She's flippant. But he's serious. And he's not asking much – only that she will assure her daughter that everything he did was done 'for love of her'. (4.4 288)

But this cuts no ice either. She replies:

Nay, then indeed she cannot choose but hate thee,
Having bought love with such a bloody spoil. (4.4.289-290)

Richard takes this as his cue for a long speech (4.4.291-336) in which he sets out his full plan for 'making amends'. It starts with what hardly amounts to an apology, let alone an expression of remorse -

Look what is done cannot now be amended:
Men shall deal unadvisedly sometimes
Which after-hours give leisure to repent. (4.4.291-293)

Elizabeth's joy in her daughter's advancement, he says, will console her for the loss of her sons. When the girl marries him and gives him an heir she'll become the proud grandmother of the heir to the throne. What's more, her son Dorset will be able to return from exile to find high favour at court. All the old griefs and grudges will be forgotten. 'What!' Richard exclaims, 'we have many goodly days to see!' (4.4.320)

Richard believes that if only she's prepared to subordinate her subjective feelings to objective facts she'll feel the force and appreciate the benevolence of what he's saying. As he paints the picture of a happily re-united royal family we wonder if he's getting through at last. When he calls Elizabeth 'mother' (4.4.325) we gasp at his infernal cheek, but she doesn't actually slap his face.

When Elizabeth replies we notice that she's switched from argument (which defies the interlocutor to reply) to questioning (which invites him to). As if asking for his advice, she begins: 'What were I best to say?' (4.4.337) Is she about to do a Lady Anne? But then she extends her question into another devastating rebuttal of everything he's been saying. What were I best to say to my innocent young daughter if she asked me whether marrying her uncle would be incestuous?

Richard has nothing to say to this and steers the conversation (for the moment) away from love, happy families (and incest) to patriotism. Tell the girl, he replies, that it's all for the good of the country. *Raison d'état*. 'Infer fair England's peace by this alliance.' (4.4.343) Mothers with the best interests of their daughters, and their country, at heart may sometimes have to advise them to 'think of England'.

This encounter – and it's not over by a long chalk yet! - holds us enthralled, partly because we have a sense that it marks a pivotal point in the action and partly because of the quality of the arguments. It interestingly recaps the earlier 'keen encounter of wits' in Act 1, Scene 2, although here the wits prove to be more evenly balanced than they were between Richard and Lady Anne. But the business that Richard and Elizabeth have to discuss isn't at all complicated: he simply wants her to persuade her daughter to marry him, while she tells him that she'd rather not, thanks very much. The confrontation runs for no less than 230 lines and as there's no more than this at stake there's a risk of it eventually becoming long-drawn-out and repetitive. The reason why it doesn't lies in Shakespeare's artful rhythmic structuring and variations of tempo. Up to this point (i.e. up to 'fair England's peace'), extended speeches have been interspaced with more rapid 'hand-to-hand' repartee, and now the general tempo accelerates as the protagonists reel off a succession of two-line exchanges in each of which Richard advances a brief argument for Elizabeth to parry. For example:

Richard: Say I will love her everlastingly.
Queen Elizabeth: But how long shall that title 'ever' last?
Richard: Sweetly in force, until her fair life's end.
Queen Elizabeth: But how long fairly shall her sweet life last? (4.4 349-352)

Done at the right pace this is literally breathtaking stuff. And the impression grows that Elizabeth is not only holding her own but beginning to get the upper hand. It isn't that Richard's serve is faltering but that her return of serve is at least equal to it. If the actors want to underline this point they can have her returns coming back faster and faster while he needs more and more time between serves. His 'your reasons are too shallow and too quick' (4.4.361) can sound like a loser's plea for a breather. But Elizabeth's not in a sporting mood. The words 'shallow' and 'quick' trigger her most telling return so far. 'O no,' she flashes back, 'my reasons are too deep and dead.' (4.4.362) She never forgets that she's talking to the man who killed her sons.

Richard still lacks traction. So far, he's sworn by love and making amends but they don't seem to have cut the mustard. What other 'sacred' and 'honourable' things can swear by now? There's royal prestige, of course. What could be more sacred and honourable than the symbols of kingly power? 'Now by my George,' he protests, 'my Garter and my crown.' (4.4.366) But Elizabeth knocks all three down in one swipe -

Profaned, dishonoured, and the third usurped. (4.4.367)

Now the music changes pace again, as their exchanges accelerate into a succession of two-beat vows and three-beat rebuttals:

Richard:	Then by myself -
Queen Elizabeth:	Thyself is self-misused.
Richard:	Now by the world -
Queen Elizabeth:	'Tis full of thy foul wrongs.
Richard:	My father's death -
Queen Elizabeth:	Thy life hath it dishonoured.

Richard:	Why then, by God –
Queen Elizabeth:	God's wrong is most of all.

(4.4.374-377)

Richard's invocation of 'God' draws her into a more extended speech. (4.4.377-387) She asks Richard how he can dare to invoke God when he blasphemously killed the Princes – her sons, whom God Himself had placed before him in line for the throne? She morally strip-searches him and exposes his irreparable credibility gap.

What can'st thou swear by now? (4.4.387)

But Richard, *nil desperandum*, always comes up with something. He finishes her line, adding his own two-beat reply to her three-beat question, with: 'The time to come!' (4.4.387)

So this, if anything, is what he **really** believes in. 'The time to come' - the nation saved and prosperous and himself still in charge. He will be justified by 'History', which always justifies politicians who promise 'goodly days', provided they survive to deliver them.

Elizabeth doesn't allow him to develop this point, and she's in no mood for more repartee. She has a serious point to make (requiring nine lines) which culminates in:

Swear not by time to come, for that thou hast
Misused ere used, by times ill-used o'erpast. (4.4.395-396)

This is where Queen Elizabeth marks herself off decisively from Lady Anne. The past can't just be air-brushed away. Richard's criminal past must be paid for - by **him**. Why believe that 'the time to come' will be any better than the time before if the same man remains in power? He calls on

'Heaven and fortune' (4.4.400) to destroy him if he doesn't make her daughter a good husband and manage to avert the dangers threatening the nation. But by the time he begs her to

Plead what I will be, not what I have been;
Not my deserts, but what I will deserve (4.4.414-415)

we feel that he's beginning to repeat himself, as he is when he appeals to her to put aside her 'peevish' (4.4.417) personal feelings in favour of seizing her political opportunity and doing her patriotic duty.

When Richard finishes this speech there needs to be a pause, to emphasise the magnificent musical 'shaping' of the scene, before Elizabeth opens a new sequence of one-line exchanges with:

Shall I be tempted of the devil thus? (4.4.418)

There's a distant echo of Lady Anne's 'O wonderful, when devils tell the truth' (1.2.73) here, which reminds us of how her resistance crumbled. It makes us wonder why Elizabeth is switching again from argument to questions, as if **her** mind is still not made up. We hope that her 'Thus' is ironic, as if to say: are these same-again arguments the best that a crafty devil like you can come up with? But there's nothing else there to confirm that ironic reading. The whole issue continues to hover before our eyes. At one moment it looks as if Richard's beginning to run out of arguments; in the next we seem to hear Elizabeth asking him for advice. Shakespeare juggles with hints and uncertainties and possibilities. - one of which is that although she was **genuinely** diffident at the beginning of the encounter, she may now only be **feigning** diffidence.

Richard has a question to answer and he answers it. Of **course** she should take the advice of the devil – if that's who she thinks he is, and why should he bother to deny it - 'if he tempt you to do good.' (4.4.419) She picks up on Richard's own use of the word 'self' a moment earlier when he promised to change – 'myself myself confound,' (4.4.399) which can be construed as: one of my two apparently identical selves will overcome – and/or be confused with – the other, and the change will be for the better. Elizabeth now follows exactly the same thought-process by asking: 'Shall I forget myself to be myself?' (4.4.420) But by framing of the words as a question she leaves it uncertain whether the forgetting or the forgotten self is her true and better self. Richard sees immediately how the (arguably) better practical **outcome** promised in his 'myself myself confound' phrase is being confronted by the issue of personal **integrity** in Elizabeth's phrase about 'forgetting'. He needs to muddy the waters again: 'Ay, if your self's remembrance wrong yourself.' (4.4.421) In other words, if it's in your (worldly) interest to change your mind, just change it. Don't worry about personal integrity.

Richard's logic is beginning to look like hair-splitting and Elizabeth seems to have given up arguing. Her next line starts with 'yet', as if she's asking him to help her overcome one last reservation before she gives in: 'Yet thou didst kill my children.' (4.4.422)

That's not 'one last reservation' at all, is it? It's the crux of the matter. Richard doesn't know whether she's weakening or not but he senses that he needs to deliver one devastating, now-or-never knock-out blow. Stand back! Here it comes!

But in your daughter's womb I'll bury them,

Where, in that nest of spicery, they will breed
Selves of themselves, to your recomforture. (4.4.423-425)

As Richard sees it, these three powerful lines are the
clincher. They address all of Elizabeth's three objections:
1) The idea of the royal heirs 'breeding selves of
themselves' is a witty and conclusive-sounding pick-up of
the 'self' topic. 2) The idea that they should do it in their
sister's womb is neat, too. 'Nest of spicery' (i.e. the nest
where, in Arabia, dead phoenixes re-incarnate themselves)
is a honey'd poetic phrase that should suffice to overlay
any gross associations. 3) Elizabeth, not knowing where
her sons' bodies are, can now rest assured that they'll be
buried with suitable honour. (He remembers that his
promise to give Lady Anne's dead relatives honourable
burial had the desired soothing effect on her.)

There's an element of outrageous humour in these three
lines but if you find yourself chuckling maybe you should
go and see a shrink. They give us a straight unobstructed
view of Richard's madness and monstrous abnormality.
He knows how to manipulate and control people, but he
doesn't really 'get' human feelings, moral or emotional, at
all. All the women, and most of the men, in the play come
to the conclusion that he's not just wicked but a devil
whose true nature falls outside the pale of humanity. In the
end he simply makes their blood run cold.

Elizabeth, with terrifying self-possession, taunts him with
one last question: 'Shall I go win my daughter to thy will?
(4.4.426) Again, the words cut both ways. Richard may
well hear them as an indication of her imminent
capitulation. But they may equally carry a silent tag-on of
irreducible defiance – 'because I won't do it, whatever you
say!'

Is she feinting again when she promises to let Richard know what her daughter says? He assumes that this means he's won and celebrates by calling her 'mother' – again! - and giving her a gallant farewell kiss, asking her to pass it on to her daughter as 'my true love's kiss.' (4.4.430) But as she takes her leave he says, just out of her hearing:

Relenting fool, and shallow, changing woman! (4.4.431)

What are we supposed to make of all this? Is this a last-minute victory for Richard? Or does Elizabeth hold out, in spite of her last words, while Richard's mind veers into delusion?

You decide.

For the first two-thirds of the play Richard's career unfolds rapidly, with each episode following the previous one in apparently unstoppable 'what-he-did-next' succession. But in Act 4 there's a sequence of four scenes that cuts right across the line and rhythm of that sort of action and shows the tide beginning to turn. The tell-tale women appear in the first and the fourth of those scenes.

In Scene 1 they appear 'in committee', submitting dire reports on what Richard has done to them and their families.

In Scene 2 we see Richard, having just graduated from Lord Protector to King, asking, with a new note of uneasiness:

.....shall we wear these glories for a day?
Or shall they last, and we rejoice in them? (4.2.5-6)

- and organising the murder of the princes in the Tower to make himself feel a bit more secure.

In Scene 3 the women remain off-stage but their complaints are powerfully side-lit by Tyrell's heart-breaking account of the 'tyrannous and bloody act' (4.3.1-22) in which the Princes die in the Tower.

In Scene 4 the women are back in force again, initially in a long passage of choral-competitive grieving and recrimination and then, in the even longer confrontation between Richard and Elizabeth where she becomes their spokeswoman. We always knew that Richard's behaviour was indefensible, and that things couldn't go on like this. Now the women have loosened his hold over us and got us prepared for his downfall. We recognise the lineaments of a political cliché: with whatever compelling self-assurance the villain begins, and however he keeps us entertained by his crimes along the way, his career will end in a big crash. He'll be more a warning than a joke.

The PC doctrine of the day insisted on true title in kingship. Richard's two-year reign defied this doctrine but never undermined it. There was always a true king – Richmond - waiting in the wings, even if he isn't mentioned until late in Act 4 and doesn't set foot on stage until Act 5, Scene 2. The doctrine was part and parcel of an overwhelmingly Christian mediaeval religious culture where the characters refer continually to oaths, curses, prayers, invocations, devils, angels, saints, heaven, hell, and God. For most of the characters these are features of the faith that binds society together but for 'godless' Richard they are matters for light, hypocritical or even blasphemous comment. In addition to his casual oaths, like 'by Saint Paul' (1.2.36 and 3.4.75) and 'by God's holy Mother' (1.3.305) we see him in his confrontation with

Elizabeth recklessly but unavailingly summoning up all sorts of 'holy' things to swear by. We also recall the brazen cynicism with which he tries to get the London public to believe that he has an aversion to loose language! In Act 3, Scene 7 we find him surrounded by conniving bishops and priests testifying to his moral integrity as he pretends to reject Buckingham's offer of the throne. This is the game they've agreed to play and they play it for all it's worth. When Buckingham flounces off-stage with: 'Come, citizens. Zounds! I'll entreat no more', (3.7.218) he gives Richard his cue for a neat bit of moral one-upmanship. ('Zounds' - God's wounds - was a pretty mild, widely-used oath which only someone who'd lived a very sheltered life would be likely to jib at.) But Richard looks deeply pained and draws a deep breath before gently rebuking him for profanity: 'O do not swear, my lord Buckingham'. (3.7.219)

Here we joined in the joke, but later, when nobody's laughing, Buckingham finally has to draw the line at killing the Princes. Richard has created a world in which, however ruthlessly he acts, he can never feel, or actually be, safe. He trusts nobody, and nobody trusts him, and the lack of trust is politically, as well as morally, disastrous because it weakens his purchase on events. It's not just a matter of ingratitude; he **needs** to keep co-villains around him for practical purposes. Without them he's down to paying hirelings to do his dirty work.

Facing execution, Buckingham ends his final speech with:

Come lead me, officers, to the block of shame.
Wrong hath but wrong, and blame the due of blame.
(5.1.28/29)

He isn't simply disillusioned; he's **contrite**. He acknowledges not only that he's been wronged but that he's done wrong himself. And in this, along with Clarence and Hastings, we can see he's part of a pattern. They, too, are far from innocent, but they die not merely disappointed but **repentant**. We may speculate whether Richard's final far-from-innocent victim – himself - will follow the same course. Obviously the answer, leaked in advance by 'history', is no; but Shakespeare doesn't want it to look too much of a foregone conclusion. In Act 5, Scene 3 he gives us an important scene in which Richard's fate in this world and the next, hangs in the balance. He awakes from a deeply dismaying dream crying, 'Have mercy, Jesu!' (5.3.178) and there's nothing to suggest that he's speaking in his usual light, hypocritical or blasphemous way this time. He means it! This is a prayer, not just another oath. It shows how profoundly shaken he is, and it confirms what we may have suspected throughout, that Richard's an enemy of God, not a disbeliever in Him. (cf the atheist Aaron in 'Titus Andronicus'.) He's set himself against the will of God by dedicating himself to the acquisition of kingly power, to which he has no legal or moral right and which he can only accomplish by crime. It's a lonely, high-risk project, which puts him at odds not only with the divine will but with the will of more or less everyone whose path he crosses. His rule has to be consistently 'me, not them', rather than 'me and them' - which rules out love, pity, respect, and even the acknowledgement that he possesses a soul that's akin to that of other human beings. But if that's the price of success he's willing to pay it.

We get so caught up in Richard's scheming and 'bustle' that at first we hardly notice his lack of inwardness. Sooner or later we realise that he's not made of the same psychological material as Clarence with his tortured 'dream and death' visions in Act 1, Scene 4. He can be self-conscious in a theatrical way, but that's quite a different thing. He dresses up and acts the part of a merry thriving lover (Act 1, Scene 2), a sentimental and unsuccessful soldier 'in rotten armour, marvellous ill-favoured' (Act 3, Scene 5) and, in clerical black, a pious, unworldly scholar (Act 3, Scene 7); but these are the impostures of a man 'designing' himself for specific purposes and judging his effects from the outside. He doesn't – perhaps he daren't – look within.

Or so it's been so far. But now, just before Shakespeare puts him back into the historical box that the Tudor propagandists have built to keep him in for ever and a day, he allows us a quite different view of him.

Conscience, which Richard had more or less convinced himself, and us, that he would have no truck with, suddenly returns. He's beset in his sleep with the ghosts of his victims calling for vengeance.

As a matter of fact, ghosts are fewer and farther between in Elizabethan-Jacobean drama than we often suppose. Four non-Shakespearean examples spring to mind. In 'Woodstock' (an anonymous history play that appeared within a year or two of this play and which covers the part of Richard II's reign that precedes the part covered by Shakespeare' in his 'Richard II') Thomas Woodstock, about to be murdered at the behest of the king, is visited in his sleep by the ghosts of his brother, the Black Prince, and his father, Edward III, who want to warn him of the danger he's in. There's also the ghost of Don Andrea in Kyd's 'The Spanish Tragedy', who figures as both client and patron of Revenge. Then there are ghosts in two less familiar plays: George Peele's 'The Battle of Alcazar' (1588) and the anonymous 'Locrine' (1595). No doubt there are others but not so many as to invalidate my general point that ghosts are rather few and far between in the 450-odd plays that have survived from the period.

By comparison ghosts are relatively numerous in Shakespeare's plays. The ghost of Hamlet's father, like the ghost of Banquo in 'Macbeth', is there to demand the settlement of old scores, as is the rather cryptic ghost of Caesar in 'Julius Caesar'. These plays get one ghost each. But in 'Richard III' we get a full-scale parade of them – so many that we realise that they don't speak merely for various wronged individuals but express something like a national consensus of anti-Richard feeling and 'desire for change'.

It's worth asking who gets to see and hear these ghosts and who doesn't. In 'Hamlet' the ghost of old Hamlet is seen first by the soldiers keeping night-watch, and by Horatio. But these characters are just go-betweens, not directly involved in the crimes with whose detection and redress the play is concerned. The ghost remains wordless until his son Hamlet comes to the battlements to be told what he has to do. In 'Macbeth' Banquo's ghost is the unsettled spirit of a murder victim, coming to plague the conscience of - and perhaps expose - his killer, so only Macbeth sees him. Lady Macbeth, 'innocent of the knowledge' (*Macbeth* 3.2.45) - of Banquo's murder, at least - sees nothing, and nor do the dinner-guests. We may be inclined to agree with Lady Macbeth that Banquo's ghost is nothing but a figment of her husband's guilty imagination and that he ought to pull himself together. The same might be said of Caesar's ghost, which appears only to the mind-wracked Brutus who (like Richard!) is alone in his tent the night before a fateful battle. Nothing but 'a figment of a guilty imagination'? Well, that's how a ghost might appear to a *compos mentis* 'realist' safely outside the experience, but if you can actually **see** it 'reality' redefines itself for you, in very different terms, before your eyes. This is what happens to Richard. When the ghosts appear his construction of rational and egoistical 'reality' collapses – albeit only temporarily.

Ghosts, Shakespearean and non-Shakespearean, are to be understood as manifestations of the dead who can't or won't 'let go' of uncorrected injustices on earth. According to traditional Christian teaching the souls of the dead that weren't cast down into Hell forever weren't necessarily swept straight up into Heaven either. They still needed to atone for their sins in a place of suffering, i.e. Purgatory, before they became fit to enter into the presence of God. But sometimes these souls broke out of Purgatory for a while and came to haunt the living. But by the 1590s this teaching was officially out of favour. The official Protestant line now was that Purgatory was an unscriptural superstition, a papist misteaching, and that the idea that the troubled spirits of the dead returning to earth to offer warnings or demand vengeance for unpunished wrongs was theological nonsense. No, death was the moment of settlement one way or the other, when the departed, wherever they were heading, became categorically incommunicado with humanity on earth and when for good or ill they had become 'past praying for'. Be that as it may, the old belief in Purgatory lingered on, together with belief in ghosts, in the popular mind - and evidently in Shakespeare's mind, too.

Hitherto, Queen Margaret had figured as a sort of ghost-and-no-ghost challenging Richard's supposed 'conscience'. He wasn't afraid of her, but facing the procession of indubitable ghosts that come to haunt him in Act 5, Scene 3 it's a different matter. There are no fewer than eleven of them! - Prince Edward, the Prince's father Henry VI, Clarence, Rivers, Grey, Vaughan, Hastings, the two princes murdered in the Tower, Lady Anne and Buckingham. Each addresses Richard and Richmond in turn, floating wraithlike from one tent to the other. Their words to Richard always end with 'despair and die': to his rival Richmond the message is 'live, prosper and save the country', or words to that effect. Their verdict is final and unanimous. Yorkists and Lancastrians, alive and dead, are now of one mind. Richard must go. There's agreement on this, whatever they disagreed about before. Providence can work in surprising ways. Richard, villain though he is, has served to reconcile a previously internecine nation!

When the ghosts depart Richmond (presumably) settles down for a good night's sleep, while Richard, half-awake and in a cold sweat, lies peering into the shadows to assure himself that they really have gone and won't be coming back. That panicky: 'Have mercy, Jesu!' (5.3.178) may have sprung to his lips when he was still more unconscious than not, but his usual sense of 'reality' has still not reassembled itself. The 'timorous dreams' that Lady Anne spoke of, thoughts that he'd scornfully brush away in the daylight, still hang about him.

Richard's final soliloquy (5.3.177-206) tends to command less attention than the two other great set-piece monologues in the play – Richard's opening one (1.1.1-41), and Clarence's 'dreams and death' one (1.4.9-74) - although technically speaking this isn't a monologue because the Keeper throws in a few questions to keep him going. They are very different speeches and invite comparisons to be made. Richard's first soliloquy, in which he declares that he's 'determined to prove a villain' and explains how he intends to go about it, is worth recalling at this point because it launches the over-reacher upwards into his trajectory, which he's at the downward end of now. Clarence's quasi-monologue is similar to

Richard's last soliloquy in that it, too, is an end-of-life self-reckoning, a 'moment of truth'. Like Richard, Clarence speaks in the aftermath of a nightmare, reporting ghastly encounters with the dead whom he's wronged - Warwick, his father-in-law, and the young Prince Edward whom he (allegedly) stabbed to death at Tewkesbury. He says he 'could not but believe that he was in hell.' (1.4.62) His harrowing dream prompts him to repent his sins, and it may be taken as a sign of divine forgiveness, which he himself hasn't recognised as yet, that he ends by asking to re-enter the realm of unconsciousness where he has recently undergone such suffering. In other words, Purgatory.

Keeper, I prithee sit by me awhile;
My soul is heavy, and I fain would sleep. (1.4.73-74)

The Keeper replies, 'I will, my lord; God give your Grace good rest.' (1.4.75)

It's from that dark realm of suffering and atonement, associated in Shakespeare's imagination with Seneca's Hades as well as with Christian Purgatory, that Clarence now returns, with the other ghosts, to haunt Richard on the night before Bosworth. And it's that dark realm that Richard now struggles to avoid.

Richard's Act 5 soliloquy reveals an aspect of his character that he's been hiding. The style is quite different from his confident, fluent, audience-directed, style at the outset of the play. Only the note of relentless argumentativeness is still unmistakably 'him'. The difference between the style of this soliloquy and Clarence's is equally marked. Clarence's language is image-rich, with syntactical stretching and swaying and lunging movements which act almost as 'gestures' indicating his intellectual and emotional discomposure. Richard's language – although there's no mistaking that he, too, is in acute distress - is image-bare, terse and relentless in its question-and-answer self-analytical dialectic. Another difference isn't a matter of style but of content: in his speech Clarence comes to the point of penitence, whereas Richard.....well, let's see.

The first thing he must do, he knows, is steady himself, collect his wits and try to restore 'reality' to its throne, resisting the treacherous attempt of rebel conscience to overthrow it.

........Soft, I did but dream. (5.3.178).

Note that 'but'. It's only a dream, isn't it? It's not 'real'! It's irrational. He ought to be able to shrug it off. But that's easier said than done. He's been profoundly shaken in a way he thought he could never be shaken. He wails:

O coward conscience, how dost thou afflict me! (5.3.179)

We've seen that Richard, in his absolute egoism, has destroyed all trust between himself and others. Now the ghosts have left in his mind the dreadful suspicion that he can't trust **himself**. His mind splits into two and a bewildered Richard starts to interrogate a terrified Richard.

Cold fearful drops stand on my trembling flesh.
What do I fear? Myself? There's none else by.
Richard loves Richard, that is, I and I.
Is there a murderer here? No. Yes, I am.
Then fly! What, from myself? Great reason why?
Lest I revenge? What myself upon myself?
Alack, I love myself. Wherefore? For any good
That I myself have done unto myself?

O no. Alas, I rather hate myself,
For hateful deeds committed by myself.
I am a villain. Yet I lie; I am not!
Fool, of thyself speak well! Fool, do not flatter.
My conscience hath a thousand several tongues,
And every tongue brings in a several tale,
And every tale condemns me for a villain…….
I shall despair. There is no creature loves me,
And if I die, no soul will pity me.
And wherefore should they, since that I myself
Find in myself no pity for myself? (5.3.181-195; 200-203)

There are nine vehement single-stride questions here, each followed by equally vehement single-stride answers. They create a sense of a powerful mind thrashing around in a space which is intolerably confined but impossible to escape from. In that excruciating space Richard's 'self' proliferates. Totting up examples - let me do this one myself - I find no fewer than 14 'I's, 9 'myself's, 1 self-referencing 'thyself', 3 'me's and 1 'my' in the nineteen lines quoted above!

That blurted prayer, 'Have mercy, Jesu!', so hastily retracted in 'I did but dream' are the words of a self-nullified man. In panic and despair he continues to fend off hope, or even human sympathy. 'No soul will pity me', he says, 'but wherefore should they, since that I myself find in myself no pity for myself?' He expects nothing more nor less than pitiless punishment. One after another, his victims – Clarence, Hastings, Buckingham - sinners all – have ended up repentant, asking and presumably receiving something more merciful, but Richard's not about to follow suit. He won't ever say, like those lesser men, and like the weak Second Murderer: 'How fain, like Pilate, would I wash my hands…' (1.4.271) He ends his speech with a curiously flat summary of what we all know, but bereft of anything like a conclusion:

Methought the souls of all that I had murder'd
Came to my tent, and every one did threat
Tomorrow's vengeance on the head of Richard. (5.3.204-206)

In that 'methought' – compare it with what follows Clarence's 'methoughts' after 1.4.9. 1.4.18. 1.4.21, and 1.4.36! - he disposes of his conscience and 'gets outside' himself again.

However the actor playing Richard chooses to speak these words they only tell us what we already know. With them he finally 'refixes' himself in the world of facts. He's in control again. He turns back with relief towards the positive business of 'bustle' and violence where he's more comfortable - and where he's finally lost. He's never going to repent, that's for sure. Shakespeare's taken the moral-psychological investigation of his hero-villain as far as he intends to take it. Now only the public political lessons remain to be hammered home.

In Act 5. Scene 3 Richard and Richmond are matched in rhetorical rivalry, addressing their battle-ready ranks of soldiers on the day of Bosworth. We hear from each of the protagonists one more time before they are frozen forever in their destined historical postures. Shakespeare follows the party line approved by the regime of the current sovereign, Elizabeth 1, the granddaughter of Richmond, who became Henry VII on Bosworth field. Their speeches contain no nuances reflecting the complexities of historical evidence as we moderns understand it, and there's no pretence of impartiality. This is Tudor propaganda, the winners' version of history. Richard presents himself as the arrogant, sneering, bloody-minded desperado, due for damnation as well as defeat, while Richmond is the modest hero with an unblemished record, come to save his long-afflicted homeland from tyranny. His victory is 'providential'. It represents the return of 'grace' to the kingdom after the tumults and usurpations of the Wars of the Roses.

Have we all got that straight now?

Addressing his troops Richmond puts Richard down in the national historical record as 'a bloody tyrant and a homicide' (5.3.246) and a usurper 'falsely set' (5.3.251) upon the English throne. He's very PC. When he assures his men that 'God, and our good cause, fight upon our side' (5.5.240) he's making a point that was virtually an article of religious faith, that only a king of true title holds his throne with the approval of God, and that usurpers like Richard are in defiance of the divine will. So as sure as eggs is eggs God can be relied upon to favour those who fight against usurpers.

Richmond is unmistakably the 'good guy', the soul of honour, God's favourite, etc, but he knows - and he needs to show that he knows - that virtue, while necessary, may not by itself be sufficient in a king. Unworldly, green-behind-the-ears kings – the most recent example being Henry VI, of course – are bad news! It's a tough world and a king needs to be tough, too – for everybody's sake. Richmond must be able to counter Richard's 'milksop' (5.3.326) sneer. He needs to display argumentative bite and a degree of toughness. Without descending to Richard's level of knockabout abusiveness he needs to show that he can attack as well as defend himself. In fact, he rises to the challenge well, with a telling point about the moral isolation into which Richard's career of crime has led him. Even his followers, he alleges, are less than half-hearted in their support for him.

Richard except, those whom we fight against
Had rather have us win than him they follow. (5.3.243-244)

This may not be entirely true, or even plausible, but the punch lands, and it's the right stuff to give the troops.

Although he has to get them worked up for a tough fight (historically, Richard had the bigger army) Richmond chooses to appeal not to his men's bloodthirsty instincts but to their more decent sentiments. Or so he makes it seem. He asks them to think of the beauty of their homeland and to remember the wives and children whom they will be fighting to protect.

If you do fight in safeguard of your wives,
Your wives will welcome home the conquerors.
If you do free your children from the sword,
Your children's children will quit it in your age. (5.3.259-262)

The appeal to 'family values' enables his followers to identify with him in a morally self-approving way; but just below the surface he's stirring a deep-seated 'biological' fear of having your women and children fall into the hands of your enemies.

Psychologically, it's neatly done!

But he isn't always so subtle. There's nothing ambiguous about his references to the rewards of victory.

If you do fight against your country's foes,
Your country's fat shall pay your pains the hire. (5.3.257-258)

And just in case they missed that - as if they would! – he repeats the point a little later:

…….if I thrive, the gain of my attempt
The least of you shall share his part thereof. (5.3.267-268)

Yes, this Richmond's a 'good guy' **and** a man with his feet on the ground - just the combination of qualities the country needs! And that's not all. As the moment of battle draws near, he's also a military hero. It goes without saying (but he says it anyway) that he will die in battle rather than concede to Richard. But he confidently expects to win, so

Sound drums and trumpets boldly and cheerfully.
God, and St George, Richmond, and victory! (5.3.269-270)

Now it's Richard's turn to speak. Although he's the crowned monarch he conspicuously omits to make any claim of right over the man who proposes to remove him from the throne. For him it all comes down to 'might is right'. The will of God expressed in terms of moral and legal right simply doesn't come into it, and he knows it's much too late to try to convince anyone that he believes otherwise. So he might as well say what he thinks:

Conscience is but a word that cowards use, *(where did we hear that phrase before?)*
Devised at first to keep the strong in awe.
Our strong arms be our conscience, swords our law! (5.3.309-311)

Richard can appeal to his men's patriotism, but it's the sort of patriotism that reminds us of Samuel Johnson's comment about 'the last resort of the scoundrel' – as opposed to the ethical, humane patriotism that Richmond has appealed to. Where Richmond speaks of love of one's homeland Richard simply appeals to xenophobia. The enemy aren't Englishmen at all, he mendaciously asserts, but

A scum of Bretons and base lackey peasants,
Whom their o'er-cloyed country vomits forth
To desperate adventures and assured destruction......
Let's whip these stragglers o'er the seas again,
Lash hence these overweening rags of France,
These famished beggars, weary of their lives.
Who, but for dreaming on this fond exploit,
For want of means, poor rats, had hanged themselves.
(5.3.317-319 + 327-331)

We can imagine his apprehensive army breaking into laughs and cheers at this splendidly derisive sally, and we may even smile ourselves. No, he's not a nice man, but he's more fun than Richmond!

There's another comparison to be made. Richmond has mentioned the 'safeguarding' of the soldiers' wives and children, referring only glancingly to the abuse they'd be at risk of were their menfolk to lose the coming battle. Richard doesn't beat about the sexual bush. Shall these filthy aliens, he asks:

.....................lie with our wives?
Ravish our daughters? (5.3.336-337)

Richard's failure to claim royal legitimacy is one remarkable omission. His failure to invoke God – or mention Him at all – is another. When we recall his earlier brazen religious hypocrisy we wonder what deters him now. Could it be that he feels a touch of spiritual inhibition, which he'd like to dismiss as silly superstition but which after the hauntings of the night before he now can't quite manage to do? Perhaps. It's more likely, though, that he realises that he simply hasn't got the moral credibility to 'go religious' now. Everybody would laugh. So he's forced at last into a sort of sincerity.

He makes no claim on God. No claim to royal right. No claim to represent the national cause. But Richard is still Richard and at least he can make a bloody good fight of it. So 'March on,' he cries,

………..Join bravely, let us to it pell-mell,
If not to heaven, then hand in hand to hell. (5.3.312-313)

After the battle, when 'the bloody dog is dead' (5.5.2) Richmond solemnly spells out for posterity the national significance of it all. 'England hath long been mad, and scarred itself', (5.5.23) he says, referring to the long-drawn-out Wars of the Roses to which Richard's reign has provided a nasty, brutish but at least fairly short *coda.* He intends to marry Elizabeth, the daughter of Edward IV, - the girl whom Queen Elizabeth so desperately defended from Richard's political plotting - thus uniting 'the white rose and the red' (5.5.19) symbolising the Houses of York and Lancaster respectively. This will reconcile all contending interests and re-integrate the kingdom. Richmond can claim to have both Yorkist and Lancastrian blood in his veins, which makes him look suitable, but we now recall that although he denounced Richard as a usurper in his pre-battle speech he didn't have much to say about his own title to the crown. In fact, he's a member of a new dynasty, the Tudors, whose claim is somewhat indirect. There are other things to recommend him, of course. He doesn't belong to either of the old warring factions; he's a likely-looking young man (*aetate* 28 in 1485); and, most important, he's won the battle and can impose his will. He also represents England's much-needed new start.

At the end of the play Shakespeare has Richmond sending a prayerful message about the Tudor dynasty to following generations, i.e. to his audience:

………let their heirs, God, if Thy will be so,
Enrich the time to come with smooth-faced peace,
With smiling plenty and fair prosperous days. (5.5.32-34)

We don't know how many in the audience would have felt that this prayer had been fully answered. The current worry, a little over a century after Bosworth, was that the Tudor dynasty was now coming to its end - although as a matter of fact it turned out that it still had almost another decade to run after the first appearance of this play. The childlessness of the 'Virgin Queen' Elizabeth made the succession look fraught with danger for the nation. The references to 'traitors' (5.5.35) and 'treason' (5.5.39) betray the growing nervousness of the time. The Catholic Mary Queen of Scots had the strongest title but after her execution in 1587 there was no clear successor. English Catholics suffering persecution under Elizabeth naturally continued to hope and pray – and even sometimes to plot – that the next monarch would either be a Catholic or at least someone willing to mitigate the persecution. He or she would probably have to come from abroad, though, and that would be politically unpopular. It's these Catholics who are being referred to as 'traitors'. Many of the audience would have responded heartily to Richmond's/Henry VII's rousing final 'God say amen!', taking it seriously as a prayer rather than just another bit of dramatic rhetoric, although the Catholics amongst them, even if they didn't dare to make it clear in public that they **were** Catholics, would have had other thoughts. In that 'smooth-faced peace', they belonged to a large religious minority officially regarded as traitors.

We wonder what Shakespeare, with his lifelong connections with that minority, would personally have felt about that.

THE MERCHANT OF VENICE

At the start of 'The Merchant of Venice' we find a man surrounded by a group of friends who are at a loss to account for his state of depression. He can't account for it either.

In sooth I know not why I am so sad,
It wearies me, you say it wearies you:
But how I caught it, found it, or came by it,
What stuff 'tis made of, whereof it is born,
I am to learn:
And what a want-wit sadness makes of me,
That I have much ado to know myself. (1.1.1-7)

(It's quite different from the way that 'Richard III' begins - with the soliloquizing Richard hogging the limelight, putting us in the political picture and drawing up his plans.)

Two of the group, Salerio and Solanio, suggest that their friend, a merchant, is sad because he's worried about the risks to his ships at sea. Salerio comes up with a vivid image of one of them fetching up on rocks, which

….scatter all her spices on the stream, (and)
Enrobe the roaring waters with silks. (1.1.33-34)

If it **is** disaster at sea that's preying on his mind such descriptions won't put his mind at ease, will they? But the merchant (identified as Antonio at line 40) patiently waves it away. He doesn't take any silly business risks. Things have been going well, and he hopes his good fortune will continue. 'My merchandise makes me not sad.' (1.1.45)

Solanio comes up with an alternative explanation. If he's not oppressed by business worries, he declares, 'why then you are in love' (1.1.45)

- to which Antonio replies: 'Fie! Fie!' (1.1.46)

'Fie! fie!' seems to be more defensive than dismissive – a gentle way of telling him to mind his own business. It's enough to make Solanio aware that he's overstepped the mark, but he needs to keep up the tone of high-spirited banter because to drop it now would be to acknowledge, and thus aggravate, the offence. So he changes tack again. He comes up with an 'insight' from the psycho-babble of the day:

> …………..then let us say you are sad
> Because you are not merry. (1.1.47-48)

There are two kinds of 'strange fellows' around, he explains. The first are manic: 'they…. laugh like parrots at a bagpiper'. (1.1.53) The second are depressive:

They'll not show their teeth in way of smile
Though Nestor (*i.e. the grim-toothed old Greek commander in the Trojan Wars)* swear the joke be laughable.' (1.1.55-56)

The pre-packaged advice that comes with the babble is presumably that Antonio should split the difference between the parrot and Nestor - though leaning a little more, perhaps, towards the first than the second. But Solanio never gets the chance to spell it out. Three other friends - Bassanio, Graziano and Lorenzo – turn up, giving the two S's their cue to leave. 'I would have stay'd till I had made you merry,' Salerio says, 'if worthier friends had not prevented me. (1.1.60-61)

We get the point. The two S's are talkative young men about town who've got - or think they've got - a talent to amuse. In their jokey way they've been trying to get Antonio to 'snap out of it'. But they're out of their depth. Antonio knows they mean well, in their way, and he bids them a courteous farewell.

Your worth is very dear in my regard.
I take it that your own business calls on you,
And you embrace th' occasion to depart. (1.1.62-64)

Will the 'worthier friends' who've just arrived have more to offer?

The S's have each put one foot in it. Now Graziano jumps right in with both feet. When Antonio pictures himself on a stage

.........where every man must play a part,
And mine a sad one (1.1.78-79)

Graziano accuses him of putting on a display of sadness in order to draw attention to himself. He's like an actor who

.... with a willful stillness entertain(s)
With purpose to be dressed in an opinion
Of wisdom, gravity, profound conceit. (1.1.90-92)

In his opinion, what Antonio needs is a robust 'come off it' talking-to from a friend who isn't afraid to speak his mind. But Antonio doesn't seem to be reacting positively to this idea, and Lorenzo and Bassanio are shuffling their feet in embarrassment. Suddenly Graziano breaks off for dinner, promising to come back and finish his 'exhortation' (1.1.104) afterwards! Lorenzo goes out with him, mumbling that he never gets a word in edgewise with his loudmouth friend. Graziano isn't in the least abashed. He's convinced that his garrulous outspokenness is the hallmark of personal sincerity and he has no intention of changing his ways. 'Well keep me company but two years moe,' he tells Lorenzo, 'thou shalt not know the sound of thine own tongue'. (1.1.108-109)

So far the friends have done much more of the talking than the dejected Antonio. But now he makes two remarks which, though brief, seem to promise to tell us more about himself. The first is to the departing Graziano: 'Fare you well, I'll grow a talker for this gear.' (1.1.110) But what are we supposed to make of this remark? One interpretation is : 'the verbal beating up (*gear*) that you've just given me has convinced me that my withdrawn behaviour **is** silly play-acting, as you say, and that I'd do better if I tried to be as loquacious as you.' If this is right, Graziano misses the irony and takes it as Antonio's *mea culpa*. He replies:

Thanks i'faith, for silence is only commendable
In a neat's tongue dried and a maid not vendible. (1.1.111-112)

Antonio makes the second remark to Bassanio, the friend who remains behind when the others have gone. 'It is that anything now, *(sic).*' (1.1.113) Unless we regard the words as a corruption in what is otherwise an exceptionally good text and are prepared to accept an editorial amendment we have to try to make sense of them as they stand. One reading might be: 'What do you make of all that then?' There's no question mark in the text but Bassanio treats Antonio's words as a question and answers it with, 'Graziano speaks an infinite deal of nothing'. (1.1.114) Another possible reading is that 'It is' has Antonio picking up on Graziano's description of silence as 'only commendable in a neat's tongue dried, and a maid not vendible' (i.e. otherwise of no earthly use), to which he adds - although there's no punctuation to support it here, either - the question: 'Bassanio - you look like the next friend queuing up to give me advice - do you have anything to add to what the others have said?'

No, we're going down blind alleys here. Antonio is still a puzzle.

At this point we're a hundred and twenty lines into the play. Antonio remains a baffling figure and there's still no sign of the plot. However, three themes - **friendship, sadness** and **hazard** – have emerged. Let's 'trail' them further into the play and see what becomes of them there.

First, then, **friendship**.

When we come across the two S's again in Act 2, Scene 8, they are mocking Shylock's loss of his daughter and his ducats. We're not entirely surprised. We recognize the insensitivity that Antonio generously overlooked in the opening scene. Here it is again, raised to the power of ten, in their mimickry of the Jew's distress – 'O my ducats! O my daughter!' (2.8.15) No doubt the original audience would have enjoyed it; they might even have joined in the chorus! But this sort of anti-semitic hostility will soon be shown up for what it is by Antonio, himself not exactly a fan of Shylock, who in Act 4, Scene 1 treats the defeated Jew with Christian consideration.

Likewise with Graziano. OK, his heart is more or less in the right place. He's accepted as one of Antonio's inner circle (as the two S's never are) and at the end he gets to marry Portia's servant/confidante Nerissa. But his friends often find him a pain in the butt. Bassanio has misgivings about including him in the party he's taking with him to Belmont to woo Portia. It will be a mission requiring discretion, and having a chap like Graziano around could well prove embarrassing, or worse. But he absolutely refuses to be left at home. 'You must not deny me, I must go with you to Belmont.' (2.2.170)

Bassanio decides that he needs of a bit of straight talking from a friend who isn't afraid to speak his mind. 'Hear thee,' he tells him,

Thou art too rude, and bold of voice,
Parts that become thee happily enough,
And in such eyes as ours appear not faults –
But where thou art not known – why there they show
Something too liberal. (2.2.171-176)

Graziano says he will behave

Like one well studied in a sad ostent
To please his grandam (2.2.187-188)

but his words hardly sound repentant, let alone abject, do they? True, he commits no gaffes in Belmont but his 'boldness of voice' is certainly heard, fortissimo, in his outbursts against Shylock in the trial scene in Act 4. High indignation at the Jew's wicked plot against Antonio is perfectly understandable but he goes right over the top. Shylock, outwitted by Balthazar/Portia, now faces unforeseen legal penalties for plotting to kill Antonio, and he looks as if he might accept conversion to Christianity as a condition of leniency. In Graziano's opinion, though, that would be too good for him. He's absolutely infuriated by the sort of pussycat treatment that Antonio, personally, and the Duke, officially, are offering him. Christians are supposed to want to see everyone given a chance to repent and be forgiven, but if it were down to Graziano the villain would be brought 'to the gallows, not to the font.' (4.1.396)

The friendships that are displayed in the first scene open up a sustained consideration of the issues of love, trust, forgiveness and generosity that continues throughout the play. Shylock makes an important dramatic impact in the middle acts, of course, but he's essentially there for contrast with the values and virtues that the 'best' Christians represent. But their affirmation never loses its critical bite. Some very tough things are said not only about the Jew who hates both the mercy (and the mercilessness) of Christians but also about hypocritical Christians who fail to live by the precepts of their own faith. Shortfalls of sympathy and compassion on the individual level are found, writ large, in the wider context of religious and economic conflict.

Second, **sadness**.

What exactly **is** bugging Antonio?

He asks Bassanio to tell him about the new woman in his life.

Well, tell me now what lady is the same
To whom you swore a secret pilgrimage. (1.1.119-120)

Yes, it's true. There is a lady. But before he tells him about her Bassanio has to confess to the fact that recently he's been living beyond his means. He's a gentleman, a 'soldier and a scholar', (1.2.108) keeping company with the likes of the Marquis of Montferrat. So he's used to living liberally. It's expected of a man of his rank. He shares his money by spending it – as one does. He offers no excuses for what meaner souls might describe as extravagance and Antonio, who is one of his creditors, offers no reproach. But now he recognizes that he needs to 'abridge' his expenditure 'from such a noble rate.' (1.1.126-127) He has a plan and Antonio hastens to assure him that he'll make him a loan to cover any expenses he incurs in carrying it out. Antonio's attitude to money is 'noble', too. In his world there's plenty of the stuff around, and plenty of people who are quite willing to lend it or give it to friends in need – not like those miserable Jews on the Rialto who are only interested in accumulating as much of it as they can. 'Be assured', he tells Bassanio,

My purse, my person, my extremest means
Lie all unlocked to your occasions. (1.1.138-139)

That's Antonio for you, Bassanio thinks. A thoroughly good egg. He'll back your plan before he even asks you what it is. He'll even buy your debts! 'In pure innocence' (1.1.145) Bassanio tells him how a new loan will enable him to get out of arrears and live on Easy Street for the rest of his life. When he was a boy, he explains, he used to try to find a lost arrow by shooting a second one in the same general direction. No, it didn't always work but it showed the right, trusting attitude to life. And his plan? He'll go to the island of Belmont to woo and marry the fabulously wealthy heiress who lives there. Her name's Portia and she's an absolute stunner. Suitors from all corners of the world are besieging her there. Antonio's eyebrows don't even flicker but we know what he must be wondering: what makes you so sure that **she** will want to marry **you**? No problem, Bassanio assures him. He's met the lady before, and

.....sometimes from her eyes
I did receive fair speechless messages. (1.1.163-164)

It's a bit vague, but he trusts the 'messages'.

But the wooing needs to be done in style and it'll cost
money.

Of course Antonio's perfectly aware that the second arrow
could just be throwing good money after bad. But who
cares? He's going to help his friend anyway. That's what
friends - and money - are for, aren't they?

But Shakespeare always leaves room for other takes.

There's a religious take. This is a play that casts long
Christian shadows. We can choose to see in Antonio the
silhouette, as it were, of a 'saviour' willing to put himself
in harm's way for the sake of his friends, regardless both
of their deserts and of the extent of the sacrifice it will
require of him. This will go beyond merely striking a
'*lacrimae Christi*' posture; he'll put his own flesh and
blood – literally - on the line.

There's also the love-triangle take. Is Antonio afraid that
the close emotional bond between him and Bassanio will
be threatened by the arrival of Portia on the scene? No, the
funding he's providing Bassanio with is to help him **win**
her, not to see her off. He's generously helping to set up a
love-rival to himself. But could he also be laying the
ground for a touch of emotional bribery later on - i.e.
'marry the woman if you must, but never forget that it's
me you must thank for it?' The play doesn't ask whether
Antonio is gay or not, so we have no need to try to decide.
If we did it wouldn't solve any questions of interpretation.
Certainly, as in the Sonnets for example, Shakespeare can

show himself to be fully alive to sexual complexities within the two-men-one-woman triangle, but that's not what this play is about. The application of modern socio-sexual categories like 'gay' to figures in Elizabethan drama tends to obscure rather than illuminate our view of what actually happens on stage. Nevertheless, the possibility may alert us to the fact that Antonio's the only major character (apart from Shylock, of course) who's not personally involved in the marital love-fest at the end, and that he does shows signs of feeling sidelined in the Bassanio-Portia story.

Perhaps Solanio picks up an element of sexual jealousy when he describes Antonio bidding farewell to Bassanio as he sets off on his love-mission to Belmont:

……even there (his eye being big with tears),
Turning his face, he put his hand behind him,
And with affection wondrous sensible
He wrung Bassanio's hand, and so they parted. (2.8.46-49)

Bassanio should be back in a matter of days and there's no reason why their friendship shouldn't continue as before, but Antonio seems to feel that he's saying goodbye forever.

When in Act 3 Portia learns that Antonio finds himself cash-strapped to a life-endangering degree she's eager to come to his rescue. Because he's her husband's best friend she unquestioningly regards herself as his friend, too, and feels bound to help him if she can. 'In companions'…. she says,

There must be needs a like proportion
Of lineaments, of manners, and of spirit;
Which makes me think that this Antonio

Being the bosom lover of my lord,
Must needs be like my lord. If it be so,
How little is the cost I have bestowed
In purchasing the semblance of my soul
From out the state of hellish cruelty! (3.4.11-21)

Her concern for Antonio, a man she's yet to meet, shows a lack of self-regard which established friends like the two S's and Graziano conspicuously fail to show. As far as she's concerned, of course, sexual competition doesn't come into it. Her role is to expand and share, not to divide, love. Antonio isn't there to hear her generous, and dutiful, words, but if he had they might have eased him of any underlying fears that he was about to be neutralized as Bassanio's 'lover'.

In the trial scene (Act 4, Scene 1), as Shylock sharpens his knife, Antonio makes his farewell speech to Bassanio. He has funded the trip to Belmont and is entitled to think of himself as the sponsor of the marriage, but now it looks as if his fate is to be no more than a tragic memory for the happy couple to cherish after his death. He accepts it, but says, wistfully:

Commend me to your honourable wife,
Tell her the process of Antonio's end,
Say how I loved you, speak me fair in death;
And when the tale is told, bid her be judge
Whether Bassanio had not once a love... (4.1.269/273)

He wants Portia to regard him, after his death, as a partner, rather than a competitor, in the emotional triangle. He uses the word 'love(d)' twice, to be sure that Portia understands: I'm Bassanio's lover, just as you are!

Near the end of the play Portia welcomes Antonio to her home in Belmont and hands him a letter which she knows has good news for him, though she doesn't say who's written it. He reads it to himself, standing outside the circle of the couples who have at last thrashed out their remaining misunderstandings. (5.1.273-307) He seems to think it's an 'anonymous' letter from her and that the good fortune it announces is her gift.

Sweet lady, you have given me life and living;
For here I read for certain that my ships
Are safely come to road. (5.1.286-288)

She makes no comment. Nobody does.

So how do we see Antonio at the end? A 'silhouette' saviour who is undaunted by any cost or risk to himself? Or a 'bypassed' male friend in a story always destined to end in marriage? Both, surely.

Third, **hazard.**

Any dealings Antonio has with Shylock are bound to bring him into the hazard zone.

Shylock's first words to Antonio are chillingly insincere:

Rest you fair, good signior,
Your worship was the last man in our mouths. (1. 3. 54-55)

True enough! A moment before, in a risk-free aside which only the audience overhears, he was muttering: 'I hate him for he is a Christian.' (1.3.37)

Antonio wants to get this business over with as quickly as possible but when he mentions the three-month duration of the loan Shylock pretends to be vague. 'I had forgot, - three months.' (1. 3. 62) Actually, he's anything but vague. Nothing's going to be straightforward with this Jew.

The theological debate that follows is designed to clarify the difference between the Jewish and the Christian attitudes to uncertainty and risk. Shylock tries to throw Antonio onto the back foot:

Methoughts you said, you neither lend nor borrow
Upon advantage *(i.e. usury)*. (1. 3. 64-65).

Antonio can only prevaricate. 'I never do use it.' (1.3.65)

Well, what's he doing now, then? we wonder.

Shylock now cites a story in Genesis (30: 27-43) which he thinks he can use to push home his point. He interprets the story of Jacob grazing Laban's sheep as an example of 'creative' business practice (like usury) which God approves and rewards:

This was a way to thrive, and he *(i.e. Jacob)* was blest:
And thrift is a blessing, if men steal it not. (1.3.85-86)

The Old Testament is Antonio's book, too, and he takes up the Scriptural cudgels with the Jew. Putting a different interpretation on the story he says:

This was a venture sir that Jacob serv'd for,
A thing not in his power to bring to pass,
But sway'd and fashion'd by the hand of heaven. (1.3.87-88)

In other words, Jacob was serving as an instrument in God's hands, not acting as a profiteer on his own behalf. He challenges Shylock by asking:

Was this inserted to make interest good? *(i.e. to justify usury)*
Or is your gold and silver ewes and lambs? (1.3.90-91)

It cuts no ice with Shylock. Rejecting the ancient Christian accusation that usury was 'unnatural' because it made money – an inanimate thing - breed like sheep, he defiantly replies: 'I cannot tell, I make it breed as fast.' (1.3.92)

Ordinarily, Antonio spreads his risks -

My ventures are not in one bottom trusted,
Nor to one place; nor is my whole estate
Upon the fortune of this present year (1.1.41-43)

- but he believes that risk has to be lived with and he places his faith in Providence to make things turn out all right in the end. The Jew, though, believes that God teaches him that 'the way to thrive' is to try to leave nothing to chance. His concern to 'make sure' shows in his usury.

There's no reference to this story from Genesis in any of the sources of the play. Evidently Shakespeare introduces it off his own bat to strengthen Antonio's ideological hand in his disputation with Shylock.

A definition of a merchant/capitalist who voluntarily risks variable results for his investments would apply equally to Antonio and his counterparts today. Without going quite as far as Bassanio with his faith in the second arrow Antonio knows that sometimes you are wiser to follow your heart rather than your head but he recognises that gains and losses can be more than merely marginal matters. There are no absolutely copper-bottomed guarantees - for merchants, or anyone. Bassanio, did he but know it, will also have to face up to 'hazard' when he takes a deep breath and makes his fateful choice of casket. And these aren't risks you run just for your own sake. The happiness of others is involved.

The Christians' acceptance of hazard is the opposite of the Jew's selfish risk-aversion. Shylock hates Antonio not simply because he's a Christian but because in the market place he lends money free of interest. When Antonio comes to him to borrow money he spots an opportunity to get rid of a competitor who has been undermining his own usurious business methods. He makes him an offer he can't refuse. He'll lend him the three thousand ducats interest-free, and in 'merry sport' (1.3.141) have a pound of his flesh if the loan isn't repaid on time. It's a very odd deal, but Antonio accepts it. In fact it has the unlooked-for advantage of letting him off the moral hook. The two men have just been arguing about the rightness or wrongness of usury but it now turns out that usury isn't the issue at stake here. There's no interest to be paid, only the price of Antonio's life if he defaults. And what's wrong with that? Shylock has come up, not just with the cash needed, but with the solution to the Christian's moral dilemma.

These terms look favourable enough to make Antonio wonder whether Shylock is turning over a new leaf. As the Jew goes off to the notary's to get the bond written up he says to Bassanio: 'The Hebrew will turn Christian, he grows kind.' (1.3.174) Ironic or not, it's more than a passing thought.

Shakespeare's audience wouldn't have believed for a moment that Shylock was 'growing kind'. And hitherto Antonio would never have trusted the Jew any further than he could throw him. Only recently he said:

Mark you this, Bassanio,
The devil can cite Scripture for his purpose, -
An evil soul producing holy witness
Is like a villain with a smiling cheek,
A goodly apple rotten at the heart.
O what a godly outside falsehood hath! (1.3.93-97)

But since then he's heard Shylock's passionate protest (1.3.102-124) against the hostility that Antonio and the other Venetians have 'many a time and oft' shown him, and his plea that his 'no interest' loan offer should be regarded as an invitation to improve their relationship in future. 'I would be friends with you,' the Jew says, 'and have your love.' (1.3.134) Antonio accepts the loan but not the offer of friendship, except to say, with whatever degree of underlying mistrust, that 'there is much kindness in the Jew'. (1.3.149) Bassanio, though, is more hard-bitten. Rhyming, but certainly not chiming, with his friend's words about 'growing kind' he says: 'I like not fair terms, and a villain's mind.' (1.3.175)

Shylock's second appeal for sympathy, in 3.1.53-66, is quite a different kettle of fish. It's an outburst of anger and grief spoken to the two S's (who seem to ignore it) and beyond them to the audience. It's an appeal to their sense of common humanity. The language is suddenly unguarded and heartfelt; the Jew, in his distress, is saying things which normally he'd be too cautious or too proud to risk saying. We're on the lookout for his usual hypocrisy but for the moment at least we don't see it. If he's 'up to something', goodness knows what it might be. What is clear is that he's expressing long-pent-up and perfectly understandable feelings. What's upset him so much is not anything that his usual enemies have done to him – that's par for the course – but the discovery that his daughter Jessica has eloped with a Christian suitor and helped herself to a substantial dowry of jewels and ducats from his treasure chests. An aggravating factor is the cruel delight that Salerio and Solanio and the street-boys of Venice have been taking in rubbing salt into his wounds by mimicking his loud lamentations for 'my ducats!' and 'my daughter!' But we need to keep our wits about us. The speech begins and ends with his desire for revenge, and it's only in between that he gives space to his argument that ordinary human solidarity entitles Jews to sympathy in their sufferings.

The speech is in prose but it generates great rhythmic force. A succession of 'physical-sensational' words – 'eyes', 'hands', 'organs', 'fed', 'hurt', 'healed', 'warmed', 'cooled', 'prick', 'tickle', 'poison' - demand the most immediate kind of human identification. Seven well-timed rhetorical 'if's – each intended to prompt an unreserved inward 'yes!' in the listeners - draw us along a path of ready assent. It's one undeniable challenge after another – 'hath not a Jew eyes', etc. He carries us irresistibly with him, at least as far as: 'And if you wrong us shall we not revenge? If we are like you in the rest we will resemble you in that.' (1.3.60-61)

But it's here that we have to pause to ask ourselves exactly where Shylock's trying to take us with this succession of 'ifs'. When he returns to the topic of revenge we sense that we need to jib at the word 'resemble' and re-distance ourselves from him. Jews and Christians are on a moral par, he argues, when they seek to get even with those who have done them wrong. But we know that two wrongs don't make a right. True, in the Old Testament (common property of by Jews and Christians alike) even God seemed to 'exact revenge' on those who annoyed Him. But the New Testament (owned only by Christians and regarded by them as the last word on the subject) teaches that God, having sent His own Son down to earth to redeem mankind, now seems to be more merciful than He was before, and that we're morally bound to reflect this by showing mercy to others. Shylock's assertion that revenge is as rife amongst Christians as Jews may be true, but it's at this point that he loses us. Yes, in practice Christians aren't always forgiving towards those who have done them, or their friends, wrong. But they **should** be. They ought not to laugh and jeer along with Solanio and Salerio, however tempted. Christians may have divided hearts but Shylock doesn't. When he hears that Antonio's ships have gone astray he has no qualms about taking his long-delayed revenge on him. That's what he's hell-bent on doing.

Just as Antonio has no truck with usury – unless it's the only way to save his friend; the risk-averse Shylock has no truck with gambling – unless it offers him the chance to destroy his business rival. The bond offers fair odds, though admittedly it's a long shot. He stakes three thousand ducats. If Antonio's ships come home safely he gets his money back – all of it but with no interest, sadly – but that's a small price to pay for the opportunity of killing him, legally, if they don't come home. Earlier, when asked by Salerio what, if he struck lucky, he'd do with a pound of human flesh, he answered, 'to bait fish withal, - if it will feed nothing else, it will feed my revenge.' (3.1.48-49) Antonio also thought the risks of the deal were worth taking. He reckoned that they lay somewhere between acceptable and remote - although the laws of probability are notoriously unreliable at sea and in stage comedies -

but now, in Act 3, it suddenly looks as if Shylock's long shot may be about to come off. No sign of the boats.

At the time that 'The Merchant of Venice' appeared in 1596 Britain had a population of about five million, including Scotland, Wales and Ireland. Her main language, English, co-existed with a range of Celtic languages in the northern and western extremities of the islands; its international - eventually imperial - reach lay in the future. But the picture of national insularity and isolation shouldn't be overemphasised. There were ancient religious, cultural and commercial connections with Europe and the Mediterranean. London was a busy sea-trading centre, not yet on a par with the magnificent city-state of Venice, but beginning to be roughly comparable in terms of its economic significance and ethnic diversity.

English literature and drama had long been under strong classical, French and Italian influences. In the case of 'The Merchant of Venice' Shakespeare might have got the story of the villainous Jew demanding his pound of flesh from several sources but mainly, it seems, from *Il Pecorone*, a book of popular tales collected by Ser Giovanni in the 14th century and published in Milan in 1558. There was no English translation at the time so it looks as if he read it in Italian. He got the casket story – or more exactly the casket 'idea': he made big changes to it – from another anthology of ancient tales, the *Gesta Romanorum*, the second edition of which, translated by one Richard Robinson, was published in London in 1595.

Shakespeare's audience had no regular supply of international news, but that doesn't mean that it was altogether ignorant of the world beyond their own shores. Many of them would have had some sort of broad but sketchy geo-political-historical-religious outline of the Mediterranean and European region. They knew that England had once been a part of the Roman Empire. They would also have been aware that more recently the Christian Crusaders had been expelled from Jerusalem, the birthplace of Christendom, by Saladin's Muslim army in 1187; that in 1453 the great Christian city of Constantinople ('the Rome of the East') had been taken by the army of the Ottoman Turkish Sultan Mehmet II, and that this had led to the Islamification of a large slice of the Eastern Mediterranean. In 1492 – the year that Columbus 'discovered America' - the Spanish monarchy had finally made Iberia safe for Christendom by establishing a Catholic religious and political hegemony there, driving out the Jews and taking over the last Muslim-ruled territories there. However, the long-term trend was still for Christianity to retreat and entrench itself in the north and west of Europe while Islam continued to press from the south and east. In 1565, for example, the Ottoman Sultan Suleyman, known as 'the Magnificent', only narrowly failed to capture Malta, which he planned to use as a springboard for the conquest of Italy. Another 'fall of Rome' – this time not to the Vandals and the Goths but to Islam - seemed to be on the cards. There were other Muslim encroachments in the Balkans and other parts of south-east Europe, including Hungary. These invaders came from what we now think of as the Middle East, although many Western Europeans continued to describe all Muslims as 'Moors', as if they were North Africans.

For all her economic power and prestige Venice's position in the 16th century was felt, in the long term, to be under threat. Sometimes she defended herself by straightforward military-naval confrontation. At other times, putting trade above other considerations, she made political and commercial accommodations with Muslim powers, earning herself a reputation as a somewhat ambivalent supporter of the Christian cause. Another ambivalent player was England in its island fortress in the north-east of Europe, standing at a safer distance from the immediate points of conflict. In the 1590s her policy was to reach trading and military understandings with the great Middle Eastern Islamic powers. Diplomatic exchanges took place in both directions. In 1598, for instance, the Sherman brothers made a well-publicised visit to Isfahan, promising arms in exchange for silk and furs. As a Protestant nation England had no wish to make life easier for the Catholic nations directly tied down in the struggle with Islam.

Shakespeare would have had much of this in mind when he staged 'The Merchant of Venice' - and so would many in his audience. In the first casket scene the Prince of Morocco's bid to win the hand of Portia would be understood in the context of centuries of Christian/Muslim conflict, and no-one would have missed the significance of his scimitar, which

… slew the Sophy, and a Persian prince
That won three fields of Sultan Solyman. (2.1.25-26)

(This could have happened in the 1530s when Suleyman was in Jerusalem reinforcing the defence walls.)

Likewise, in the next casket bid, Shakespeare's audience would have seen the Prince of Arragon as a representative of another, nearer, hostile power. Spain was National Enemy No 1. As recently as 1588 the Spanish Armada had sailed into 'the narrow seas that part the French and English' (2.8.28/29) on a mission to invade and bring Protestant England back into the Catholic fold. The weather had driven the ships off course and destroyed most of them, but Spanish sea-power was still formidable and there was every reason to expect further attempts. That was only eight years before 'The Merchant of Venice' was staged in London in 1596.

We see suitors of various nations, ethnicities, and religions (but no Jews, of course) rallying to Belmont to claim the hand of the millionaire heiress Portia. Her father, since deceased, has set out the arrangements to be followed. Three caskets – one gold, one silver and one lead – have been prepared. One of these has a certain 'affinity' with her which the successful suitor had somehow to twig. A riddle-like inscription attached to the gold casket reads: 'Who chooseth me shall gain what many men desire.' (2.7.5) On the silver casket it says: 'Who chooseth me shall get as much as he deserves.' (2.7.7). And on the leaden casket there's a warning: 'Who chooseth me must give and hazard all he hath.' (2.7.9) It'll take more than luck to get it right; spiritual insight into the meaning of the riddles is required. The suitors have one choice only. Losers must depart immediately and never marry anyone else. Some - those from England, Scotland and Germany - have been deterred by this penalty clause and the short-list is now down to two: the Prince of Morocco, a North African Muslim, and the Prince of Arragon, a Catholic Spaniard. But then a last-minute candidate turns up, a Venetian gentleman called Bassanio who doesn't throw his hat into the ring until the others have played and lost. Bassanio, as we already know, is after the lady's money as well as the lady herself, which to us may look a bit suspect, although Renaissance people were often more open-minded on that score. What's more, he's the one that Portia herself, who's met him before, would choose - if she were **allowed** to choose.

These caskets are the stuff of folk stories, you may think,

but they carry a serious moral message. Nerissa, Portia's servant-confidante, assures her mistress that her father's rules and procedures are providentially designed to produce the right result. 'Your father', she says, 'was ever virtuous, and holy men at their deaths have good inspirations, - therefore the lott'ry that he hath devised in these three chests of gold, silver and lead, whereof who chooses his meaning chooses you, will no doubt never be chosen by any rightly, but one who you shall rightly love'. (1.2.26-31)

Portia will need to hold on to that idea. It may look like a 'lottery' but Mr Right won't just be the suitor your father wants. He'll be the one **you** want. Promise!

The casket scenes give us more than a series of isolated choices revealing the social and moral characters of the individual suitors. They are spread out over no less than thirteen scenes (from Act I, Scene 2 - to Act 3, Scene 2) – more than half the play – and interwoven with other events occurring around them. Elements of action and ideas derived from two very disparate sources – Gesta Romanorum and Il Pecorone – are merged in a varied and fast-moving plot which unfolds in two locations, Venice and Belmont. It's a remarkable feat of dramatic synthesis.

Suspense is the driving force of the play. In Act 4 the suspense is about saving Antonio's life from the merciless Jew who believes that he's got everything buttoned up with his bond. In the last act the suspense lies in the difficulties the lovers have in settling the painful misunderstandings that have arisen between them. But in the first three acts – which is where we are at the moment - the suspense is about the outcome of the casket tests.

Let's look at each of these scenes in turn, and indulge in a couple of digressions to shed light on them.

Shakespeare gives Morocco **two** scenes with Portia, which adds to the suspense. In Act 2, Scene 1 he has a 'let-me-tell-you-about-myself' initial chat with her in which he immediately raises the question of his 'complexion'. (2.1.1) He doesn't beat about the bush. 'This aspect of mine' (2.1.8), he boasts, terrifies his enemies and it makes 'the best-regarded virgins of my clime' (2.1.10) fancy him no end. But now, wooing Portia, 'the fairest creature northwards born', (2.1.4) he hopes that she won't count his colour against him.

>..........I would not change this hue
> Except to steal your thoughts my gentle queen. (2.1.11-12)

Portia assures him that her personal feelings are beside the point.

>.............the lott'ry of my destiny
> Bars me the right of voluntary choosing:
> But if my father had not scanted me,
> And hedg'd me his wit to yield myself
> His wife, who wins me by that means I told you,
> Yourself (renowned prince) then stood as fair
> As any comer I have look'd on yet
> For my affection. (2.1.15-22)

Morocco is a soldier. He expects to win Portia by killing his rivals.

> Let us make incision for your love,
> To prove whose love is reddest, his or mine. (2.1.6-7)

He doesn't quite grasp that this is a test of moral insight, not of military prowess. All he has to do is choose the right casket: it's not for Portia to choose him. But doesn't that mean, he protests, that the outcome will be decided by mere chance? Should a throw of the dice rather than a trial of strength decide whether Hercules is a better man than his lackey? Well, she replies, that's how it is. She's just following her dad's rules. Morocco can step down if he's not happy about it, but if he decides to proceed and chooses the right casket – she'll be his, as sure as eggs is eggs. Morocco wants to try his luck at once but Portia hospitably – or perhaps nervously? - invites him to have dinner with her first. It's a very long dinner – six scenes long!

Morocco's previously compared himself to Hercules/Alcides (2.1.32/34) and now, when he returns in Act 2, Scene 7, he continues in the same vaunting style.

From the four corners of the earth they come
To kiss this shrine, this mortal breathing saint.
The Hyrcanian deserts, and the vasty wilds
Of wide Arabia are as thoroughfares now
For princes to come view fair Portia. (2.7.39-43)

This doesn't impress Portia as much as he hopes. It simply embeds him even deeper into the 'exotic alien' stereotype. It's the kind of far-flung imagery that makes you think of the frantic Othello in his 'Pontic Sea' vein, or of Tamburlaine plundering the world. The Lady of Belmont is well aware that it takes all sorts in this life, including Moroccan princes, but can she really believe that with a providential father looking after her from above, she may have to marry one of them?

Morocco ponders the inscriptions on the caskets. He dismisses the leaden one out of hand, considers the silver one unworthy and goes for gold. Only gold is good enough for her - or him.

It's not clear whether Portia already knows which is the right casket. The actress (or director) has a decision to make. Will it be with confidence or in trepidation that she hands him the key to the golden casket? -

>   ....if my form lie there
Then I am yours! (2.7.61-62)

Inside the casket Morocco finds a skull, 'carrion Death'. (2.7.63) In one of its empty eye-sockets he finds a versified rejection slip informing him that 'all that glitters is not gold'. (2.7.65) He's been fooled by appearances. The glamour of gold, he reads, leads only to death and corruption. It's a moral cliché, which any right-minded Christian would have taken as a warning rather than a promise. It's not 'blind Fortune' (2.1.36) that's let him down. He's made the wrong **moral** choice. But he takes it like a sportsman. His last words to her are: 'Thus losers part'. (2.7.77)

No doubt Portia's thinking 'thank you, daddy!' but what she actually says - to herself (since the text omits Nerissa from this scene) - is:

A gentle riddance. Draw the curtains, go.
Let all of his complexion choose me so. (2.7.78-79)

Pause for thought –

(and cue for the first digression).

Portia had referred to Morocco's 'complexion' (2.1.1) before she even clapped eyes on him, and like him, she doesn't beat about the bush. 'If he have the condition of a saint,' she tells Nerissa, 'and the complexion of a devil, I had rather he should shrive me than wive me.' (1.2.124-126) Evidently his colour weighs more with her than any moral qualities he may or may not have, but as she's a lady - and he's a prince – she'll handle the matter deftly. All she has to do is follow daddy's casket procedure, which doesn't discriminate in terms of Equal Opportunities (Race). Her own views are irrelevant. She can say with a clear conscience that she doesn't discriminate against him in any way.

We already know that she's dead set on Bassanio, although he's not yet a 'comer' and for all she knows he may never be. If she were allowed an opinion Morocco certainly wouldn't 'stand as fair' as Bassanio. What she tells him is true, although she knows he'll be deceived by it.

Portia's our heroine. She's utterly wonderful - beautiful, wealthy, with an IQ of 203, with oodles of generosity thrown in for good measure – as well as a bit of a 'racist'. But should that bother us? Not if we don't let it. After all, we all know that the play's not taking place 'now' but 'then'. Unless we're prepared to criticize it, anachronistically, as 'politically incorrect', or try to make it say what it's plainly not saying, we'd better just take it as it comes. We should bear in mind that neither Shakespeare nor his audience would have thought any the worse of her for not wanting to marry a Moor. So it might be more appropriate for us to exercise a 'multi-cultural' acceptance of values of 400-odd years ago than to object to them because we don't share them these days.

Portia's words should alert us not primarily to her 'racism' but to the possibility that however wonderful she is, she's not without contradictions and conflicts and that she doesn't always say exactly what she means. Her mood when we first see her in Belmont invites comparison with Antonio's 'sadness' in Venice. She says, 'By my troth, Nerissa, my little body is aweary of this great world.' (1.2.1-2) Nerissa, explaining that this is because she's 'surfeited' (1.2.5) with an abundance of good fortune, goes on to offer the sort of advice about the cultivation of mood moderation that we suspect Solanio was about to give Antonio before he was interrupted. 'It is no mean happiness ....' she tells her mistress, 'to be seated in the mean.' (1.2.6-8) Easier said than done, Portia replies, and in a rather wild speech she explains that she wants a husband to share her good fortune with but, thanks to daddy, she faces unusual difficulties in finding one. 'The brain may devise laws for the blood, but a hot temper leaps o'er a cold decree, - such a hare is madness, to skip o'er the meshes of good counsel the cripple; but this reasoning is not in the fashion to choose me a husband, - O me the word 'choose'! I may neither choose who I would, nor refuse who I dislike, so is the will of a living daughter curb'd by the will of a dead father: is it not hard, Nerissa, that I cannot choose one, nor refuse one?' (1.2.17-25) Is this how models of virtue are supposed to talk, even in private? We never cease to admire her but there are moments when we're much more aware of her as interestingly human young woman than an inhumanly perfect one. We have to question some of the things she says and does. As we'll soon see, there's room to doubt whether she's playing it entirely straight in the casket scene with Bassanio in Act 3, Scene 2. There's also a momentary spark of unfounded jealousy in the trial scene when, as 'Balthazar', she hears Bassanio expressing his overwhelming love for Antonio, whom he expects to die any minute under Shylock's knife. (4.1.278-283) We may also wonder if her tantalising handling of Shylock in the same scene isn't a touch cruel. And later there's the 'where's-the-ring? *contretemps* in the last act, where she seems to enjoy tormenting the husband that she knows is (more-or-less) innocent a bit longer than is strictly necessary. It's a complex and shifting picture but her essential goodness is never seriously in doubt. Like Antonio she occasionally casts the shadow of a religious 'silhouette'. In her 'quality of mercy' speech (4.1.180-201) she seems almost to impersonate Christ's mother in her call for universal forgiveness. Elsewhere she may remind us of a slightly less up-market religious 'silhouette' – Eve – in challenging the rules set down by her providential father. Like Eve, she has a mind of her own. She's sorely tempted to disobey his rules and it's quite possible to watch or read the play and feel that she actually does. It isn't only her suitors who are morally tested. She is, too.

(End of digression.)

When the Prince of Arragon comes in we can just imagine what Portia's thinking. Daddy, you can't be serious! You can't let this aged Spaniard blight my life! He's got silver hair!

Portia never forgets her manners, though. And she's also the soul of generosity. She gave Morocco dinner and so, fair dos, she'll give Arragon a few helpful hints. She greets him as one of the suitors who's 'come to hazard for my worthless self'. (2.9.17) 'Hazard', 'worthless' - do hints come any broader than that? But Arragon isn't a man who takes hints. He may think that in describing herself as worthless she's just being maidenly-modest. Charming, but nice girls are brought up to say things they don't mean, aren't they? And he fails to connect Portia's 'hazard' with the word jumping out at him from the inscription on the leaden casket: 'Who chooseth me must give and hazard all he hath'. (2.9.20) 'You shall look fairer ere I give or hazard', (2.9.21) he tells her. Such gallantry!

Turning to the gold casket, Arragon reads the inscription referring to 'what many men desire' and he jibs at that, too. Gold would be an obvious, vulgar choice. He's a prince and he's not going to

.............jump with common spirits,
And rank with the barbarous multitudes. (2.9.31-32)

Which leaves him with the silver casket. He's drawn to the inscription there which promises him 'as much as he deserves'. Silver, in fact, will match the colour of his hair.

The silver key, please.

(Hooray! Thank you, daddy!)

In the casket Arragon finds a picture of a 'blinking idiot' and a scroll mocking his illusions.

Some there be that shadows kiss,
Such have but a shadow's bliss.
There be fools alive (Iwis)
Silver'd o'er, and so was this.
Take what wife you will to bed,
I will ever be your head:
So be gone, you are sped. (2.9.65-71)

Shakespeare, you may notice, 'nods off' here. He forgets (cf 2.9.69) that suitors who don't get to marry Portia are all sworn not to marry anyone else. But Arragon, man of honour at least, hasn't forgotten. As if mesmerized by the scroll's rather folksy four-beat-a-line rhythm, he takes a rather jaunty leave of her:

Still more fool shall I appear
By the time I linger here.
Sweet adieu, I'll keep my oath,
Patiently to bear my wroth. (2. 9. 72-77)

Yes, he's got 'as much as he deserves'.

Portia ought to be confident by now that daddy isn't
playing Russian roulette with his beloved daughter's future
happiness. She's spotted the hidden hand of providence in
what he's done so far. 'O these deliberate fools!' she
muses,

......when they do choose,
They have the wisdom by their wit to lose. (2.9.79-80)

(Cue for digression No 2.)

As we noted above, Shakespeare borrows the casket idea
from a translation by Richard Robinson of 'Gesta
Romanorum'. In this work (in History 32, to be precise)
there's only one test, not three. A princess undergoes it to
find out if she's worthy to marry the Emperor's son. There
are inscriptions attached to the gold, silver and lead
'vessels' placed in front of her, and it's not by guess-work
but by making the right moral deductions that she must
reach her decision. The inscriptions are pretty
straightforward. The one on the leaden vessel reads: 'who
so chooseth me, shall finde that God hath disposed for
him'. Bingo! All Christians must choose 'what God hath
disposed'. It's obvious. What else **could** be right?

As in Shakespeare's play there's a commentary inside
each vessel as well as an inscription on the outside. In this
case it says: 'By the third vessell of lead full of (hidden)
golde and precious stones, we ought to understand a

simple life and a poore, which the chosen men choose, that they may be wedded to our blessed Lorde Jesu Christ by humilitie and obeysance, and such men beare with them precious stones, that is to saye, faith and hir fruitfull works, pleasing to God.'

(And yes, for those of you who need to know, lead is the right answer and the princess does get to marry the Emperor's son.)

It's the casket/vessel device, not the story-line, that Shakespeare's interested in. He replaces the princess with three male suitors and introduces a teasing element of chance – or what appears to be chance. The suitors are more perplexed than the princess was by the clues in the inscriptions and they are inclined to wonder whether luck may be the deciding factor. If so, they are mistaken, of course. Daddy's 'providence' hovers over all. Nevertheless, 'luck', or 'hazard' – or more precisely people's spiritual attitude to uncertainty - is an important concept in itself. Shakespeare was thinking of this when he rewrote the inscription on the Gesta Romanorum lead vessel, replacing 'what God has disposed for him' with 'who chooseth me, must give and hazard all he hath.' The meaning he gives it is just as Christian, but less of a dead give-away. 'Hazard' links his casket sequence with the main plot, in which Antonio runs risks for Bassanio's sake and doesn't even regret it when everything seems to have gone wrong. Shylock, by sharp contrast, isn't one to trust to luck; he reckons that he's got everything signed, sealed and about-to-be-delivered in the bond.

When Nerissa (1.2.28) and Portia (2.1.15) call the casket business a 'lott'ry' they draw attention to the element of hazard in it (especially as there's a penalty clause for the losers) but both of them realize that that's not the whole truth. Portia waits tensely to see how (whether?) the spirit of her father will deliver the goods, although all the appearances are that the outcome might be quite chancy. The casket and her father's intention may appear to be two separate things – image and reality - but they aren't. Both things express a single meaning. Portia herself suggested this in her words to Morocco:

One of them contains my picture prince,
If you choose that, then I am yours withal (2.7.11-12)

- and she uses the same formula when she tells Arragon:

Behold, there stand the caskets noble prince.
If you choose that wherein I am contained
Straight shall our nuptial rights be solemnized. (2.9.4-6)

Arragon guesses wrong. He's deceived by appearances.

(End of digression No 2.)

Portia's been courteous and correct – and typically generous - with the other suitors. She gave Morocco dinner. She gave Arragon heavy hints. And now that Bassanio has belatedly materialized as a suitor she immediately invites him to be her houseguest! 'Pause a day or two', she says, 'before you hazard, for in choosing wrong, I lose your company'. (3.2.1-3)

With the previous suitors she took refuge, thanks to daddy, in neutrality. With Bassanio her partiality is blatant. Within a few lines she extends her offer of hospitality from a day or two to 'some month or two.' (3.2.9)

This is exceptional treatment, but Portia's an exceptional young woman. She stands amidst the grandeur of her palace but makes no effort to be grand herself. She's in a sort of elegant tizzy, caught between the urge to express her excitement and to show the kind of maidenly caution that daddy would have expected of her. She's asked Bassanio to stay because

There's something tells me, (but it is not love)
I would not lose you, and you know yourself,
Hate counsels not in such a quality. (3.2.4-6)

Come off it, dear girl, we think. What else could that 'something' be but love?

Portia's has her own version of the problem of divided trust and loyalty. When Jessica replaces the authority of her father with the authority of her new Christian husband a sense of betrayal was no doubt in the mix of her feelings, whatever other reasons she had to run away. Gobbo, too, in an age when loyalty to one's master was regarded as a moral bond, believes that it must be the Devil tempting him to escape from the miserable Jew who keeps him starved and to attach himself to a better one – Bassanio, as it happens. (See 2.2.1-30) In Portia's case the question is whether she's going to put all her trust in daddy's supposedly all-wise providence or see if there's anything she can do to tip the odds in Bassanio's favour in his casket test. Spending time with him will give her an opportunity to 'teach him how to choose right'. (3.2.10-11) Hang on a minute, though! What did she say? **'Teach'** him? Daddy's rules don't allow for teaching. No, she didn't mean 'teach', even if she said it, because that would make her 'foresworn', and 'so I will never be'. (3.2.11) After the elimination of Morocco and Arragon she must be aware which is the right casket, so she could help him if she chose. But she can't just tell Bassanio the answer, can she? On the other hand she knows that if she doesn't help him and he fails the test she won't be able to stop herself sinfully wishing, ever after, that she **had** foresworn herself.

There don't seem to be any absolutely right answers here. Maybe she'll have to go for one of the wrong ones. In turmoil she looks into Bassanio's eyes. He's in turmoil, too. Neither of them can tell the other what to do. 'Beshrew your eyes,' she says,

They have o'erlook'd me and divided me,
One half of me is yours, the other half yours, -
Mine own I would say: but if mine then yours.
And so all yours. (3.2.14-18)

She's caught between the state of maidenly independence and that of wifely devotion, expressing her readiness, in both states, to 'dispense with the meum-tuum sense'. Not that Shakespeare needs any help from Robert Graves (whose phrase that is) to give Portia the right words here. He has her condense her feelings into these thirty-four 'everyday' words (i.e. between 3.2.14-18), most of them single-syllable, to remarkable effect.

Her thoughts turn next to the imagery of commerce and property law. The faint nod they got in 'hazard' (3.2.2) and 'venture' (3.2.10) becomes a deep bow of recognition in

..........O these naughty times
Put bars between the owners and their rights! (3.2.18-19)

She already possesses Bassanio by right of love, and anything that gets in the way of that is a 'bar', an injustice. So why should she be expected to stand by and do nothing to remove any obstacles to it? Obviously she can't just give the whole game away by telling him which casket to choose. Apart from making herself 'forsworn' it would leave him unvalidated and demeaned. The example of this kind of solution in Jean Cocteau's 'La Machine Infernale' might serve as a warning. The Sphinx spells out her riddle to Oedipus, leaves him scratching his head in perplexity for a few minutes, but then tells him the answer and gives him a test a little later to check that he's remembered it. She **wants** Oedipus's downfall and this is quite enough to bring it about. She's *'du sexe qui dérange les héros'* (of the sex that undoes heroes) and her aim is to demonstrate his helplessness and undermine his freedom of choice. She's looking forward to watching him *'courir d'un piège dans un autre, comme un rat écervelé'* (run about from one trap to the next like a brain-damaged rat). But Portia's no Sphinx. She loves Bassanio, so she's **not** going to give him the right answer. 'So though yours, not yours', (3.2.20) she says. It's for him to prove himself. She's not going to forswear herself. 'Let Fortune go to Hell for it, not I.' (3.2.21)

Although Bassanio's 'on the rack,' (3.2.25) he feels that she's already helped him -

O happy torment, when my torturer
Doth teach me answers for deliverance! (3.2.37-38)

There's that word 'teach' again. She's done nothing (yet?) to tip him the wink but her love helps him to put 'that ugly treason of mistrust' (3.2.28) - lack of faith and fear of failure - behind him. His own love for her will guide him.

The casket business is not the lottery that it seems to be. It's a test, not of wisdom or worth, but of love. If there's love, all the luck, wisdom and worth you need will be added unto you. But Portia's belief that 'if you do love me you will find me out' (3.2.41) still sits uncomfortably alongside her unwillingness to leave anything undone that might help Bassanio. There may be a grey area between spilling the beans and dropping a helpful hint or two. Wrong'uns don't spot hints – remember Arragon! - although she would expect Bassanio to cotton on better than that. She calls for music to express either grief or rejoicing, depending on how things turn out. Still full of misgivings she addresses him as Hercules, herself figuring as Hesione, the chained and trembling sacrificial victim waiting for him to rescue her. Citing the story mentioned by Ovid in Metamorphoses Book 11, lines 211-213 (Loeb) she cries:

Go, Hercules!

Live thou, I live – with much, much more dismay,
I view the fight, than thou that mak'st the fray. (3.2.60-62)

We can take it that amongst all her other excellent qualities Portia's well-read, so she'll be aware that this story provides an unhappy analogy. Yes, Hercules rescues the princess, but not because he loves her. He's after the king's reward – chariot horses in this case. In addressing Bassanio as Hercules she's issuing a challenge rather than bestowing a compliment. She's calling his love into question – as, come to think of it, she does right up to the end of the play. Things are easier for him because, feeling encouraged by her love, he can now decide and act, while she remains fraught with pessimistic premonitions.

To the dramatic suspense – drawn out to full length by Portia's anguished speech (3.2.40-62) and Bassanio's decision-making *rationale* (3.2.73-107) – an element of mystery is now added. The play starts to run along parallel tracks. As we hear a doleful voice singing 'Tell me where is Fancy bred?' we also follow Bassanio's thoughts as he makes his decision. (3.2.73-107) It tests our listening skills to the limit.

155

Tell me, where is Fancy bred?
Or in the heart, or in the head?
How begot, how nourished?
All. Reply, reply.
It is engend'red in the eyes,
With gazing fed, and fancy dies
In the cradle where it lies:
Let us all ring Fancy's knell.
I'll begin it. Ding, dong, bell.
All. Ding, dong, bell. (3.2.63-72)

This description of the short life of Fancy as a speed-blurred sequence of birth, infant mortality and parental grief, leading directly to the tolling of funereal church bells, is entirely appropriate. Fancy represents all the error, emotional and intellectual, that arises from confusing transient earthly appearances with permanent spiritual truth. Listening to Bassanio's initial reasoning –

So may the outward shows be least themselves.
The world is still deceived with ornament (3. 2. 73-74) –

we are ready to join our voices to the singer's call for Bassanio to 'Reply, reply'. (3.2.66) In fact, he's **already** replying, and he's on the right track. Our view of truth and reality, he argues, is blocked by worldly shows and deceptions. All that glitters is not gold, etc. Don't be deluded by appearances.

Bassanio opens the leaden casket.

The caskets (like tabernacles, treasure-chests and coffins) are 'appearances', but the one he has chosen now stops concealing, and begins to reveal, the truth within. As he gazes at the portrait inside he finds a marvellous, though still apparently contradictory, 'matching' between outer and inner, form and content. It's as if we see Shakespeare's imagination tracing the pattern of 'outward sign of inward grace' that characterizes the Christian sacraments - the two things being unified, in spite of appearances to the contrary. In 'fair Portia's counterfeit' (3.2.115) he sees both a false image of Portia (all images are false, by definition) and a true image (which hardly falls short of her actual beauty, it's so well painted). This is an exceptional case, though, miraculously contrived by her father. In the normal run of things appearance and reality remain at treacherous loggerheads.

Many a man his life has sold
But my outside to behold. (2.7.67-68)

The virtue that lead symbolizes is humility, of course, as it did in the 'Gesta Romanorum' source. It's his recognition of this that liberates Bassanio from worldly illusions and gives him the counter-intuitive wisdom to say:

thou meagre lead *(casket)*
Which rather threaten'st than dost promise aught,
Thy paleness moves me more than eloquence,
And here choose I, - joy be the consequence! (3.2.104-107)

The difference between him and his rivals is now clear. Morocco and Navarre, in their worldly pride, thought they were worthy of her. Bassanio doesn't. He's humble.

Bassanio and Portia show humility to each other as they become a married couple. When he asks her to confirm that she's his – he won't take the casket's word for it – she says:

Myself, and what is mine, to you and yours
Is now converted. But now I was the lord

Of this fair mansion, master of my servants,
Queen o'er myself: and even now, but now,
This house, these servants, and this same myself
Are yours, - my lord's! (3.2.166-171)

Humility and generosity - they're theologically 'married'.

So Bassanio has passed the casket test. But has Portia also passed **her** test? In her anxiety to make things work out right has she bent the rules in some way?

Here's the evidence for the prosecution. The rhymes of the first three lines of the 'Fancy' song – 'bred', 'head', 'nourished', like 'fed' three lines lower down - all happen to rhyme with 'lead', (and with 'dead', for that matter). To an alert listener 'lead' (and 'dead') are like spare rhymes hanging in mid-air over the verse, as if waiting to descend upon it. Coincidence? Scarcely. Portia has stage-managed the music, not just to set the background mood but to give Bassanio a clue. Maybe it's meant to reach him 'subliminally' but that doesn't alter her intention. She either wrote the words herself, or had them written to order. Either way, though…

In Portia's defence we can point to her anguished aside in which she acknowledges the

…doubtful thoughts, and rash-embrace's despair,
And shudd'ring fear, and green-eyed jealousy (3.2.109-110)

that gripped her just as Bassanio was about to make his fateful decision. Obviously she didn't feel that she'd 'fixed' the outcome (Shylock-style), but that doesn't mean that she didn't interfere at all. We can't know for sure, so she has to be given the benefit of the doubt. The case against her wouldn't stand up in court, and her 'good character' would stand her in good stead. At the worst, in Scotland, the verdict might be 'unproven'. Shakespeare seems to have wanted the uncertainty to linger. It raises the question of whether good ends can justify dubious means, which comes up again in the legal effort to rescue Antonio. If Bassanio believes that Portia bent things a bit in his favour earlier he may think he's only taking a leaf from her book when, just before the trial gets under way, he says to her (though thinking he's talking to the lawyer Balthazar, of course):

………..I beseech you
Wrest once the law to your authority,-
To do a great right, do a little wrong
And curb this devil *(i.e. Shylock)* of his will. (4.1.210-213)

When push comes to shove and correctness of procedure threatens rightness of outcome, which side are we on? Was Antonio 'right' to borrow money from a despicable usurer to rescue his friend? Was Portia 'right' to (try to) help Bassanio choose the leaden casket? Now the question is: would Balthazar be 'right' to bend the law if it served to foil Shylock's wicked machinations? After all, we'd only be talking about 'little wrongs', and come to think of it, what is mercy but slightly bent justice?

But Balthazar has no intention of bending anything.

It must not be, there is no power in Venice
Can alter a decree established:
'Twill be recorded for a precedent,
And many an error by the same example
Will rush into the state, - it cannot be. (4.1.214-218)

This is what you'd expect a lawyer to say. S/he already

knows – unlike the rest of us, who are in an agony of suspense - that she's going to win the case. It was different in the casket scenes, wasn't it? She couldn't be so sure then. But she's sure now. In spite of everybody's misgivings, she can see how to combine legalistic scrupulosity with mercy.

At the trial in Act 4, Scene 1 Shylock, brandishing the bond, believes he has a water-tight case. His insistence on a pound of Antonio's flesh rather than interest on the money he's lent him does nothing to enhance his moral prestige in our eyes. But he can deploy ethical arguments to support his case, too. Why, he asks, if the law allows Christians to keep slaves to do with as they like, shouldn't he be allowed to claim one pound of Antonio's flesh to do with as **he** likes? (4.1.88-102) The Christians don't notice - let alone answer – his question. They have other things on their minds. In a moment they'll have to watch helplessly as the cruel Jew vivisects Antonio before their eyes. Graziano, shouting across the court-room, expresses their feelings: 'O be thou damned, inexecrable dog....' (4.1.127, etc.)

It's all water off a duck's back, of course. The more hatred and contempt his enemies shower on him the more determined the Jew is to have justice. 'I stand here for law,' he says. (4.1.141)

The Duke himself – a magnate with great authority in Venice – has come to court to play what the Christians hope will be the trump card. Addressing the Jew directly and pulling out all the oratorical stops, he says that Antonio's plight would

.........pluck commiseration of his state
From brassy bosoms and rough hearts of flints,

From stubborn Turks and Tartars never train'd
To offices of tender courtesy;
We all expect a gentle *(gentile?)* answer Jew. (4.1.29-33)

The actor playing Shylock has options at this point. He can listen (or pretend to listen) respectfully to the Duke's speech, or be inscrutable, or look defiant. But whatever his body language says he isn't going to cave in now, is he? He implacably reiterates that he must have 'the due and forfeit of my bond' (4.1.36), but then he launches out into a very odd and ugly outburst, spelling out a sequence of rat, pig, cat, bagpipe and incontinence images (4.1.39-61) culminating in the assertion that different people want different things for all kinds of strange and obscure reasons, and that he doesn't see why he should have to give any reason for what **he** wants

More than a lodg'd hate, and a certain loathing
I bear Antonio. (4.1.59-60)

There's a fierce exchange of one-liners between Shylock and Bassanio summarising the (supposed) differences between Christian and Jewish values, and giving the Christian values a clear moral edge.

Bassanio: Do all men kill the things they do not love?
Shylock: Hates any man the thing he would not kill?
Bassanio: Every offence is not hate at first.
Shylock: What wouldst thou have a serpent sting thee twice?

At last Balthazar/Portia arrives and presents her credentials – at some length: it helps to build up the suspense. Shylock must relent, she says. When he refuses s/he makes her celebrated 'quality of mercy' (4.1.180) speech. As God's mercy 'seasons' justice, human beings must show each other mercy in their dealings with each other.

.........................therefore Jew,
Though justice be thy plea, consider this,
That in the course of justice none of us
Should see salvation: we do pray for mercy,
And that same prayer, doth teach us all to render
The deeds of mercy. (4.1.193-198)

It's not just an appeal to the Jew's better nature. Implicitly it's the first suggestion that he needs to become a Christian.

Although Jews and Christians worship the same God, Judaism (allegedly) looks to the Old Testament, which depicts God as requiring strict adherence to His commandments and punishing those who infringe them, while the New Testament portrays a more forgiving God intent on saving rather than punishing. But Shylock, scenting victory, isn't to be swayed by this sort of talk. He's after strict justice, according to the terms of the bond signed by himself and Antonio. So Balthazar/Portia must try to turn his own weapon, the letter of the law, against him. S/he acknowledges that that the bond is valid and the court is obliged to honour it - 'O noble judge!' (4.1.242) he exclaims delightedly - but then s/he begins to unravel the implications. Quietly and thoughtfully, as though they had only just occurred to her, s/he says: 'Tarry a little, there is something else.' (4.1.301)

Although the bond clearly entitles Shylock to his pound of flesh it says nothing about blood. If he sheds any of Antonio's blood as he cuts away the flesh he will find the law against him, and the penalty will be severe – the confiscation of his lands and goods. Why didn't anyone think of that before? we may wonder – especially when, a little earlier, s/he told Shylock to have a surgeon on standby 'to stop his wounds, lest he do bleed to death.' (4.1.253)

Shylock is stumped, and admits it. OK then, no pound of flesh. He'll settle for the money, 'the bond thrice' (underwritten by Portia) which Bassanio has just offered. But Balthazar/Portia rules that out: 'The Jew shall have all *(i.e. only)* justice.' (4.1.317) He's already refused money in lieu of the pound of flesh, and there's no going back on that now. He must take the flesh, but if he takes an iota too much or too little not only his property but his life will be forfeit. S/he now proceeds to dismantle him step by step, upping the penalties as Shylock lowers his demands until, in full retreat, he says: 'Give me my principal, and let me go.' (4.1.332)

But the law, once invoked, must take its course. It's the course he insisted on himself and he can't 'do a deal' now. S/he's relentless. He can't even go home empty-handed. He has

…………..contriv'd against the very life
Of the defendant (4.1.356-357)

and the penalty for that is to forfeit one half of his estate to the intended victim and the other half to the state. What's more, his life is forfeit, for plotting against the life of a Venetian citizen. If he wishes to be spared he must kneel to the Duke and beg for his own life.

A tough cookie! We're full of admiration for his/her lucidity and rigour, but what price that splendid speech about mercy now? Is this religious persecution finally showing its true face? Is s/he turning the trial into a display of judicial Jew-baiting?

The Duke had asked Shylock earlier: 'How shalt thou hope for mercy rend'ring none?' (4.1.87) But that was when everyone was thinking of Antonio, not Shylock, as in need

163

of mercy. Now the boot is on the other foot. The basic Christian *quid pro quo* is: show mercy, receive mercy, but how do things stand if you've refused to show mercy? Are you entitled to any yourself? Obviously not. But fortunately it isn't a question of what you're entitled to, even less deserve. Mercy isn't that sort of thing. It's a gift.

So Balthazar's/Portia's toughness doesn't rule out clemency. S/he's merely rubbing in the 'mercy' lesson before s/he hands the prosecutor-turned-defendant over to others for the final verdict. He isn't let off scot-free but he does escape the full rigour of the law. The Duke immediately grants him his life, saying:

That thou shalt see the difference of our spirit *(i.e. Christian as opposed to the Jewish)*
I pardon thee thy life before thou ask it. (4.1.364-365)

Shylock isn't grateful, and why should he be? He doesn't see that he's being offered a gift. He sees only that his wealth – his very **life**, he feels – is being taken from him.

When Balthazar/Portia asks: 'What mercy can you render him Antonio?' (4.1.374) the merchant still has it in his generous heart to make things even easier for the Jew. He asks that the state should allow him to keep half of his property, the other half being put in trust for Jessica and Lorenzo. When Shylock dies everything will pass to them.

And Shylock must become a Christian.

What!!!?

Modern audiences tend to gasp with embarrassment. Sometimes the line is cut out. Do our ears deceive us? There's this 'saintly' Antonio putting on a conspicuous display of mercy, when he suddenly comes up with this call for compulsory conversion, apparently expecting Shylock – and us – to think of it as a gift rather than a punishment. Actually, of course, it's worse than a punishment. It's a violation of human rights!

Again, it's important not to let contemporary attitudes obscure our understanding of what the play is telling us.

Conversion is one of the concessions being made, not one of the penalties being imposed, and it's perfectly consistent with the mercy being shown to him in other ways. Mercy is not only prescribed by doctrine but of great emotional importance in Christian culture. In stage comedies mercy and forgiveness were often integral features of the resolution of the plot. In this play they're not just features but the central theme. The 'better Christians' – Portia, Antonio, Bassanio and the Duke – are not just being soft on the wicked Jew; they feel obliged to try to bring him to salvation. Shylock's a moral disaster area. He needs to see Christ, as they do, as His redeemer, and to let go of the unyielding 'eye for an eye' attitude which causes humanity, including himself, so much grief. To help him do this would be an act of mercy in itself. He may not want it or deserve it, and he won't thank them for it (and the whole idea might prove a bit controversial four centuries on) but that's not the point. They can't leave him at the mercy – if mercy's the right word - of his own Jewish conscience. It's there that the problem lies.

Graziano gives voice to what we all feel, and perhaps **should** feel, about Shylock's calculated and unflinching cruelty. Through him Shakespeare allows us to recognise and not simply deny feelings of repulsion which can't simply be air-brushed away by morally irresponsible leniency. Although our better selves identify with the example of the 'better Christians' we still have the emotions of our worse selves that tempt us to join Graziano's lynch-mob mood. Justice pulls us one way and mercy another. No-one's perfect, or beyond redemption. The Jew, no matter how vile, can't be excluded from the universal redemption story, and if compulsory conversion is what it takes to break his wicked heart and bring him to repentance, so be it. It's tough love. And who, after passions have cooled, would see it otherwise? Graziano? If so, we can only hope that Nerissa will have a good influence on him over time.

Shylock isn't an English Jew. He's a European continental Jew imported along with the Venetian Christians, into a late 16th century play for the London stage. Some believe that at this time Shakespeare may have had a mistress, Elizabeth Lanier, the daughter of a Venetian Jewish musician at court, but apart from her he may not have met more than a handful of Jews in London, let alone in Stratford. There can't have been many of them around, at least in the circles that he was familiar with. They were legally barred from England, but provided they 'professed' Christianity, at least outwardly, they weren't hunted down or driven out. Nevertheless, we can probably assume that they were regarded with ready-made suspicion as historic enemies of Christ, doomed by God's will to wander the world with no land of their own, living by their wits.

In 1594 two things happened in London to do with Jews – one theatrical, the other political. The theatrical event was the very successful staging of Marlowe's 'The Jew of Malta'. Its central figure, Barrabas, was an outrageous and shameless Jew-villain. The political event was the scandal of Dr Roderigo Lopez, a 'converted' Portuguese Jew who got involved in dangerous high-level politics and was arrested for trying to poison the Queen, and other important people – for which he had recently been tortured, convicted and executed. Big news story!

When Shakespeare sat down to write his own play with a Jewish villain he clearly decided to keep any similarities between Barrabas and Shylock to a minimum. Both are out-and-out stage villains, there to generate righteous moral indignation in the audience rather than to make serious claims on its sympathy. (History today tells us a different story about the Jews of Europe but our concern here is to focus on the plays, not the historical 'revisions', accurately.) Barrabas occupies and dominates virtually the whole of Marlowe's play, whereas Shylock has a more incidental role in 'The Merchant'. He appears in only five of the twenty scenes in the play – 1.3, 2.5, 3.1, 3.3 and 4.1, and he doesn't appear, and is virtually forgotten, in the last act. Marlowe gives Barrabas a sensational free run in a Malta that doesn't provide a serious moral challenge to him. Shylock, though, is up against serious Christian values in Venice which will emphatically overcome him in the end. 'The Merchant' has a moral and theological depth which the atheist Marlowe wasn't interested in.

Shakespeare's play makes no reference to 'The Jew of Malta', although the earlier play had been revived to run alongside it in a theatre nearby. But 'The Merchant' does make two clear references to the Lopez case. The first, at 3.2.24-31, comes when Bassanio, bracing himself to make his casket choice, tells Portia that he sees her as his rigorous but compassionate torturer. In the second, Graziano, berating Shylock in court, says:

Thou almost mak'st me waver in my faith
To hold opinion with Pythagoras,
That souls of animals infuse themselves
Into the trunks of men: thy currish spirit
Govern'd a wolf, who hang'd for human slaughter –

Even from the gallows did his fell soul fleet,
And whilst thou layest in thy unhallowed dam,
Infus'd itself in thee: for thy desires
Are wolvish, bloody, starved and ravenous. (4.1.129-137)

These lines bring together several assorted Lopez associations. First, of course, the name Lopez translates as 'wolf'. Graziano – who has a thing about hanging, in case you didn't notice – recalls the custom of hanging man-eating wolves. Shylock has a predatory spirit which, transmigrating from the body of such a wolf, found its way into his mother's womb before his birth, fixing his character for life. His appetite for chunks of flesh out of Antonio's body runs parallel to his appetite for the exorbitant profits of usury. In one of a number of books on the subject circulating at the time, 'A Discourse on Usury', (1572) the author, Sir T. Wilson, describes usurers, in a comparison that makes no claims on originality, as 'greedy cormorant *(i.e. flesh-eating)* wolfes'. The beads on Graziano's string of associations are: Lopez (traitor) > wolf (hanged) > Shylock (usurer), and the string on which they hang is Jewishness.

Lest we indulge in an over-sentimental view of Shylock let's tot up the negatives that Shakespeare heaps on his head. There's his murderous plot against the saintly Antonio's life, his hatred of Christians *per se* and of their faith (whether they live up to it or not), his total lack of affection for others, as shown by his imprisonment of his daughter Jessica at home - 'our house is hell' (1.3.2) - and his keeping his servant Gobbo on, or below, the bread-line. He's consistently unkind, miserly, resentful, untrusting, deceitful, mean-spirited and self-pitying. Except on the few occasions when he's too angry to watch his words he's habitually insincere and manipulative. He has no sense of humour and gives no sign that he even rejoices in his own villainy, as other stage villains of the time, such as Barrabas, Aaron in 'Titus Andronicus' and Richard III, do, to make themselves more entertaining. He's a morally nasty and personally unattractive piece of work. He's repeatedly called 'devil' and 'dog', etc., by his enemies, and he doesn't seem to have any friends to speak up for him.

But doesn't he have **any** off-setting virtues or redeeming features? you may ask. His crafty intelligence and articulateness, quick-witted but not witty, hardly count in his favour, as they're mainly deployed in the cause of villainy. Maybe his wife Leah loved him, when she gave him a turquoise ring. But that's only 'maybe'. But when Jessica runs away with it he says he wouldn't have parted with it 'for a wilderness of monkeys,' (3.1.110-112) and what does that monkey image tell us? Is he grieving for the value of the jewel or the memory of his dead wife? Leah might have loved him, but that doesn't mean he loved her more than the ring.

Nevertheless, a lot of people seem to be anxious to sympathise with - even excuse - him. They – we? – feel pity as well revulsion in our hearts, so we find some satisfaction in the merciful treatment at the end. When he pleads to our common humanity to see him as a social victim he hits the mark, though he's hardly an undeserving victim, and being a victim doesn't do anything to redeem any of his particular villainies. Nevertheless, like the 'better' Christians, we'd like to see him saved. We don't identify with the Elizabethans' brassy attitude to 'minorities'. There's been the 20th century 'Holocaust' which makes us think that by now we ought to know better than that. We're uncomfortable about judging Shylock as an individual in case it makes us look as if we're anti-semitic in general. These inhibitions may account for some of the efforts in contemporary stage and film productions to give Shylock a more positive image than he had in the late 16th century. It takes various forms. Actors can confer a dignity on the Jew's key speeches which the text doesn't warrant – although, to be fair, it doesn't rule it out either. In his appeals for human sympathy his guile can be hidden behind pathos. The Christians, or more precisely the 'best' of them, can be 'ironized' by directorial decree, although they're clearly meant to be inspiring moral examples for us. Some directors even add socio-historical signals about ghettoes, costume and so on lest we forget the unjust things suffered by Jews in Venice and elsewhere. Such gestures may be meant well, but they tend to widen, not narrow, the cultural gap between contemporary consciousness and the play's still perfectly findable original meanings.

It's as silly to worry about whether 'The Merchant' is a 'racist' play as it is to ask whether Antonio is gay. The aim should be to set aside our own ideological attitudes as much as possible. But to those whose modern susceptibilities insist on being assuaged let me say this: nowhere in Shakespeare's plays do 'good' characters endorse animosity towards vulnerable social or religious minorities. (If you can think of any exceptions, please let me know.) As a man with known Catholic connections, carefully keeping his head down in the Elizabethan police state, Shakespeare had good reason to fear minority bashing. And there's one case where he has a notably **good** character speaking up in defence of minorities. He's believed on sound evidence to have collaborated on the multi-authored, never-finished and politically incorrect 'The Book of Sir Thomas More'. He contributed a couple of speeches for More, later to be canonized a Catholic saint, reproving indigenous Londoners in the early 1530s for their hostile treatment of 'strangers' in the city. 'If your king were to banish you from your own country,' More asks them, 'for some religious reason offence'

..........whither would you go?
What country by the nature of your error
Should give you harbour? Go you to France or Flanders,
To any German prince, (to) Spain or Portugal,
Nay anywhere that not adheres to England,
Why you must need be strangers. Would you be pleased
To find a nation of such barbarous temper
That breaking out in hideous violence
Would not afford you an abode on earth:
Whet their detested knives against your throats,
Spurn you like dogs, and like as if that God
Ow(n)ed you not, nor made not you? (Lines 248-259, my modernisation.)

Wandering in exile. Knives, throats. Spurned like dogs. Your common humanity as children of God denied by your enemies. Here, I think, we may be overhearing the Shakespeare of 1594 mulling over his thoughts about what Jews and other kinds of 'strangers' faced in unfriendly environments, as 'The Merchant' began to take shape in his mind.

It's Act 5. Our no-longer-dangerous villain has gone. He's only mentioned, briefly, twice more. The play has moved on, but if you think – as some people evidently do - that we've had the interesting bits and that all that remains is a perfunctory celebration of the happy outcome you should think again.

We find ourselves transported to the garden of Portia's house. Lorenzo and Jessica have been put in charge of the place while she's away. It's been their idyllic honeymoon hotel. They're expecting Portia and Bassanio, with their retinues of friends and followers, to turn up, separately, at any minute.

As usual, the mood in Belmont is in marked contrast to the mood in Venice. In Venice, in the trial scene - until Antonio (4.1.378) and Shylock (4.1.389) both declare, whatever their true feelings, 'I am content' - a tense drama was unfolding to decide whether Antonio would live or die. But now in the tranquility of Belmont the young couple are sharing a sentimental 'story-time' about lovers in classical days. Lorenzo begins a sort of love-duet with Jessica.

The moon shines bright. In such a night as this,
When the sweet wind did gently kiss the trees,
And they did make no noise, in such a night
Troilus methinks mounted the Trojan walls,
And sigh'd his soul towards the Grecian tents
Where Cressid lay that night. (5.1.1-6)

This, and what follows, is meant to hold us spell-bound - and it does. There's something lullaby-like about the off-beat rhyming of 'bright' with 'night' in the first line, and the phrase 'in such a night', repeated eight times in all, provides a hypnotic rhythmic structure and spacing for the couple's exchange of love-story 'clips'. All four – Troilus and Creseyde, Pyramus and Thisbe, Dido and Aeneas, Medea and Aeson – are borrowed from Chaucer, with a few additional details from Virgil and Ovid.

In the word-created beauty of this setting we allow ourselves to perceive the happiness of the couple, now man and wife, representing the new relationship of Jew and Christian seen in the light of love and reconciliation.

Jessica has converted to Christianity (as her father has also done) so everything should be hunky-dory from now on. But is everything really that straightforward? All the love-stories, we notice, end tragically, like the story of Hercules and Hesione that Portia remembered (3.2.53-61) in her moment of acute trepidation before Bassanio made his casket choice.

When the couple run out of old love-stories they turn to a new one – their own. 'In such a night', Lorenzo says,

Did Jessica steal from the wealthy Jew,
And with an unthrift love did run from Venice,
As far as Belmont. (5.1.14-16)

Jessica picks up on the word 'steal'? 'In such a night', she replies,

Did Lorenzo swear he loved her well,
Stealing her soul with many vows of faith,
And ne'er a true one. (5.1.16-19)

Could 'stolen her soul' refer to her conversion, as well as falling in love? Do those 'many vows of faith' carry a religious as well as a romantic meaning, and is there deception in them? Is she beginning to regret what she's done, and blaming Lorenzo for it?

No, it's alright. They're still smiling and embracing. 'In such a night,' Lorenzo continues,

Did pretty Jessica (like a little shrew)
Slander her love, and he forgave it her. (5.1.20-22)

We can breathe again. It was just a bit of lovers' badinage.

Jessica has the last word:

I would out-night you did nobody come:
But mark, I hear the footing of a man. (5.1.23-24)

In succession we've beheld the night-time tranquility
surrounding Portia's house, the poetic sting of tragedy in
the old love-stories and a hint of something precarious in
their love. The delicate transitions from one moment to the
next have been made with what seems to be a dreamlike
tread. And now, as Jessica detects 'the footing of a man', it
changes again. The approach of Portia *et al.* is announced
by a very forgettable messenger, and soon after the
approach of Bassanio and his party is startlingly heralded
by Gobbo's idiotic hunting-call imitations - Sola, sola! Wo
ha, ho! Sola, sola! (5.1.39)

At first Lorenzo's and Jessica's reaction is: 'we must go
indoors and prepare a welcome for them', but their second
thought is: 'no, let's stay here. Call the musicians into the
garden and we'll welcome our friends in the open air.
They can join **us** in this enraptured night-scene.'

So they relax, and Lorenzo instantly conjures up the 'night
atmosphere' again:

How sweet the moonlight sleeps along this bank!
Here will we sit, and let the sounds of music
Creep in our ears – soft stillness and the night
Become the touches of sweet harmony:
Sit Jessica, - look how the floor of heaven
Is thick inlaid with patens of bright gold,
There's not the smallest orb which thou behold'st
But in his motion like an angel sings,
Still quiring to the young-ey'd cherubins;
Such harmony is in immortal souls,

But whilst this muddy vesture of decay
Doth grossly close it in, we cannot hear it. (5.1.54-65)

The transitions of mood and meaning are 'pulled' by antithetical images – waking and sleeping, heavenly and earthly spheres, celestial and human beings, awaited then audible music.

Lorenzo says to the musicians:

... wake Diana with a hymn,
With sweetest touches pierce your mistress' ear,
And draw her home with music. (5.1.66-68)

'Diana', goddess of chastity (aka Selene, goddess of the moon) stands for the still virginal Portia, of course, who is being 'woken' and drawn towards her earthly married home. In case we don't make this connection immediately Portia herself will soon acknowledge her affinity with the goddess. 'Peace!' she says,

- how the moon sleeps with Endymion *(a beautiful
mythological youth),*
And would not be awak'd! (5.1.108-109)

Meanwhile, as the music plays, Jessica says, 'I am never merry when I hear sweet music.' (5.1.69) Is she simply identifying with the mood of the moment, or revealing a secret sadness? Lorenzo tells her that sweet music isn't meant to make you merry. It detaches you from the cares and temptations of earthly life and draws you upwards towards a more heavenly state. But even under the star-studded glory of the night sky, amidst the singing angels, your mortal state with its 'muddy vesture of decay' will prevent you hearing the full harmony of the universe audible only to immortals. This is a wonderful moment for them to share, but it's only **near**-perfection. Portia's house may be Paradise Regained, or near as dammit, but there may still be the odd serpent or two in the undergrowth. Music has (amongst other things) a calming power. Orpheus used it to charm savage animals as well as men - but it can only work when it's allowed to. Some men never give it the chance.

The man that hath no music in himself,
Nor is not moved with concord of sweet sounds,
Is fit for treasons, stratagems, and spoils,
The motions of his spirit are dull as night,
And his affections dark as Erebus:
Let no such man be trusted... (5.1.83-88)

(Is 'the man' here hypothetical, or could it conceivably be Shylock?)

But the prescription is more of the same - 'mark the music.' (5.1.88)

We need to keep our eyes on the moon, to follow the fluctuations of mood! For the moment it has stepped behind the clouds and the light level has gone down. As Portia and Nerissa draw closer to the house they say:

Portia: That light we see is burning in my hall:
How far that little candle throws his beams!
So shines a good deed in a naughty world.
Nerissa: When the moon shone we did not see the candle.
Portia: So doth the greater glory dim the less, -
A substitute shines brightly as a king
Until a king be by... (5.1.89-95)

We've been so impressed by Portia's brilliance that we'd almost forgotten her Christian humility, hadn't we? Her description of her rescue of Antonio as 'a little candle' reminds us of it. She falls in readily with Nerissa's comment that they wouldn't even have spotted it in the bright moonlight. What's her good deed compared with the love of God for the whole world?

But Portia still has unfinished business. In her hand she clutches the wedding ring which she gave Bassanio just before the Antonio emergency sent them hurrying off to Venice on separate paths. He swore black's white that he'd never part with it and Graziano swore the same oath to keep Nerissa's ring. But now the moment is approaching that she had in mind, just after the trial, when she said to Nerissa,

We shall have old swearing
That they did give their rings away to men. (4.2.14-15)

Bassanio and Graziano will have some explaining to do when their wives interpret their failure to produce the rings as evidence of sexual infidelity. Their story about the judge and his clerk will sound a bit thin. They're in trouble.

But two deft touches of plotting are all that's needed to get everything to work out alright. The first has the initial effect of tightening the noose around their necks. Portia tells her staff and followers to say that she and Nerissa have been at home all the time. It's a flat lie, but let's not get too judgemental here, it's only a **temporary** lie. Portia won't stick to it when it's served its purpose, i.e. of undermining their credibility when they say that they gave the rings to **men**, and making their breach of faith look worse than it really was. (Remember, the women explicitly **refused** any alternative rings or tokens of gratitude for their legal services.) The other touch of plotting (which loosens the noose) is the presence of Antonio at the end to explain that they were acting on his advice. He's a man of unchallengeable moral authority but he's willing to take the blame, casting his own 'saving' shadow over the incident.

But Portia remains unmistakably the 'judge', not one of the judged. What she says and does outweighs the questionable set-up that she contrives and leaves us feeling more, not less, morally impressed by her. For the women at least, holding all the best cards, it's become a game – albeit a necessary and instructive game - but there are no longer any serious crimes or serious punishments at issue. This 'forswearing' matter might still be a bit tricky but any outcome other than forgiveness would be unimaginable. After all, the betrothal rings are **not** lost. The women have them in their own safe keeping. But it's a good opportunity to give the men a shot across the bows.

Immediately after Lorenzo recognizes her voice in the dark Portia asks whether Bassanio has returned yet. It's the thought uppermost in her mind. She's been stopping off at various shrines on the way where, she says, 'we have bin praying for our husbands' welfare'. (5.1.114)

But what do you make of her next comment, as she hears a trumpet sounding Bassanio's arrival?

This night methinks is but the daylight sick,
It looks a little paler, - 'tis a day,
Such as the day is when the sun is hid. (5.1.124-126)

The moon is out again, but 'sick', 'pales' and 'hid' don't exactly denote unbridled joy at seeing her beloved husband again, do they? If the light of day is gold, and the moonlit night is silver, her mood is pretty leaden at the moment. She'd been looking forward to the row - another 'trial', as it were - but now she seems to be more conscious of the pain that it'll cause, to Bassanio and herself.

As she's introduced to Antonio, whose welcome she 'scants' with 'breathing courtesy' (5.1.141) a second, even less decorous, conversation breaks out nearby. 'A quarrel ho, already!' (5.1.146) Nerissa has launched her (unheard) attack on Graziano, who before the whole company protests aloud his innocence 'by yonder moon'. (5.1.142) With characteristic tactlessness he infuriates his wife by describing the wedding ring she gave him as 'a paltry ring'. (5.1.147) So why all this fuss, he asks, because he gave it to 'a scrubbed boy', (5.1.162) 'a judge's clerk' (5.1.143, etc.) who made himself useful to him in a court case in Venice?

Portia wholeheartedly supports the indignant Nerissa and rebukes Graziano. Her own husband would never do such a thing!

Oh yes he would! But as soon as the second cat is out of the bag the difference of moral quality between the two men is immediately clear. Bassanio doesn't denigrate his ring, or what it stands for. He admits that he acted wrongly in giving it away, whatever the mitigating circumstances. He would never do such a thing again. He asks for pardon and with the grace of Antonio's 'saving' intervention he is fully forgiven. It's a perfect confession.

In her declaration of love (and uneasy conscience) in the casket scene with Bassanio Portia, if you recall, declared:

    ……..Beshrew your eyes,
They have o'erlook'd me, and divided me,

One half of me is yours, the other half yours, -
Mine own I would say: but if mine then yours,
And so all yours. (3.2.14-18)

Now near the end of the play, as Bassanio begins to swear
his repentance:

……. even by thine own fair eyes
Wherein I see myself – (5.1.242-243)

she interrupts him with a new 'eye' image:

………Mark you but that!
In both my eyes he doubly sees himself:
In each eye one, - swear by your double self,
And there's an oath of credit. (5.1.243-246)

This is a statement about division within unity.

Portia wants to ensure that his experience of mercy at this
moment will always remind him of his sinful 'double'
nature. Sins can be forgiven. Sinfulness remains.

It's something for him to bear in mind in his married life.

MEASURE FOR MEASURE

'Measure for Measure' was first staged in 1604, about eight or ten years after 'The Merchant of Venice'. Shakespeare had 'moved on'. There's a 'justice and mercy' overlap – in each play the heroine makes a memorable speech about mercy– but otherwise the two plays are chalk and cheese. 'Measure for Measure' offers a very different kind of dramatic experience – albeit it's still a comedy, so it works out 'right' but it's darker and edgier in mood and its verse is generally more challenging and suggestive. And unlike 'The Merchant of Venice' it lacks the note of celebration of a prosperous Christian culture.

Whereas Venice is a well-governed city, the Vienna of 'Measure for Measure' is a city where there's corruption amongst the enforcers as well as the infringers of the law. In the two great interview scenes between Angelo and Isabella the focus is as much on standards in public life as in private consciences, and the connections between them. The same can be said of the criminal underclass material, of which there's no equivalent in the earlier play; it not only adds dramatic variety, complexity and spice but gives Shakespeare the scope to paint a fuller picture of social degeneracy.

Generally speaking, Shakespeare drew a clear moral line **between** characters like Antonio and Portia who, are unmistakably 'good', and Shylock who, although he momentarily attracts our often-misplaced sympathy, is 'bad' – the villain of the piece. In 'Measure for Measure', by comparison, the line distinguishing good from evil is less tortuous, and more often drawn **through** the characters. There's a strong element of moral contradiction in the 'good' characters - Isabella, the Duke and Claudio.

Even the bad hat, Angelo, is ambivalent – he starts and finishes the play, remember, as a 'virtuous' man.

'Measure for Measure' is a play of its time and place. Elizabeth Tudor had died in the previous year and the new regime of James 1, a Scottish Stuart, had given rise, if not to wild enthusiasm at least to a certain amount of wary optimism. In the spring of 1604, having set up his court in London, the king undertook a 'look-and-see' tour of his kingdom. There is some evidence that that James was given on occasion to snooping around incognito, but it obviously didn't include an extended trawl through the low-life of the capital. In the last gloomy years of Elizabeth's 45-year reign there had been a feeling that the Queen's preoccupation with foreign affairs and national security had drawn her attention away from the accumulating problems and abuses at home. She'd 'lost touch', as we'd say today. Vice and crime in London was a hot topic in the first decade of the 17th century, and not just with Puritans. Thomas Dekker, for example, would soon be piling into the debate with his sensationalist pamphlet 'The Seven Deadly Sinnes of London' (1606). But along with the alarm there was a hope that if matters were brought to the attention of the new ruler he might be able to do something about them.

In fact, 'Measure for Measure' wasn't the only play of the time to depict a city in moral decay. In Thomas Middleton's 'The Phoenix', staged in the same year, the Duke of Ferrara has been sitting up there on the judge's bench for so long, formulating the 'law', that he's now in dire need of a reality-check. It's not the Duke himself but his son and heir, the eponymous Phoenix, who, pretending to go into exile, disguises himself and embarks on a series of investigations into the disgraceful goings-on in the city.

Duke or Duke's son - it's a difference of detail. The idea in common – and it's by no means new or original - is that there's something rotten in society which has been festering away for a long time and which won't be righted unless the man 'up there' is prepared to come down into the midst of his people and get a direct personal take on the state of things on the ground. Playwrights watched each other's productions closely, borrowing each other's ideas and developing their own variations upon them. Jostling with 'Measure for Measure' for the attention of the Globe audience was John Marston's 'The Malcontent', which also has a Duke disguised as a hermit and an innocent young woman being sexually blackmailed by an unscrupulous politico.

It's worth mentioning that there appears to be another link between Middleton and 'Measure for Measure'. Recent research suggests that he revised Shakespeare's play for a later performance, and that some of the text that has come down to us – though precisely what is a matter of conjecture - is from his pen. No-one's suggesting, though, that the play isn't essentially Shakespeare's in design and meaning, if not in all details.

It's less fanciful than one might initially suppose to believe that in 'Measure for Measure' Shakespeare may have seen himself as conveying a message to the king, as well as keeping the Globe crowd entertained. The Revels Accounts record a performance in the banqueting hall at Whitehall on 26 December 1604 when James would have been present. Shakespeare may have made as much as he did of the discussion about the responsibilities and pitfalls of 'magistracy' because he knew that it would be of particular interest to James, who'd given a lot of thought to the subject and who rather fancied himself as a 'wise magistrate'. Such message-sending from playwright to monarch wasn't a new thing. Fifteen or twenty years earlier it had been a feature of the plays that John Lyly wrote for the court of Elizabeth, and there was an ongoing tradition of staging successful 'public' plays at court by royal command. 'Macbeth', hitting the stage a couple of years after 'Measure for Measure', is another attempt to capture James's special attention; the witch material (some of which, including the songs and dances with Hecate - is believed to have been added by Middleton, by the way) refers to a subject that the king had written a learned book about – 'Demonologie'. And the fact that soon after his arrival in England the theatre-loving king had 'adopted' Shakespeare's company, bestowing the enviable title of 'The King's Men' upon them and kitting them out in royal livery, may be taken as further confirmation that Shakespeare felt that he could catch the royal ear at this time.

During his 14-year rule the Duke has failed to curb sexual vice and crime in Vienna. Things have gone from bad to worse. Acknowledging his responsibility for this, and believing that things have gone too far for him to be able to repair the damage himself, he decides to put his deputy Angelo in charge and go into exile. Or so he says - actually he intends to stick around disguised as a Friar and keep his eye on developments. Angelo - 'a man of stricture and firm abstinence' (1.3.12) - will impose the long-overdue crackdown. The Duke has decided to promote Angelo over his senior colleague Escalus because he's still a 'new man' in public life; he hasn't had time to fall into lax ways and make those kind and easy compromises with wayward human nature that have done so much to undermine respect for the law.

He gives him carte blanche.

In our remove, be thou at full ourself. (1.1.43)

In other words, I want you to 'be me' precisely because I'm not like you.

The first case to come before the newly promoted Angelo is that of Claudio, a young man of good family and previous good name, now under arrest for getting his intended, Juliet, pregnant. The young couple sincerely love each other; they've exchanged pledges and they believe that they're morally, if not quite legally, married. Claudio speaks of their 'true contract' (1.2.134) and claims that Juliet is

> fast my wife,
Save that we do the denunciation lack
Of outward order. (1.2.136-138)

And it's not **their** fault that there's been this slight legal hiccup.

This no irresponsible fling. Hitherto the law has closed its eyes to, or imposed only a token penalty, on this kind of irregularity. But Angelo's determined to change attitudes and expectations. The law must be enforced. Public examples must be made. So here's poor Claudio – much to everybody's shock and dismay - being marched through the streets on his way to gaol – and execution! It's like a motorist having his driving licence taken away for doing 31 m.p.h. in a built-up area! OK, it's the law, no doubt. But if old-fashioned custom and practice is out of the window, we're **all** in dead trouble, aren't we?

Actually – and it's to his credit – Claudio takes the point that Angelo's making. It's a fair cop. He's been tempted, he's fallen, he's been caught and he doesn't expect to be let off. He agrees that public and personal standards of conduct are connected. People tend to copy each other's good and bad examples so it's important for the law to say what the right standards are, and enforce them. The law must repress 'liberty', (1.2.117) he says, which

As surfeit, is the father of much fast;
So every scope by immoderate use
Turns to restraint. Our natures do pursue,
Like rats that ravin down their proper bane,
A thirsty evil; and when we drink, we die. (1.2.118-122)

It's this 'liberty' – we might call it 'permissiveness' - that's led him and many others astray. It needs to be curbed. Offenders must be punished. He's ready to take his own punishment. It's just that death seems so disproportionate! He's not a rat, so why should he die? This is just Angelo's opening flourish, surely? He just wants to make him sweat for a bit, then he'll commute the sentence.

We soon find, though, from the way he talks to his friend Lucio, a man who represents the Viennese laxity, that Claudio is a more complicated man than this summary of his attitude suggests. It comes out in his language. Some of his words have an oddly 'contrary' sense. They're a bit like the verbal mishaps in which the hapless Elbow says the opposite of what he means - for example describing Pompey and Froth as 'notorious benefactors'. (2.1.50) With Elbow it's using big words so as not to appear as ignorant as he is, but in Claudio's case it must be something else. The word 'denunciation' (1.2.137) is only the first of a number of examples. It refers to the legal document needed to approve his relationship with Juliet, but of course the negative prefix conveys a sense of **dis**approval. On its own there'd be nothing to be made of this, but his use of the word 'propagation' two lines further down has a similar effect. On the face of it, it means 'production' - i.e. of the dowry needed for the legal completion of the marriage contract; but the associations of the word with pregnancy and childbirth – here with 'unlawful' associations - make it an odd choice of word in this particular context. There'll be more examples later in the scene, but already we're wondering: what's going on here? Could it be that these words carrying 'contrary' meanings are coming from another part of Claudio's mind which, as a counterpoint to his self-extenuation, insists on expressing shame? Are they the voice of bad conscience filtering through the language of excuse? Is Claudio allowing these words to 'find' him and to say what he can't quite bring himself to say himself? Is this his back-handed way of admitting his shame to his shameless friend and to a shameless society?

There are more examples which can be interpreted in this 'psychological' way, rather as if they're 'inadvertent' material. What about Claudio's image of the legitimising dowry stowed away in the friends' coffer? (1.2.140) Why should he bring in such a specific 'contained/container', 'hidden/hiding-place' image unless as an unconscious reference to the child in Julietta's womb? The thought-pattern goes like this: the 'stealth' (1.2.143) of their love-making has now been exposed to public knowledge and censure by her 'gross' (1.2.144) pregnancy, just as her (hidden) pregnancy will in due course be exposed by the birth of a child. Such thinking is clearly of an intuitive/associative, not a rational/descriptive kind. 'Good' and 'bad' things, not just disparate things, are fused together. The (good) finding of the concealed dowry is embedded in the same image as the (bad) dread of the exposure of the hidden sexual secret. Hope, worry and shame are all intermeshed. (Are we allowed to recall, by the way, that twenty years before he wrote this play Shakespeare, still in his teens, had found himself in a Claudio-like situation when he got Ann Hathaway pregnant in Stratford?)

Claudio has the bright idea of roping in his sister Isabella to plead on his behalf to Angelo. Tactically, it's a smart move, but further 'psychological' considerations arise when we notice little indications in his language that he's conscious of deploying her sexuality for his own purposes. He sends Lucio off to her with these words:

Implore her, in my voice, that she makes friends
To the strict deputy: bid herself assay him.
I have great hope in that. For in her youth
There is a prone and speechless dialect
Such as move men; beside she hath prosperous art
When she will play with reason and discourse,
And well she can persuade. (1.3.170-176)

Of Isabella's potentially useful assets – personal attractiveness and eloquence – it's the first that Claudio mentions first. 'Make friends/To the strict deputy' suggests a charm offensive aimed at relaxing his formal correctness. He's not saying anything like 'seduce him, if necessary', but that 'speechless dialect' certainly 'moves men'. He's up against it, it's worth a try, and the risk to Isabella looks remote: she won't be aware of any sexual effect she might have on Angelo (he supposes), and even if he did find himself drawn to her he's a Puritan - he wouldn't show it, let alone do anything about it. But let's take a closer, more suspicious, look at some of Claudio's words. 'Assay' was commonly used in the military sense of laying siege to a defended position, but it was also a cliché-metaphor for sexual advances. What about 'prone', 'move', 'play' and 'art'? None of them quite amounts to a double - entendre but they all have sub-erotic associations in the speech of the time, and together they create a certain impression. No, it's not the impression of Claudio as an outright bounder, but rather of a distraught man across whose mind the shadow of the possible sexual implications of what he's asking his sister to do has fallen, but who wants to ignore it. This is iffy stuff, but we can be quite certain that we're meant to pick up on the 'pimp' implication here because it will tie up directly with Isabella's accusations against her brother later on. If, when the language is nudging us towards suspicion, we don't register it, or dismiss it as unlikely in such a nice young man, we'll fail to see that the ground is being laid for Act 3, Scene 1 in which the incandescent Isabella lets rip against the brother she's been trying to save. There, to the pimp charge she will add a surreally shocking charge of incest:

Wilt thou be made a man out of my vice? (3.1.137) –

and for good measure speculate, not shirking the aspersion on their mother's honour, that he must be a bastard. Her parting shot –

Thy sin's not accidental, but a trade;
Mercy to thee would prove itself a bawd;
Tis best thou diest quickly - (3.1.148-150)

will fling him down into the underworld of prostitution which, in her view, is his proper moral milieu. If we hadn't already considered Claudio in the ambivalent light cast by his language in this scene, Isabella's fit of rage (which, we note, isn't the only one that this 'thing enskied' has in the play) would be less intelligible, or cause us to revise our opinion of her steeply downwards. Anger may not be particularly virtuous but Isabella has plenty of reason for it. In his panic, Claudio **does** eventually ask her to barter her body to save him, and even before that he **did** understand, as his sex-tinted words betray here, the sort of risk, or at least indignity, that he was prepared to expose her to with Angelo.

In Act Two, Scene 1 the two magistrates, Angelo and Escalus, spell out the differences between them. It's a matter of temperament as well as conviction. Angelo is 'tough'; Escalus is 'tender'. Neither tendency is entirely correct or incorrect, or even generally preferable to its opposite. The good magistrate, one supposes, is one who can combine tough with tender in the right proportions, case by case and consistently over time. (Are you listening, Your Majesty?) Angelo, as we'll see, believes that in the long run his tough approach will reduce the quantum of human suffering; contrariwise, Escalus will put on a show of toughness (well, makes tough noises perhaps) when necessary but hope to give the benefit of the doubt and show leniency wherever possible. They both get it wrong. It may be an impossible job. Things swing too far this way towards mercy, then that way towards rigour, and it's very difficult to get, or keep, the balance exactly right. All you can do is swing back to leniency when the law is felt to be too harsh, and back again to severity when things have got too slack. But currently, it's more rigour that the Duke sees Vienna in need of, and that's why he's put Angelo in charge.

Angelo holds his own well in the discussion he has with Escalus about the condemnation of Claudio. Escalus's view seems to be based on an interpretation of the scriptural injunction: 'Judge not, lest ye be judged'. We must be jolly careful when passing judgement on others, he argues. We're all sinners. Any of us - even Angelo! -

190

could find ourselves in Claudio's shoes! Angelo doesn't see it that way at all. Escalus's attitude is a part of the problem, not the solution. Our sense of common human fallibility, he says, shouldn't reach the point where magistrates feel disqualified from using the law to punish crime. That only serves the interests of wrong-doers, the results of which we can see all around us. One-off lapses become repeat-behaviour; offenders get a sense of impunity, settle comfortably into lives of crime and society goes to hell in a handcart. The only concession to the principle of moral equality that Angelo's prepared to make is this: if he himself were guilty of the offence that the prisoner in front of him is convicted of he'd expect exactly the same punishment:

When I that censure him do so offend
Let mine own judgement pattern out my death. (2.1.29-30)

People like Escalus and Lucio – and the audience, if they don't know the play already – might feel that it's easy for Angelo to say this because he's immune to 'the wanton stings and motions of the sense'. (1.4.59) But if so they'd be mistaken. He's tempted all right, but

'Tis one thing to be tempted, Escalus,
Another thing to fall. (2.1.17-18)

Mm…noted! We'll remember that later.

Anyway, the moral calibre of judges and juries isn't the point. All they have to do is apply the law strictly, objectively and impersonally, and not be distracted by ethical relativities of the sort that Escalus is trying to introduce. When all's said and done it's not they who are being judged. To insist that if they aren't personally perfect they shouldn't be passing judgement on others would be to bring the whole law-enforcement show to a grinding halt. That would be irresponsible.

Escalus still prevaricates. What sort of justice is it, he asks, if you make a dire example of the few you catch while so many others get away with it?

Some run from brakes of (v)ice and answer none
And some condemned for a fault alone. (2.1.39-40)

(Lever's Arden text gives 'ice', but here I accept Rowe's emendation 'vice', which gives the most straightforward meaning: i.e. 'some habitual criminals escape the law entirely'. When the line's spoken aloud you can see that the two readings sound almost the same, anyway.)

Angelo points out that Escalus is indicating an inequity that the law ought to correct, not accept and accommodate. It comes of patchy, as distinct from overlax, enforcement. In the coming crackdown not only will sentences be tougher and send a stronger deterrent message but more offenders will be caught and sentenced. When few if any wrongdoers get away with it that'll be another much-needed improvement in the justice system.

The discussion between the two magistrates, occupying only 40 lines, sets out the opposing arguments and gives Angelo, at this point at any rate, the logical edge. But this is the theory. What about the practice? The remainder of the scene give us a demonstration.

Elbow, a constable, brings two accused men, Froth and Pompey, into the courtroom and introduces them to Angelo as 'notorious benefactors'. (2.1.50) Whatever his name might suggest, Elbow isn't 'bent'; he's just a complete nitwit. As we soon see, he has a particularly hapless way with words; what he says tends to come out the opposite of what he means. (It's a comic version of what we saw happening in some of Claudio's speeches.) The effect is ludicrous, of course, but it isn't long before we realise that Shakespeare's showing us the kind of unlikely-truth-telling with which 'pure' fools can be inspired. When Elbow says of the accused: 'If it please your honour, I know not well what they are. But precise villains they are, that I am sure of, and void of all profanation in the world, that good Christians ought to have' (2.1.53-56) the words seem to apply as much to the two judges as to Froth and Pompey. And this isn't just a passing thought. It's confirmed when Pompey denies the charges against him – though exactly what they are isn't clear – and Elbow challenges him with: 'Prove it before these varlets here (i.e. Angelo and Escalus), thou honourable man, thou, prove it.' (2.1.85-86)

'Precise villains' – the Duke has already used 'precise' to describe Angelo. (1.3.50) 'Varlets' – well, if Pompey's an 'honourable man' that might well make his judges 'varlets', wouldn't it? Escalus appears to be quite relaxed about Elbow's verbal and moral topsy-turvydom. He (presumably) knows Elbow of old, he's seen it all in his time and he's not one to get all het up about seeing the law being made an ass of. Angelo, though, shows signs of irritation. He isn't comfortable about finding himself on the receiving end of blame-words, even if the speaker's a blatant idiot. And he certainly doesn't enjoy seeing courtroom proceedings descend into low farce.

The story that now unfolds is hilarious, but rather horrible. One day Elbow's wife, in state of advanced pregnancy (cf Juliet!) drops into the 'Bunch of Grapes', Mistress Overdone's tavern/whorehouse, where Pompey's employed as tapster and general factotum and where Froth is a regular customer. She's beset with a great longing for a dish of stewed prunes - a speciality of such houses, apparently. Whether or not she gets her prunes is never established, but something untoward evidently befalls her while she's there. Elbow, who's very indignant about it, has run them in for whatever it was.

As the case proceeds Pompey somehow manages to slip out of the role of defendant into the role of witness for the defence for Froth. Impervious to any direction or restraint from the bench he starts revelling in the limelight, spinning out the story in his own jokey and insolent way and giving Escalus, who's supposed to be in charge, the complete run-around. Angelo can't stop the performance, or take charge, or bear to watch, so he walks out indignantly, saying to his fellow-judge:

This will last a night out in Russia
When nights are longest there. I'll take my leave,
And leave you to the hearing of the cause;
Hoping you find good cause to whip them all. (2.1.133-136)

Escalus keeps trying to find out what actually happened to Mrs Elbow and it gradually emerges that the charge - never clearly formulated, let alone proved - is that she was grossly insulted by the drunken Froth and perhaps even 'put to the uses of trade' by him. Pompey, now promoting himself from defence witness to counsel for the defence, earnestly asks Escalus to look long and hard at Froth and then say whether 'your honour see(s) any harm in his face'. (2.1.151) No, says Escalus, submitting to answering questions when he ought to be asking them, I don't. Well, says Pompey, 'his face is the worst thing about him,' (2.1.153-154) so he can't have done Mrs Elbow any harm, can he?

Escalus buys this 'evidence'. Forgetting or ignoring Angelo's advice that bawds and their customers should all get at least a whipping before they go home, Escalus judges that in this case a wigging will suffice. He dismisses Froth with a quip about tapsters and 'hanging and drawing' which is meant to establish his street cred and tell the accused that although the law has fearsome punishments at its disposal this particular representative of it – aren't you lucky? – is too nice to want to inflict them on him, this time at least. He prefers to appeal to people's better natures, give them a second chance, etc. So we've got Escalus's number, and no doubt Froth has got it, too - this magistrate fancies being known in the taverns of Southwark as 'a decent old beak'. He advises him not to frequent places like Mistress Overdone's establishment in future if he doesn't want to be drawn into bad ways. Then it's 'go and sin no more.' His dismissal of Pompey is just as flippant. He treats him as a 'card' who doesn't need to be taken, or treated, seriously; he's already made a joke from the bench about his surname, Bum, and the unusual size of that feature of Pompey's physique which corresponds to it. Very amusing. Now he thinks that a bit of rather more learned, upper-class wit is what's called for. Assuming a 'but-seriously-though' air, but still with a twinkle in his eye, he says: 'I advise you, let me not find you before me again upon any complaint whatsoever…If I do, Pompey, I shall beat you to your tent and prove a shrewd Caesar to you. In plain dealing, Pompey, I shall have you whipped. So for this time, Pompey, fare you well.' (2.1.242-248)

Pompey's reply is polite enough: 'I thank your worship for your good counsel' (2.1.249) but we know what he must be thinking: Ha, bloody ha! What a wag! What a wanker!

There's no contrition, no gratitude, just scorn and defiance.

In an aside he says:

Whip me? No, no, let carman whip his jade;
The valiant heart's not whipped out of his trade. (2.1.252-253)

The text is full of shadowy cross-references, contradictions and ironies, linking lower with upper Viennese life. In the course of his defence of Froth, for example, Pompey seeks to discredit Elbow as a witness by accusing him of having had intercourse with Mrs Elbow before they were married. It's the 'you're-no-better-than-us-so-who-are-you-to-object' argument that gets several outings, in various guises, in the play. Picking up on Elbow's misuse of the word 'respect' to mean something like its opposite, he says: 'She was respected with him before he married with her.' (2.1.167-168) Claudio and Juliet come to mind, and they're meant to.

Although freeing the accused is the only option a judge has when the charge isn't proved we all know what a travesty of the law we've been watching. A serious offence (rape?) has been committed. We know who did it and who was complicit; the guilty men show no signs of remorse and are going unpunished. Judge Escalus knows this, too, of course. Of the two magistrates he's the 'nice' one, but we're jolted by the cynicism of the words he uses to dispose of Elbow's complaint: '...because he (Pompey) has some offences in that thou wouldst discover if thou couldst, let him continue in his courses till thou know'st what they are.' (2.1.182-185) Shakespeare adds an extra sting to this by having the poor wronged constable reply: 'Marry, I thank you worship for it' (2.1.186) and then, turning to the grinning Pompey, say: 'Thou seest, thou wicked varlet now, what's come upon thee. Thou art to continue now, thou varlet, thou art to continue.' (2.1.186-

187) We remember Elbow calling Escalus and Angelo 'varlets' earlier in the scene. Well, about Escalus he wasn't far wide of the mark, was he?

The Duke has got one thing right, at least – appointing Angelo over Escalus.

We're shown this scene of legal incompetence and moral frivolity as we worry about the fate of Claudio. Will he, too, get off with a warning? We doubt it, although he's much more deserving than Pompey, because Angelo is in charge of his case and if there's any erring with him it'll be in the opposite direction.

In Act Two, Scene 2 Angelo has condemned Claudio to death and given orders for summary execution of the sentence. There's not much time to save him! The Provost expects there to be a reprieve, but when he says so to Angelo he's firmly put down and threatened with the sack. So we see what sort of mood this new broom magistrate is in when Isabella arrives, with the rakish Lucio in a supporting role, to plead for her brother's life.

Earlier Isabella had told Lucio (1.4.**88-89**) that she was confident of saving her brother. Now she's not so sure. Her spirit, tuned to the quiet purlieus of the convent she longs to enter, is unsettled by the 'corridors of power' environment where she now finds herself. She's understandably discouraged by Angelo's 'what-do-you-want-then?' manner, and she begins very diffidently.

Her opening argument amounts to this: punish the crime, spare the criminal. It cuts no ice. She seems to be ready to give up and retire but Lucio urges her to try again – and harder. She does. She admits that Claudio has done wrong – he admits it himself – and deserves to be punished, but must he needs die? (2.2.48)

Put so briefly this hardly amounts to an argument. It's a yes/no question, which Angelo needs no more than the three-beat remainder of the same line to answer:

Maid, no remedy. (2.2.48)

So far, no contest. But why, we're beginning to wonder, isn't Isabella putting up more of a fight? We've already seen that she's articulate and not especially shy, but she certainly seems to be very inhibited at present, just when she can't afford to be. Lucio tries to urge her out of it by complaining, twice, that she's too 'cold'. (2.2.45 and 2.2.56) She needs to show more passion. So why doesn't she? What's holding her back?

Isabella's a very proper, well-brought-up young woman. Her life has been sheltered from the Viennese version of 'Sex and the City' going on around her but she's not altogether oblivious to it and it may to some extent represent 'the devil, the world and the flesh' which she hopes to get away from in the nunnery. But it would be a mistake to see her as a prude. Lucio may regard her as 'a thing enskied and sainted' (1.4.34) but he also sees her as distinctly fanciable, and that doesn't seem to bother or surprise her in the least. Nor does she jib at his earthy language when he breaks the news to her about what Claudio's been up to:

Your brother and his lover have embrac'd;
As those that feed grow full, as blossoming time
That from the seedness the bare fallow brings
To teeming foison, even so her plenteous womb
Expresseth his full tilth and husbandry. (1.4.40-44)

Her matter-of-fact response to this is: 'Someone with child with him? My cousin Juliet?' (1.4.45)

-- which, when he confirms it, she follows up with the perfectly sensible: 'O, let him marry her!' (1.4.49)

So she's not **that** unworldly. Proudly virginal herself she knows the facts of life and isn't shocked that men – and women – have sexual desires. Of course she disapproves of their indulging those desires except in marriage, but she knows that such things do happen and she sees no reason to disown either her brother or Juliet, her friend from schooldays, just because they've strayed from the strict path of virtue.

Nor, I would imagine, is Isabella altogether too naïve to understand what Lucio's driving at when, urging her to go to Angelo to plead for Claudio's life, he says:

> when maidens sue,
Men give like gods. (1.4.80-81)

She knows what he means. She'll have to be a bit careful, that's all.

Which brings us back to Act 2, Scene 2, where Isabella is now the maiden doing the suing.

Angelo a worldly-wise seducer? Isabella an unsuspecting virgin? Forget it. The truth is that Isabella is less sexually 'repressed' than Angelo. She's more realistically aware of the sexual factor in human relations and she's readier than he is to acknowledge – though only to herself, of course - that the forthcoming interview might, if wrongly handled, become a sexual encounter. She can read the subtext, and she's anxious to keep it 'sub'. But she also knows that

Lucio, constitutionally impatient with all forms of repression and restraint, has a point when he reproaches her for the 'coldness' of her address to Angelo. It's a dilemma. Is she to stay cold and correct, and so lessen her chance of saving her brother? Or is she to warm to the task of persuasion, displaying more animation and feminine appeal, at the risk of getting into deep water? She knows what men are like - even if Angelo has a bit of a blind spot about what he's like. She's pure and modest, but that doesn't mean that she doesn't know she's an attractive young woman.

So it's with misgivings, but for her brother's sake, that she now goes to work to make up for her faltering start with Angelo. She decides to 'go for it'. Of course, the last thing the actress playing Isabella should do is exert any kind of charm other than maidenly modestly; but she does need to show that she has decided to make Angelo sit up and take proper notice. Diffidence and self-effacement won't do it. She must bring her eloquence and force of personality to bear. She must start arguing and persuading, though in a way that is still safely formal and 'distanced'. 'Well, believe this,' she says,

No ceremony that to great ones longs,
Not the king's crown, nor the deputed sword,
The marshal's truncheon, nor the judge's robe,
Becomes them with one half so good a grace
As mercy does. (2.2.58-63)

This falls well short of a 'personal appeal', doesn't it? It's a general moral sentiment which everyone – everyone being Christian, of course - would presumably share.

Angelo doesn't argue back. It's for the actor and/or director to decide whether he remains off-hand and inscrutable or chooses this moment to betray the first signs of disturbance when he says:

Pray you be gone. (2.2.66)

At the beginning of the interview this curt dismissal would have been enough to send Isabella backing meekly out of the door. But now she's gripped by thoughts and emotions which, however generalised, she fervently believes in, and which she feels are too true and important for Angelo to be allowed to brush aside. She stands her ground, and decides to advance into less abstract territory, even risking a touch of 'ad hominem'. 'I would to heaven I had your potency,' she says,

And you were Isabel! Should it then be thus?
No; I would tell what 'twere to be a judge,
And what a prisoner. (2.2.67-69)

This definitely strikes a much more personal note. Isabella's referred to herself by name – 'Isabel'. There's also something almost intimate about this notion of swapping roles and identities; it shrinks the adversarial distance between them, almost as if she's saying: that's enough wary sparring, how about some close combat? Does Isabella understand the possible effect on Angelo of such an invitation? Lucio certainly does. He enthuses: 'Ay, touch him: there's the vein.' (2.2.70)

Lucio may be encouraged, but we're beginning to worry.

If Angelo's 'touched' he doesn't give any sign of it. He knows that the advantage of his inscrutable and dismissive manner is that it keeps the onus on Isabella to make the running and keep the interview going. He doesn't need to say anything much, or new. He can afford to repeat himself:

Claudio is forfeit of the law
And you but waste your words. (2.2 71-72)

But Isabella's now firing on all cylinders. Ignoring the 'waste your words' bit she pounces on 'forfeit', a word full of meaning for the devout novice nun, which gives her the cue for a directly religious appeal to Angelo. What she now says is her version, very differently but equally beautifully worded, of Portia's plea for mercy in 'The Merchant of Venice'.

Alas! Alas!
All the souls that were, were forfeit once,
And He that might the vantage best have took
Found out the remedy. How would you be
If He, which is the top of judgement, should
But judge you as you are? O, think on that,
And mercy then will breathe within your lips,
Like man new made. (2.2.72-79)

Needless to say, Isabella isn't making this reference to the Saviour's forgiveness and mercy merely as an argumentative ploy. Her words stem from a passionate conviction deep in her faithful Christian heart, and they're meant to reach deep into Angelo's heart. This is Christian speaking to Christian. We're all sinners standing in need of mercy - which God freely gives us - so it behoves us to show mercy to others. If we do we're promised a new creation, Adam redeemed.

An appeal couched in such terms can't easily be ignored or rejected, but it can be deflected – and this is what Angelo does. Maybe he's mindful – as we might be ourselves – that Escalus, a follower of the Isabella line, has been giving mercy a bad name in Vienna. However that may be, it's the inspired messenger rather than the inspiring message that he fastens on to. Shakespeare leaves us to guess the precise moment – if there is one - when Angelo falls for Isabella, but for my money it's here, at the moment when he recognises her spiritual radiance. There's no evidence for this yet, but it'll come in his soliloquy at the end of the scene, where he says:

> Most dangerous
> Is that temptation that doth goad us on
> To sin in loving virtue. Never could the strumpet
> With all her double vigour, art and nature
> Once stir my temper; but this virtuous maid
> Subdues me quite. (2.2.181-186)

Opposites attract. Isabella is what Angelo isn't. She possesses in full measure the qualities that he lacks - not only to remedy but to **complete** his being. The virtue and generosity of spirit that animate her - and how animated she is now! - are the opposite of his own rigid severity, just as her expressive femininity is the opposite of his tense masculinity. It's her moral beauty – as much as her physical beauty – that makes her an object of desire for him. It's lust, all right, but of an existential as well as a sexual kind.

But what, if anything, is Isabella making of the situation? The text doesn't tell us, so the actress playing her has to decide whether she's baffled by Angelo's stone-walling or whether she thinks that she's beginning to get him on the run. Either way, she needs to show her bracing herself to take more risks, and say some pretty challenging things to him.

The actor playing Angelo has decisions to make, too.

Whether or not he was 'touched' before there probably needs to be some signs now that something's going on behind that mask of non-admission. They don't have to be many, or too blatant. Perhaps all that's needed is a bit of body language to suggest that the interview has now become a bit of a trial for him and that he wants to end it as quickly as possible. Abruptly he says:

Be you content, fair maid;
It is the law, not I, condemn your brother.
……………He must die tomorrow. (2.2.79-80 and 2.2.82)

So - decision made, reason given, temptation resisted. Now go away, Isabella.

But that's not what happens. 'Tomorrow' simply galvanises Isabella into something approaching panic.

Tomorrow? O, that's sudden.
Spare him, spare him! (2.2.83-84)

It's at this point that the scene, so far characterised by caution and constraint with the two protagonists in fixed positions, needs to break into physical movement. Isabella, let's say, takes a step or two towards Angelo, drops to her knees and looks directly into his eyes; she might reach out a hand out towards him, but pull it back just before it touches him. Whatever she does will have the approval of Lucio, who understands the effects of such things, but the effect on Angelo, struggling to master feelings he can't account for……….well, let's just say it doesn't help. Of course he has only to call a servant and have his visitor shown out but somehow the moment for that seems to have gone by. He finds he didn't really mean 'go away, Isabella'. He wants her to stay. There's unfinished business.

Were it not for the inner turmoil that Isabella's stirring up in him the interview ought to be easier for Angelo than for her. After all, she's the one who has to come up with the match-winning performance - he has only to defend. So far he's said very little – just 'no' in various ways. But now – could it be a sign that the tables are turning and that he finds that he wants **her** attention? – he has more to say. And what's more, his words start to reveal a lot about the man as distinct from the public persona. We're reminded of Claudio in Act One, Scene 2 – where we noticed the verse thickening up with imagery and references stemming from out-of-the-way, even inappropriate, thought processes. This is what happens here, too. At first it seems that he's simply going to trot out his 'much-needed-crackdown' argument again - the law has been asleep and failed to keep due watch on wrong-doing, but now it's awake again, etc – but suddenly his words start carrying striking images suffused with strong emotion. The law, he finds himself saying

Takes note of what is done, and like a prophet
Looks in a glass that shows what future evils,
Either new, or by remissness new conceiv'd,
And so in progress to be hatched and born,
Are now to have no successive degrees,
But ere they live, to end. (2.2.95-100)

This imagery is almost dreamlike. 'Glass', meaning foresight, suggests a pagan wizard with his crystal ball rather than a Biblical figure. And those fearful 'future evils' that must at all costs be prevented are actually images of new but still-hidden life. 'Hatching' is a recurrent image in Shakespeare. In 'Julius Caesar' it occurs in association with snakes. Depicting Caesar as a growing political threat Cassius says:

Think him as a serpent's egg,
Which, hatch'd, would, as his kind, grow mischievous,
And kill him in the shell. (JC: 2.1.32-34)

Angelo makes no mention of snakes, but 'hatch'd' suggests that the unborn life he's so afraid of is an unconscious fusion of human and snake life. (Garden of Eden! Fall of Man!) The chain of associations seems to be: human conception, gestation, 'mischief' threatening to emerge, and a sort of wizard/prophet who carries out a kind of (legal) abortion. Would it be excessively 'psychoanalytical' to diagnose an 'anti-life' complex in Angelo? I don't think so. As in the case of Claudio earlier, Shakespeare lets obscure and unadmitted feelings poke far enough through the surface of the words to allow us 'special recognitions' which, however putative - and even if we don't fully register them - shape our understanding of the speaker's state of mind.

But whatever's bubbling up from the subconscious level Angelo's ability to rationalise remains unimpaired. He knows what he's doing. He can't show the 'pity' that Isabella's pleading for in this case but he has a judicial strategy which will vindicate his wisdom and compassion in the long run.

I show it *(i.e. pity)* most of all when I show justice;
For then I pity those I do not know,
Which a dismissed offence would after gall. (2.2.102-103)

The problems of neurosis don't stem directly from the unacceptable contents of the undermind per se, but from the way that consciousness beautifies them with reasons, excuses and good intentions. Self-deception is the danger. Christians understood this in spiritual terms long before Freud taught us to analyse it psychologically. Isabella's moral training as a schoolgirl and as a novice nun has been quite enough to make her aware that people all too readily find good reasons for bad deeds. She recognises Angelo's 'I'm being cruel only to be kind' line for what it is. The voice that the self-deceiver needs to hear is one saying: 'Come off it. You flatter yourself.' If the voice comes from **within** it's the voice of conscience and humility, but sensing that Angelo's inner voice is silent she feels that she must speak out herself to undeceive him. She's spot on about what's afoot, and what's amiss, with him. But what she doesn't realise is that the 'come off it' voice coming from **outside - from** her - isn't the voice of conscience and humility; it can only sound in his ears like the voice of disrespect and mockery.

She picks up adroitly on Angelo's 'prophet' reference (2.2.95) and, stepping back behind her Christian faith into classical culture, she invokes Jove, the ancient god of draconian punishment:

Could great men thunder
As Jove himself does, Jove would ne'er be quiet,
For every pelting, petty officer
Would use his heaven for thunder, nothing but thunder.
(2.2.111-114)

Her use of the word 'thunder' (with expansive gestures, perhaps) three times in three and a half lines has an unmistakably sardonic effect. She's got a nerve! Angelo must think. The classical reference deceives no-one. It's **him** she's talking about, no mistake, and she knows he knows it. 'Great men' - alright, he accepts **that** categorisation; but what's this about 'every pelting, petty officer'? Is this young woman, who only minutes before seemed to be so suitably overawed by him, mocking him by putting him into that category, too?

What Isabella says next removes any doubt on that point.

> Man, proud man,
> Dressed in a little brief authority,
> Most ignorant of what he's most assured –
> His glassy *(that word again!)* essence – like an angry ape
> Plays such fantastic tricks before high heaven
> As makes the angels weep; who, with our spleens,
> Would all themselves laugh mortal. (2.2.118-124)

For Lucio this is 'touché!' He hoped she'd bring Angelo round by personal charm but now it looks as if she means to do it by ridicule. But what does it matter how she does it, as long as it works? The Provost still lurking in the background mutters, 'Pray heaven she win him' (2.2.126) and we can only guess at the hope/anxiety ratio that lies behind his words. He knows Angelo and understands how he's likely to react to such phrases as 'little brief authority', 'ape' and 'fantastic tricks'. He'll see them as jeers at the sea-green incorruptibility and dignity of the magistrate's role that he identifies himself with. And the notion of heavenly spectators watching him from above, hardly knowing whether to laugh or cry, isn't one that he's likely to take kindly to, either.

Isabella has no intention of insulting Angelo. She simply thinks that it would help him to be more humble and merciful – and persuade him to change his mind – if she were to hand on a little of her own moral education to him. She innocently underestimates the degree of resistance and resentment to be expected in a man like him, full of self-esteem and with an authoritative image to maintain in public life. But now, as she feels him bristling with indignation she realises that she'd better change tack – and quickly. Casting around, the best she can come up with is a couple of pronouncements which he won't take personally and which she hopes will impress him with their trenchant worldly wisdom and searching moral insight. 'Great men', she says, (*that phrase again!*)

> may jest with saints: 'tis wit in them,
> But in the less, foul profanation. (2.2.127-129)

and then, when Lucio, more supportive than comprehending, whispers: 'more o' that', she adds for good measure:

That in the captain's but a choleric word,
Which in the soldier is flat blasphemy. (2.2.131-132)

What on earth is Angelo - or are we - supposed to make of these weighty *sententiae*? Both seem to imply a critique of moral inequality but their exact relevance in this context isn't at all clear. Are they as profoundly meaningful as they sound? Is Angelo meant to be classed as 'great men' and 'captains' or as 'lesser men' and 'soldiers'? Do they have the unanswerability of proverbs rooted in wisdom acquired over the ages, or are they just castle-in-the-air conceits? (Answers on a postcard, please.) Lucio takes them as clinchers, but Angelo evidently regards them as air-punches. 'Why do you put these sayings upon me?' (2.2.134) he asks, calling her bluff, but now it's Isabella's turn to brush aside her adversary's words and proceed regardless. She returns to her provocative and (we're beginning to fear) counterproductive 'who-are-you-to-judge-others' theme. 'Authority', she says,

……………….. though it err like others,
Hath yet a kind of medicine in itself
That skins the vice o'er the top. (2.2.135-137)

This 'unhealed – suppurating? - wound' image virtually equates authority with deception and hypocrisy, and Angelo can only see it as a further attempt to discredit his public position by putting him on a moral par with every offender that appears before him for sentence. But with a new burst of eloquence and conviction - and less sense than ever of how it might be coming over - Isabella asks if it's right for him to condemn Claudio if he's really no different or better himself? 'Go to your bosom,' she says,

Knock there, and ask your heart what it doth know
That's like my brother's fault. If it confess
A natural guiltiness, such as is his,
Let it not sound a thought upon your tongue
Against my brother's life. (2.2.137-142)

It's a powerful and moving speech, but a rather distressing one. Isabella began by trying to keep her distance from Angelo, but gave that up because it didn't work; now she's getting alarmingly close to him, 'asking his heart what it doth know' and trying to ventriloquise the inner voice with which it's supposed to give its answer. But that's not working, either. Isabella's so good and sincere: we long, and rather expect, to see her gentle innocence disarm Angelo's harsh self-righteousness, because that would be 'the right thing'. But now we see that innocence doesn't necessarily sweep all before it, and that naïveté can be disastrous in dealings with the powerful. It's beginning to look hopeless. How can Isabella possibly get clemency for her brother in a situation as politically stacked against her as this, with the eyes of the world upon Angelo, watching to see if he's as rigorous as he claims to be? How can she make good sense and compassion prevail in an argument about sexual frailty with a knotted up puritan like him? And how can she have any kind of straightforward or sincere communication with him now that she's becoming (if she isn't already) the object of his guilty sexual desire?

.

Earlier, Angelo admitted (to Escalus, not to Isabella) that he, like other men, had sexual temptations, but he was quick to turn the point to his own advantage by claiming the moral credit for resisting them. It was this that entitled him to feel superior to others. But now Isabella is crashing in where more worldly-wise angels would fear to tread. 'Go to your bosom' challenges him to find a conscience that isn't just a projection of his Mister Clean reputation, and to dwell not on the temptations that he's so praiseworthily resisted, but on the inherent sinfulness that he shares with the rest of humanity. Isabella seems to take it for granted that like everybody else he's not only sinfully inclined but a sinner in fact. Actually, he isn't, but the point is that he **could** be. He's been avoiding seeing himself in this way, no doubt supposing that the best way to resist temptation is to ignore it, but now, 'going to his bosom', as she urges him to do, he realises the truth of what she's saying. Suddenly everything looks different. He **is** a sinner, not just by inclination – his eye rests wonderingly on Isabella for a moment – but potentially in deed! With the best of intentions and telling nothing but the truth, Isabella has liberated his sexual imagination. As Nietszche says: 'Whatever we recognise in a man we inflame in him'. Without her moral tuition he might well have remained too inhibited and too proud to transgress, but now she's presenting him with a convincing picture of wayward manhood featuring her own brother Claudio and countless others and recognising him, the forbidding magistrate, in that picture, along with all the others. He only has to admit, in the safety of silence: 'Yes, that's me. I recognise myself. I'm one of the many.' He doesn't have to say anything at the moment. It's still too soon for him to declare his passion and make his body-barter proposition, but we can be pretty sure that that's the way his mind will be working from now on.

Confirmation of this crucial psychological shift comes in Angelo's dozen-word 'aside':

> She speaks, and 'tis much sense
> That my sense breeds with it. (2.2.143-144)

'Sense' is a complex word - to put it mildly - yoking together a wide range of mental and physical connotations: meaning, understanding, feeling, touch, desire. 'Breeds' is another complex word, at least in the conflicting connotations that it has for Angelo. For his 'higher' anti-life self procreation is thing loaded with feelings of fear, revulsion and disdain, but for his recently-activated 'lower' self they're now beginning to exert a pull that he's finding it difficult to resist.

Isabella - so admirable and, once she gets going, so eloquent - has got everything wrong. First she's allowed herself to become an object of desire for Angelo – which, to be fair, was probably unavoidable. Then she's thrown those startlingly disrespectful 'angry ape' and 'fantastical tricks' taunts at him which can only tempt him to retaliate by trying to take **her** down a peg or two. And now, fatally, she's taught him to recognise himself as a man like other men, free, if he chooses, to act out his sexual desires. With her help he has indeed become 'a man new made', (2.2.78) though not at all in the sense of 'Adam redeemed through mercy' that she had in mind.

In an aside the audience hears Angelo's dozen words about 'sense' and 'breeding'. Lucio and the Provost don't. They only hear him say, 'Fare you well.' (2.2.144) and make for the door.

It's a moment of crisis. Angelo's better self is still in contention; he's trying to walk away from temptation. But Isabella can't afford to let him, because if he does Claudio's a dead man. In alarm she calls out:

Gentle my lord, turn back! (2.2.144)

Her cry tells him that she's in his power, helpless, pleading. She wants another chance to appeal to his better nature; she doesn't realise that now it's only his worse nature that wants to listen. He hovers, neither moving further towards the door nor coming back towards her, not knowing how to continue the interview, or end it. Then he hears himself saying:

I will bethink me. Come again tomorrow. (2.2.145)

We wonder – **he** wonders! – whether that's just the voice of his indecision, or whether a plan has just been laid in his mind, which will need time to hatch.

Naturally, Isabella's excited by 'come again tomorrow', which is the first encouraging sign she's had from him. She wonders whether in spite of all appearances he's had a change of heart. But she's not prepared for a sudden breakthrough and her next words seem to spring from nowhere:

Hark, how I'll bribe you. (2.2.146)

Gasps all round!

In a situation like this there's bound to be a whiff of *quid pro quo* in the air, but we're shocked that anyone – especially Isabella! – should make open reference to it. 'Bribe' is the last word that anyone with any discretion would use. Lucio's absolutely aghast; a few moments ago he was urging her to speak more freely, and now she comes out with **this** – the b-word! And Angelo himself isn't merely feigning shock when he demands:

How! Bribe me? (2.2.147)

He's never relaxed his 'correct' official posture and he still has all his ethical wits about him, so his anger that anyone should dare to offer him – **him!** - a sweetener comes ready-made. Conscious that 'the public' is present in the form of the Provost and Lucio, what can he do but bristle with indignation? But at the same time we can't help wondering what wild surmises the b-word might have triggered off in his other – 'is-this-really-me?' - self that Isabella's so recently acquainted him with. Could this 'new' self, by any chance, be wondering whether this beautiful young woman, as dauntingly righteous in her own way as he is in his, might not be altogether what she seems? Could she possibly - like him! – be a bit too good to be true? Was 'bribe' a glimpse of her shadow-side? Might she even be capable of a 180-degree turn from virtue to disgrace? Bribe! What's her offer, then?

Shakespeare – and I mention him by name because at this point he seems here to be making an artistic decision of personal moral and religious significance for him – is sowing the suspicion that Isabella's purity of heart may not be completely immune from, or effective against, the impurities of the world that surrounds her. The idea of Original Sin and the Fall of Man is central to his understanding of the human condition. Isabella probably doesn't envisage **exactly** what Angelo might want from her in return for repealing the sentence on Claudio, but the b-word is a strong hint that at the bottom of her mind she's considering the 'what's in it for him?' question. In fact she seems to be a step ahead of him. She's probably found, and pronounced, the b-word before even the thought came into his mind. If so, what kind of innocence is that?

Well, that's how things appear for the moment, but the picture keeps changing.

What is Isabella offering Angelo then? She makes it quickly clear that she isn't offering money, and of course she doesn't even make a negative mention of sexual favours, though – no, because – she's probably aware that there may be something of that sort in the air. So what else is there? The answer is: 'such gifts that heaven shall share with you.' (2.2.148) She's offering to pray for Angelo. She and other 'preserved souls' (2.2.154) in the nunnery will remember him with gratitude in their prayers. Maybe it was prayers that she had in mind when she uttered the b-word; or perhaps the word just slipped out – like one of those unexpectedly revealing 'gaffe' words used by Claudio and Angelo when under psychological stress – before she knew what she was saying, and then found she had to do a quick bit of ad-libbing. Either way, the 'heavenly gifts' gloss retrieves the situation. Lucio, who a moment earlier thought she'd committed a huge faux pas, expresses the general relief when he mutters to Isabella: 'You had marr'd all else.' (2.2.149)

Fortunately, Angelo seems prepared to let the b-word pass without further comment. He doesn't withdraw his invitation; he repeats it:

Well: come to me tomorrow. (2.2.157)

Phew!

But we still have our misgivings. What got into her in that mad moment? She could have offered to pray for Angelo without talking of a bribe. We worry. Exactly where **did** that b-word spring from, and what effect has it had on him? It's hard to say anything very hard-and-fast about it, but uneasy intuitions insinuate themselves. Isabella's sense of the sexual subtext of the interview must have made her aware of the sort of possibilities that the word 'bribe' might to conjure up. She'd have absolutely no intention of fulfilling them, of course, but could there have been, lurking in the recesses of her mind, the idea that even the most oblique suggestion of sexual favours might give her some extra persuasive leverage with him? It's a question we can ask, but she can't. The very thought of using such manipulative tactics is incompatible with her self-respect. So the b-word has somehow to find its way into her head and out of her mouth in some unavowed way. The opportunity arises when the surge of panic as Angelo starts to walk out, followed by the surge of hope when he offers her another interview, momentarily skittles her presence of mind and overwhelms her with contradictory emotions. The b-word gets blurted out, in her voice, true, but in such a spontaneous and unconsidered way that it can scarcely be thought to express **her** meaning. It's as if it said *itself.* She doesn't have to 'own' it. And she's free to refute any unfortunate impression it may have given: 'I'm talking about heavenly gifts. I hope you didn't think for one moment that…….' So if there's any misunderstanding it'll be down to Angelo, won't it?

It's inconclusive and it'll have to be good enough. But the signs are persuasive that in the post-lapsarian world of 'Vienna' Eve/Isabella, like Adam/Angelo, is not altogether morally shadowless. The b-word can be glossed, defused, even withdrawn, but it can't be **un**said; and it will have its impact. Let's look at the sequence of events and draw some tentative inferences. In his first offer of a further meeting the smitten Angelo seems to have been in a state of indecision, asking for time to 'bethink me' but probably just wanting to be sure he'll see her again; but by the time he repeats the offer it looks as if he's more or less decided to corrupt her, has an embryonic plan for doing so but needs a second interview to carry it out. If that's the right reading, what's changed him? That word 'bribe' - what else?

Isabella's parting 'Save your honour' provides the first two beats of a pentameter line which Angelo, now in soliloquy mode, completes with this three-beat rejoinder:

From thee: even from thy virtue. (2.2.162)

So that's the way the wind is blowing. She's tempting him – with her virtue, true, but if he falls it won't be entirely his fault. He hasn't fallen yet, though. We were premature to suppose that Isabella's rash use of the b-word had been enough to set him firmly on the path of dishonour. He's still inwardly divided. Faustlike, he can say:

Zwei Seelen wohnen, ach! in meiner Brust (Goethe: Faust Part One, line 1112)
(Two souls dwell, alas! in my breast.)

and the outcome of the struggle between them remains hanging in the balance. He's tempted all right, but although he puts a punning spin on Isabella's words of farewell he doesn't actually repudiate her prayer that 'his honour' will be 'saved'. His inner uncertainty finds form in no less than ten questions - all left unanswered - studding the 26 lines of his soliloquy. His honourable soul is still struggling to credit the desires and intentions of his dishonourable one. The underlying questions are: what's

happening to me? and who/what am I **really**? The question: what am I going to **do** about Isabella, if anything? depends on the answers to those questions. He asks: What's this? What's this? (2.2.163) and What dost thou, and what art thou, Angelo? (2.2.173)

Like all serious crises of conscience it's also a crisis of identity.

'Even from thy virtue'. That's the nub of it in Angelo's tortured mind. He's always been strongly in favour of virtue, mainly in himself. Now, in Isabella, he's still very much in favour of it, and as he senses his own virtue falling into the shadows he wants in some way to appropriate hers. The trouble is that he can only do that by degrading it, and her. Complicated man! Not yet ready to face his villainy fair and square, he tells himself that his weakness is – characteristically - only a weakness for virtue (and what's so wrong with that?) and that in tempting him with her virtue Isabella's as bad as he is (which can't be too bad either, can it?). Yes, force Isabella to share the blame, that's the thing to do. He asks:

The tempter or the tempted, who sins most, ha? (2.2.164)

- ergo (if you can use a logical term for such an obscure and irrational thought process) she deserves what's coming to her. By focussing on Isabella's virtue, rather than directly on her desirable body, he tries to kid himself that in sinning he'll somehow remain both a lover of virtue and a figure of justice, meting out punishment to a wrong-doer, so remaining 'himself' and preserving his self-respect - something that he of all men can't bear to live without. Maybe he doesn't actually **believe** this cock-and-bull narrative, but just finds some comfort in formulating it at the back of his painfully conflicted mind. Angelo speaks in 'privy' language (2.2.170-172) about the foulness of defiling Isabella, but he still doesn't make it clear to us - or, we suspect, to himself – whether he's saying it **would** be foul to do it (so he won't) or it **will** be foul to do it (and he's going to). Maybe he won't do it, after all, but even if he does he'll be able to share the blame with the blameless Isabella. Either way, he's not altogether to blame, is he?

> Never could the strumpet
> With all her double vigour, art and nature,
> Once stir my temper: but this virtuous maid
> Subdues me quite. (2.2.183-186)

Moral pervert? Hardly. Put that way, he sounds quite a decent chap.

But we still don't know what he's going to **do**.

Shakespeare makes us wait. Before giving us the crunch follow-up interview (Act 2, Scene 4) he gives us a short scene in which the Duke, now kitted out as a friar, brings Juliet to repentance for **her** sins of the flesh. Initially it looks like a scene put in just to hold us in suspense while the necessary time elapses between the two Angelo-Isabella interviews; but in this complex and highly organised play - so full of symmetries, echoes, cross-references and contradictions – Shakespeare spots an opportunity here to cast an unexpected sidelight on the Angelo-Isabella tussle with which we're mainly concerned. He shows us the reverse side of the picture. With Angelo v Isabella we see sin seeking to undermine virtue; with Juliet and the Duke we see virtue being released from sin. It's not a pain free experience for her, but she manages to make a heartfelt and complete confession which gives us a glimpse of goodness and hope amidst the encircling gloom.

Although we can take it for granted that the devout Isabella prays before each of her interviews with Angelo we might be more surprised to learn that Angelo prays, too. But that's what we find him doing when we next see him. At the end of the first interview, approaching his moral crisis, he felt the need to pray but realised that it might not be easy.

> I am that way going to temptation,
> Where prayer's cross'd. (2.2.158-159)

And so it's proving. He's trying to pray for help in resisting temptation but finds that he can't do this without conjuring up the image of what it is that's tempting him – Isabella.

> …………………..Heaven hath my empty words,
> Whilst my invention, hearing not my tongue,
> Anchors on Isabel. (2.4.2-4)

Desire always hopes for some kind of transmigration of souls. The complete thing is mission impossible of course, but in any kind of strong yearning or identification **something** tends to get transferred. We now see that the proud Angelo, having fallen for the virtuous Isabella, is beginning to sound a bit like her. He's assimilated some of her moral understanding. Her depiction of the pretentiousness of 'virtue' as an instrument of public authority (cf 2.2.135-137) – which so rankled with him at the time - has nevertheless got into him, and stuck. He can now say:

> …………………..O place, O form,
> How often dost thou with thy case, thy habit,
> Wrench awe from fools, and tie the wiser souls
> To thy false seeming! (2.4.12-15)

Angelo's adoption of Isabella's insight is one of the many echoes and cross-references in the play. His use of the word 'habit' is another. We picture him dressed up in his fine magistrate's robes, and then we recall that only a few moments ago we saw the Duke dressed **down,** in the habit of a humble friar.

Angelo's soliloquy, beginning with a failed prayer, ends with a contradiction. OK then, he reasons, he has two souls, one real, the other 'seeming'. If Isabella's right, that's what he's been like all along anyway - a hypocrite. So why change? Why does it have to be either/or, when it can be yes/both? This is his decision then: he'll sin under cover of public virtue, corrupting Isabella but taking care to preserve appearances. 'Blood, thou art blood,' (2.4.15) he says, meaning that sexual desire is too urgent to be denied, but

Let's write good angel *(i.e. good Angelo!)* on the devil's horn –
'Tis not the devil's crest. (2.4.16-17)

Clang! Round Two! Seconds out!

Actually, the seconds aren't just out; they're not there at all. This time Angelo isn't seconded by the Provost, nor Isabella by Lucio. This is how Angelo wants it. Just the two of them in private. No witnesses.

When Isabella's arrival is announced the 'blood musters to his heart'. (2.4.20) Finally determined to make his play for her, and expecting to win, he almost faints with excitement. But then he quickly pulls himself together and by the time the servant shows her in he's able to take the initiative in a way he never did in the first interview.

Assuming the role of a judicial interrogator with the right to ask 'test questions' he starts by posing this one:

Which had you rather, that the most just law
Now took your brother's life; or, to redeem him,
Give up your body to such sweet uncleanness
As she that he hath stained? (2.4.52-55)

The body-barter proposal is suddenly out in the open, and in a form that doesn't leave her with much room for treating it as hypothetical, even though, officially, that's what it is. Isabella fences and feints. She'd be willing to die in Claudio's place (if that's what Angelo is demanding, although she knows it isn't) rather than do anything sinful. She even wins a sort of confirmation that it was only a what-if question - 'I can speak against the thing I say,' (2.4.59-60) he concedes. Then he moves swiftly on to the next question he's got lined up for her. Reminding her - as if that were necessary – of her brother's death sentence, he wonders:

Might there not be charity in sin
To save this brother's life? (2.4.63-64)

Once again Isabella's forced on to the back foot. Her best chance lies in deliberate misunderstanding. Taking it as if Angelo is volunteering out of charity to spare Claudio's life she snaps up his supposed offer, adding that if he's worried that it might be sinful for him to bend the law so far in the direction of leniency she'll herself pray that God will forgive him. Top marks for quick-wittedness, Isabella! - but not so good for plausibility and sincerity! Angelo isn't impressed. He doesn't believe that she means what she's saying – well, do **we**? - and he ticks her off for not being straightforward with him.

Your sense pursues not mine: either you are ignorant,
Or seem so, crafty; and that's not good. (2.4.74-75)

Angelo fires yet another hypothetical question at her. It's
of the 'I've got a friend' or 'I know a man' variety. 'What
would you do?' (2.4.98) he asks, 'if this 'suppos'd'
(2.4.97) had the power to spare Claudio's life but would
do so if only you were willing to 'lay down the treasures
of your body' (2.4.96) in exchange?'

Isabella can only equivocate again. She's not taken in for a
moment by that 'supposed' man of influence that Angelo's
conjured up, but her room for manoeuvre is limited. She
realises that by 'treasures' he means her virginity, but it's
not safe to acknowledge it. Again she can't afford to
'pursue his sense'.

If the text broke off there and we were left guessing what
she'd say next it would probably be something like this:
'I'm a young nun. My vocation requires me to be detached
from the concerns of earthly life and to be always death-
ready. It's death that will unite me with God, and if it
comes to me now while I'm in the prime of life so much
the better. If I'm called to martyrdom I'll rejoice in it.
'Greater love than this hath no man,' or woman, etc.'

But the text doesn't break off there, thank goodness.
Shakespeare does introduce the 'martyr' theme, but the
words that he puts into his heroine's mouth have a
complexity and fascination (not to say obscurity) that
could have come from no-one but him. She takes
'treasures' to refer to 'life' rather than 'virginity' or
'honour', and picks up on Angelo' phrase 'lay down' as a
trigger for two vivid but contradictory images: in one she
is on a bed of love and/or sickness, in the other on a torture

rack or execution block. 'Were I under terms of death,' she says,

Th'impression of keen whips I'd wear as rubies,
And strip myself to death as to a bed
That longing have been sick for, ere I'd yield
My body up to shame. (2.4.100-104)

Here's yet another case, surely, of the language scooping up 'repressed' images and associations from the unconscious mind. A fleeting image of Isabella undressing for bed is fused with an image of her under condemnation, bleeding from a whipping and facing cruel execution. Her rejection of Angelo's body-barter proposal is clear enough; she won't give her body up to shame. But she might give her body up in another way - as a martyr – and the figure of Isabella choosing martyrdom as a response to judicial oppression casts a long and crooked shadow across the poet's imagination. It bestirs more unresolved reflections about religious persecution than he can make use of here, although some of them make themselves partly-visible in this almost hallucinatory imagery.

For Shakespeare, martyrs weren't just figures from distant church history. He was brought up in an at least partly Catholic household, though we don't know how pious it was or whether he was an observing Catholic at any time of his life. But what we do know, because scholars have filled out and clarified the picture in recent years, is that in the eyes of contemporaries close to him personally, however circumspect his behaviour and ambivalent his feelings, he must have appeared to be connected with the officially persecuted Catholic party. The martyrs of his day were in some cases men that he knew at first or second hand through his family's Warwickshire social network; they were involved in the Catholic resistance movement, some as priests, some as terrorists. Whether he identified himself with the persecuted Catholic minority, or tried to distance himself from it we aren't clear. Maybe a bit of both, according to circumstances. Perhaps he had something like the range of feelings that a non-radical Muslim might be expected to have in today's world of Islamic terrorism. He'd sympathise with people persecuted for their (his!) faith. He'd admire those willing to die defending or promoting it. He might feel ashamed that he himself lacked such faith and courage and had opted for safety. He'd resent the injustices of a persecutory government and accept the justice of opposition to it, although he'd be appalled at the lengths that the militants and plotters were prepared to go to, shedding innocent as well as guilty blood. He'd feel horror at the spectacular brutality of their deaths, but also feel that they'd volunteered for it. He'd venerate holy, non-violent martyrs, but have mixed feelings about the terrorists and those that egged them on.

Isabella is a holy, non-violent martyr, of course, but this 'terms of death' imagery does seem to be projecting some of Shakespeare's ambivalent feelings about martyrdom on to her. If it crosses our mind it probably crossed his, too, that the heroic virtue of Isabella-as-martyr is a bit bogus; after all, it's a self-chosen pose and she doesn't really think that it'll cost her her life. It's not fair – as if fairness ever comes into such things! – but this has the effect of making her a slightly puzzling, even suspect, figure. She uses language that seems to suggest that a (female) martyr's death is sexy, and that sexual beauty ('rubies'), linked as it is with extreme suffering, is a subject of sadistic fantasy, but there's certainly more to her than meets the eye. She has a 'shadow side' – the side of themselves that people don't want others to see - and this speech gives us a glimpse of it. Even Shakespeare's most virtuous characters have at least a hint of a shadow side – remember Portia? It's one of the things which, for all the dramatic and verbal artifice by which they explain themselves, makes them so intriguing and humanly convincing.

Angelo makes no joinder to Isabella's 'terms of death' speech, except to say: 'Then must your brother die.' (2.4.104)

But no doubt he's thinking – and who's to say he's wrong? - that the tantalising glimpse he caught of Isabella's shadow side has revealed something of her womanly sexuality. So it is there! That's the side that he'll be trying to reach from now on.

But Isabella, sensing danger, comes to a hard decision. Yes, she'd give her life to save Claudio's but if, as she realises, that's not an option, and the price demanded is her honour, Claudio will just have to die. Better for him to lose his earthly life than for her to lose her eternal life.

When the interrogation continues with:

Were you not then as cruel as the sentence
That you have slander'd so? (2.4.109-110)

she's ready with a perfectly formulated reply:

Ignomy of ransom and free pardon
Are of two houses: lawful mercy
Is nothing kin to foul redemption. (2.4.111-113)

Well said, Isabella! That should give him pause for thought. But it doesn't. No, the side of her that says things like that isn't the side that Angelo's concentrating on now.

He comes back to the lack of straightforwardness he complained about before. He senses her uncomfortable tension between saying what she believed about chastity and making the case for her brother. Hadn't she been guilty of talking down the gravity of Claudio's offence and 'slandering' the law that condemned him? (2.4.114) How did that square with the value she claims to attach to chastity as a moral principle and, for that matter, to her own chastity? It's a clever ploy, which Isabella's innate truthfulness makes it difficult for her to resist. What can she say? She can't deny it. Yes, in her concern to save her brother she's been bending things a bit. She just owns up, bless her heart!

O pardon me, my lord; it oft falls out
To have what we would have, we speak not what we mean.
I something do excuse the thing I hate
For his advantage that I dearly love. (2.4.117-120)

We think: well, love and mercy **do** involve bending things a bit. But the unbending Angelo is probably thinking: Aha! we're getting there! She admits she's fallible!

We are all frail, (2.4.121) he says, enjoying the unexpected and undeserved view from the higher moral ground. But isn't this the kind of thing that people say as they announce that they intend to show mercy? There even seems to be a hint of 'who-am-I-to-judge-others' in it. So is he going to relent after all? No. Isabella may hope that all this talk about frailty will lead to clemency for Claudio, but Angelo means it to lead in quite a different direction.

She says:

Else let my brother die,

If not a foedary *(i.e. inherited substitute)* but only he
Owe and succeed thy weakness.

The gist of this is: If Claudio's unique in his frailty, i.e.
different from you, then let him die; but if he isn't – as
your 'all frail' phrase implies - why should he die and not
you? Isabella puts it very obscurely, and perhaps it needs
to be very obscurely because the underlying argument
hardly bears scrutiny - the fact that we're all weak doesn't
mean we're all **equally** weak and deserve the same
rewards or punishments. Angelo may or may not follow
Isabella's meaning but he isn't in the least fazed, or
diverted, by it. Yes, men are frail, he says. We agree on
that. But what about **women**?

As we saw, if Isabella's 'terms of death' speech was meant
to put Angelo off it could hardly have been worse judged.
It showed him a 'flash of ankle', as the Victorians might
have said. Now she does it again. She could say something
like: 'yes, women are frail, too, but not all equally frail;
some – like me – aren't particularly frail at all, if by frail
you mean what I think you mean.' But no, honest
Christian girl to a fault, she now gives the whole game
away. 'Ay', women are frail, she admits,

…as the glasses where they view themselves,
Which are as easy broke as they make forms.
Women? – Help, heaven! Men their creation mar
In profiting by them. Nay, call us ten times frail;
For we are soft as our complexions are,
And credulous to false prints. (2.4.124-129)

The wrong message comes through loud and clear;
'glasses' (= virginities), 'easy broke' (say no more), 'make
forms' (= bear children) - all have clear sexual

connotations which the elliptical imagery, double meanings and jumpy syntax can't conceal from Angelo. It's almost as if her shadow side has captured her voice and is giving him the come-on! This is women for you, she says – sexually fragile, 'soft', 'credulous' – and I'm one of them. You didn't actually believe all that dedicated saint and unassailable virgin stuff, did you? It was just a front, like your own incorruptible magistrate front. I'm as vulnerable as anyone. So spare me, good sir! I appeal to your better nature!

The really poignant thing about this is that the shadow side of Isabella that Angelo is now getting a straight view of isn't really a **bad** side (as his own shadow side certainly is). It's just the rest of her humanity. We're all sinners, she admits, but she fails to add that some are more sinful than others and that it doesn't have to stop us trying to be saints, as she does herself. It's not a question of moral fraudulence, of pretending to be better than you are. But Angelo, scenting victory, isn't bothered with what Isabella could or should have said. Predatorlike, he takes any sign of weakness as an incitement. Finally dropping the guise of a judicial interrogator (though perhaps there's one ironic last trace of it in his use of the word 'arrest' in line 134) he asks Isabella, now she's admitted that she's a woman like other women, to start behaving like one towards him:

…from this testimony of your own sex –
Since I suppose we are made to be no stronger
Than faults may shake our frames – let me be bold.
I do arrest your words. Be that you are,
That is, a woman; if you be more, you're none.
If you be one – as you are well express'd
By all external warrants – show it now,
By putting on the destin'd livery. (2.4 130-137)

The cat's definitely out of the bag now and Isabella can no longer pretend it isn't. But she has one last go at trying to put it back in. In the course of the interview they've each had to retract something they've said. Now Isabella hopes to get Angelo to unsay his last speech. 'Gentle my lord', she says – perhaps in a defeated, pleading way? but the actress will have to decide on that –

Let me entreat you to speak the former *(i.e. 'whatif', hypothetical)* language. (2.4.138-139)

But it's going to take a lot more than that to stop him now. He's seeing green light, not red. 'Plainly conceive, I love you,' (2.4.140) he says.

Isabella's reply, when it comes – perhaps after a tense and prolonged pause in which she has to fight down a rising panic - seems well judged to stop him in his tracks:

My brother did love Juliet
And you tell me that he shall die for it. (2.4.142/3)

But it doesn't. He simply sidesteps the moral force of the comparison - the time for ethical debate is over - and spells out his offer:

He shall not, Isabel, if you give me love. (2.4.144)

Shameless bastard! we think, but at the same time we can't help noticing that his newfound directness confirms not only his tactical but a paradoxical moral ascendancy over Isabella. His 'baddy' bluntness plays better than 'goody' prevarication. Her insincerity is painfully obvious when she can only counter by pretending that she can't believe that he means what he's saying, and that he's still only trying to test her. And of course it doesn't work.

'Believe me, on mine honour,' he replies, 'My words express my purpose.' (2.4.147-147)

Isabella can't challenge his frankness, but she can and does pick him up on that word 'honour'.

Ha! Little honour, to be much believ'd,
And most pernicious purpose! (2.4.148-149)

In a way Isabella's seen this coming all along, but now he's finally come out with it she's absolutely outraged. The impudence of the man! How dare he proposition her - **her!** - like that! We sympathise, of course, but can't help noting that she's now making herself an exception from the ill-advised generalisations she's just been making about her sex. (2.4.124-129)

Virtue - humanity having inherited all kinds of moral complications from Adam's Fall – can be importantly deficient in wisdom, and in any case it's never entirely pure. Whatever else, it's always liable to contain an element of pride. (And it's pride, we may reflect, that the Duke in his friar's garb is currently trying to give up.) What is it if it's not pride that's kicking in with Isabella now? She's furious that after all her efforts to fend him off, she - a novice nun, no less, on the eve of taking her vows! - doesn't command more respect. She knows perfectly well what men - her brother, for instance - are like, and she knows, too, that other women have to deal with them as best they can; but she really thought she herself would be spared this sort of indignity! She shouldn't be reduced to having to say: 'How dare you, sir!', as other women might (or might not) have to. But nuns are supposed to follow a rule of personal as well as sexual modesty, and not take offence on their own behalf, so she feels the need to convert her anger at Angelo's disrespect for her into a rather more 'displaced' anger at his **hypocrisy.** Angelo, a pillar of rectitude? No, he's a contemptible fraud!

'Seeming, seeming,' (2.4.149) she hisses at him.

Angelo's transformation from correct magistrate to sexual blackmailer is truly breathtaking. No trace of the alarm and compunction that he articulated in his soliloquy (2.2.162/187) remains; apparently his inner conflict is completely resolved in favour of right-on villainy. He doesn't try to excuse or ingratiate himself (as Richard did with Anne) by telling Isabella that her beauty has entirely overpowered him, that he can't help himself, etc. He's perfectly clear and unapologetic about what he wants, and confident of getting it.

Isabella's naïveté is political rather than sexual. She knows what 'men' are like, even relatively decent ones like her brother, but she seems to have had no inkling how men in positions of power can do disgraceful things and still preserve their moral credibility in the eyes of the world. For one silly moment she thinks she's got him where she wants him; she'll blow the whistle on him unless he pardons Claudio. But of course Angelo's seen this one coming a mile off.

Who will believe thee, Isabel? (2.4.154)

If it's her reputation against his, he'll win. He rubs in the lesson: in this world 'seems' trumps 'is'.

Say what you can: my false o'erweighs your true. (2.4.169)

She's got no answer to that. Or to this:

.....redeem thy brother
By yielding up thy body to my will,
Or else he must not only die the death
But thy unkindness shall his death draw out
To ling'ring sufferance. (2.4.162/166)

He leaves her to think things over.

At the end of the first interview it was Angelo who had a
soliloquy. At the end of the second it's Isabella. She has to
face facts – facts that are new to her. She knew about
sexual corruption in Vienna and this may have been a
factor in her decision to enter the convent. But now
Angelo's behaviour as an enforcer of justice seeking to
enforce his own injustice against her has opened up a new
dimension. 'O perilous mouths,' she says,

That bear in them one and the self-same tongue,
Either of condemnation or approof,
Bidding the law make curtsy to their will,
Hooking both right and wrong to th'appetite,
To follow as it draws. (2.4.171/176)

Her pluralisation of 'mouth' make this a political
statement. It's not just Angelo, it's all of them. There's
something rotten in the state – as well as in the population
- of Vienna. Angelo has the whip hand and there's no-one
she can turn to. If deceit is what works in the world, and
there isn't anything that she can do about it except what
would be shameful, it can only confirm her decision to
turn her back on the world and put herself in a place where
a life devoted to truth and virtue has some sort of chance.
It's the convent for her – tomorrow. Claudio will
understand. She's done her best. She offered her life to
save him but the offer was refused. He'll have to pay with

his own life after all. He'll die with courage. He'd rather be beheaded twenty times

Before his sister should her body stoop
To such abhorred pollution.
Then, Isabel live chaste, and brother, die:
More than our brother is our chastity. (2.4 181-1840

She'll be off to the nunnery tomorrow to pray for all concerned, and to thank God that there's a place where she can go to escape from this 'injurious world'.

We may be a little surprised that Isabella reaches her decision so swiftly. After all, this is 'Measure for Measure', where notoriously nothing's simple and straightforward. But perhaps that's the point. Shakespeare might have made her soliloquy more agonised and hanging-in-the-balance, but here perhaps he chooses to make less say more. Isabella's decision is undoubtedly irreproachable, but in this play Shakespeare seems to be determined to cast a mistrustful eye on everything that has the look of moral certainty and virtue. It seems to be the corollary of casting a compassionate eye on vice, which he also does. Nothing can be taken at face value. The unquestionably 'right' decision may have motives which aren't absolutely pure; pride, cowardice, etc may have their part in it, or it may be too simplistic a response to a complicated situation and so contribute to an unsatisfactory outcome. For justice to be done it requires worldly wisdom, even guile perhaps, as well as good intent. This is where the dodgy Duke comes in. If the outcome of 'Measure for Measure' were down to the likes of the saintly Isabella poor Claudio would be a dead duck and there'd be no just or happy ending. What seems to be called for in 'the real world', where deceit is so fatally effective and where Isabella so innocently malfunctions, is someone like the Duke, capable of bending the moral universe a little and working through, as well as against, the failings of human beings in order to achieve (more or less) good ends. Isabella is, up to midway in the play when she becomes the Friar/Duke's accomplice in his slightly sordid intrigues, a part of the problem rather than the solution.

So let's take first a backward and then a forward look at this Duke Vincentio who's the one who has to come up with the answers in the end.

In the first scene of the play, we remember, Duke Vincentio announced his departure from Vienna (though that, we soon saw, wasn't exactly his intention) and expressed his confidence in his two right-hand men, Escalus and Angelo, one of whom he'd be appointing to replace him in the top job. The senior man, Escalus, has the advantage of experience and has evidently been working closely with the Duke in governing Vienna for the last 14 years. Angelo is the 'new man', full of virtue and promise and although still something of an unknown quantity more likely to bring about change than continue in the current unsatisfactory way of things. The Duke appoints Angelo, with full powers, with Escalus second-in-charge.

But what exactly lies behind the Duke's abdication? Act 1, Scene 2 gives us an idea of how things are in Vienna. We hear Lucio's flippantly irreligious chat with the two gentlemen, followed by the appearance of Mistress Overdone, the brassy and utterly shameless manageress of one of the many disease-spreading whorehouses in the city. Then we meet Claudio, on his way to prison – and execution - 'for getting Madam Julietta (his betrothed) with child' (1.2.70). We now know two important things: just how licentious and decadent Vienna has become under the Duke's rule, and that Angelo's crackdown has already begun. Judicial severity has begun to bear down on immorality that's grown used to a sense of impunity. The question is how to 'measure' the punishment against the offence. Without such a 'measure' how can true justice be distinguished from the making of spectacular and disproportionate 'examples' of offenders like Claudio? And how can true mercy be distinguished from the kind of permissiveness that has so degraded life in Vienna?

Act 1, Scene 3 gives us a private close-up of the Duke. We find him in mid-conversation with a Friar - his face hidden under his monastic cowl, let's say – who's there as a confidant/confessor and who speaks, briefly, only three times. The Duke is sharply rebutting what the Friar, accustomed no doubt to the usual routines of the confessional, has evidently just suggested – that the Duke is in love. 'No, Holy father', he says,

...........throw away that thought;
Believe not that the dribbling dart of love
Can pierce a complete bosom.' (3.1.1-3)

There's a mediaeval/Renaissance ethical cliché here, which isn't altogether unfamiliar to us these days. The sort of man that people look to for moral authority ought to be free from sexual passion. It's a matter of self-command and maturity. It helps if a ruler's old enough to be past 'that sort of thing', so that he can dedicate himself without distraction to responsibilities and purposes

More grave and wrinkled than the aims and ends
Of burning youth. (1.3.5-6)

So the Duke's the very model of the wise and detached magistrate, is he? Well, he'd like to think so, although he has to admit that his track-record hardly confirms it. It's been on his watch that moral standards in Vienna have collapsed. The laws were there, but he's failed to enforce them.

We have strict statutes and most biting laws,
The needful bits and curbs to headstrong jades,
Which for this fourteen years we have let slip. (3.1.19-21)

It's reached the point where crime and vice now have the upper hand over law and order.

Liberty plucks Justice by the nose. (3.1.29)

When the shadowy Friar Thomas, speaking for us all perhaps, suggests that it might be better for the Duke to clear up his own mess rather than get Angelo to do it for him the reply he gets is pretty unconvincing. Having been slack for so long it would be, or at least might appear to be, inconsistent for him to start punishing things now which previously he'd cast a blind, or lenient, eye on. The crackdown now required, the Duke argues, must be draconian and it will inevitably arouse opposition, so he'd prefer the opprobrium to fall on his deputy Angelo! Now he's actually spelt it out he realises how lame, even dishonourable, this explanation must sound, and conscious of what Friar Thomas may be thinking (but too deferential to say) he promises 'moe reasons' (1.3.48) when they have more time to talk - though the present moment would seem to be as good as any to say what needs to be said. But no, the Duke allows no pause for a rejoinder and turns abruptly to practical matters. Would the good friar be so kind as to lend him a monastic habit, so that he can go about Vienna in disguise, finding out at first hand what's going on – and keeping an eye on Angelo?

So doesn't the Duke trust Angelo, even though he's placed his dukedom in his hands? Well, yes and no. He's certainly the right man to impose a crackdown on vice – a man of rigid principles, and willing to apply them unsparingly. He's the sort of man that Londoners who frequented not only the Globe but the bear-and-bull-baiting pits, taverns and cheap brothels nearby would recognise and hate as a Puritan, a thorough spoilsport. The Puritans regarded the whole South Bank - with more than a little reason - as a den of vice, which they wanted to close down and redevelop. (In 1642, when the Parliamentarians took over they got their way, at least with the theatres.) But in 1604, whatever the Globesters thought about vice in Vienna, they didn't want their entertainment district cleaned up, thank you very much. They would have breathed a heartfelt 'yes!' at the Duke's first hint of a suspicion that his deputy might just possibly be too good to be true, and that he intended to keep him under observation until he could be shown up as what everyone knows every Puritan is - a hypocrite.

But a word more about the Duke's disguise. Paradoxically, it's intended to deceive, of course, but it's also a means of establishing the truth – not just the truth that he'll discover about the city he's been misruling but a truth about him personally. He'll be more authentic as a humble, unobtrusive man of God than as a man of worldly power and public position:

> I have ever loved the life removed,
And held in idle price to haunt assemblies.
Where youth, and cost, witless bravery keeps. (1.3.8-10)

As a 'character' the Duke consists of his high position in the Viennese world, which (rather like Lear) he never really abdicates, and the values that he holds, but has difficulty applying, with regard to justice and mercy. He hardly appears as a unitary psychological 'self' in the way that Iago - to pluck an example out of thin air – does. He appears as a series, or set, of selves, linked as much by contradiction as by congruence. One self is the failed liberal ruler. Another is the unworldly man of prayer and reflection now seen pulling the friar's habit over his head. Another is the realpolitical man who sets up Angelo to 'be him' in a way he ought to be but fails be:

> we shall see
> If power change purpose, what our seemers be. (1.3.53-54)

In this play Shakespeare is well into the 'is'-versus-'seems' vein that preoccupied him so much at this stage of his career. It plays all ways, for good and ill. Although we're shocked by the revelation of Angelo's hypocrisy, nobody ever really wanted him to be as virtuous as he seemed, did they? And we can see why the Duke is resorting to 'comic' deception though some of the fast ones he pulls are pretty unnerving. In the paddock before the race Angelo 'looks good', though something tells us not to put our money on him, as the Duke – with reservations - does. By comparison, the Duke has definitely not 'looked good', and he still doesn't. A self-confessed moral and political failure, he's now going underhand as well as underground. Lucio, better at spotting flaws in others than in himself, picks out this dodginess in the Duke when he tells Isabella that

> His givings-out were of an infinite distance
> From his true-meant design. (1.4.54-55)

So, straightforward this Duke **isn't** – in any sense of the word. He looks morally under-powered compared to Isabella who, handicapped by her own integrity, innocently but comprehensively goofs things up in her encounters with Angelo. He's a 'deep one', and he doesn't exactly inspire confidence. Evidently it's down to him to sort things out, but is he the man to do it?

Lucio sees only the Duke's vulnerable side, but we're more fair-minded than him and we recognise his underlying honesty of purpose. He's a man of great seriousness, as he takes on the role, as well as the garb, of a friar. But when he comes

to visit the afflicted spirits
Here in the prison' (2.3.4-5)

he meets the repentant and visibly pregnant Juliet who's been making a prison-visit to her betrothed Claudio. He takes the opportunity to reprove her for her sin and seems to come within such a thin whisker of giving her absolution that we suspect that she may be going away thinking she **has** received it. The Duke seems to assume that if he dresses up as a friar he really **is** a friar. But he doesn't come over as a particularly compassionate one, as we see from the way he informs her, without offering any sympathy or comfort, that the father of her unborn child 'must die tomorrow' (2.3.37). What sort of man is this? we wonder. He's obviously determined to save Claudio by hook or by crook but he's a bit short on 'person skills'. Did it really help Juliet to pull that now-you-see-it-now-you-don't stunt with the sacrament of confession? And a few kind words, with prayers to God to alleviate her distress, wouldn't have done any harm either, surely?

There are several other occasions when the Duke seems to be in danger of getting carried away by his holy friar role. One, perhaps, isn't of much significance. When he tells Claudio: 'I am confessor to Angelo,' (3.1.165) we aren't expected to believe that the Duke has really been hearing Angelo's confessions and is now passing on what he's learned; it's just another example – though a fairly hair-raising one, especially for Catholics - of his 'tactical' lying. In Act 4, Scene 3, there's an altogether more serious case. Here he's up against a hardened criminal, Barnadine, whose eternal soul he regards it as his duty to try to save. Earlier, Juliet had willingly accepted his spiritual ministrations, which had also had the desired effect on the panic-stricken Claudio – for a while, at least. But Barnadine is a much tougher nut. He's permanently drunk and literally doesn't give a damn about anything or anybody, himself included. He hardly lets the Duke/Friar get a word in. What's needed, of course, is for Barnadine to repent his sins quickly, so that he can be beheaded without any further ado. The matter is urgent because Angelo is demanding to see Claudio's severed head, and the plan is to fool him by sending him Barnadine's head instead. But the Duke/Friar finds Barnadine 'unfit to live or die' (4.3.63) and when the Provost orders the jailers to bring him, repentant or not, to the block at once he insists that the execution be delayed until the old villain is spiritually ready to die. It could be a long wait, and he's well aware that without anybody else's head to send to Angelo it might have to be Claudio's at any minute. But the Duke believes, and it's part and parcel of his Friar role, that even if the law condemns a man to death you mustn't send him to the block with all his sins upon him. Eternal damnation is a much more important matter than life or death. It's a question of 'measure'. Just as the sentence on Claudio's unjust because the punishment's out of proportion to his crime, so it would be wildly disproportionate to dispatch a criminal to Hell – whatever he's done - by not allowing him enough time to repent. If there's anything you can do to save him from that fate a Christian's plain duty is to do it. Barnadine, he declares, is

A creature unprepared, unmeet for death;
And to transport him in the mind he is
Were damnable. (4.2.64-66).

In other words, to execute him now would mean damnation not only for Barnadine but for the man who ordered his death! This tells us a lot about this Duke. His Christian principles don't sit too well with the effective administration of the law. Apparently he's been waiting for people to repent their sins before executing them, and they've been taking advantage of his hesitancy. Later on he has a tell-tale exchange with the Provost which confirms this sort of interpretation:

Duke: How came it that the absent Duke had not either delivered him *(Barnadine)* to his liberty, or executed him? I have heard it was ever his manner to do so.
Provost: His friends still wrought reprieves for him; and indeed, his fact *(i.e. guilt)* till now in the government of Lord Angelo came not to an undoubted proof.
Duke: Is it now apparent?
Provost: Most manifest, and not denied by himself. (4.2.130-137)

We've had an earlier take on the Duke's failure as a magistrate in Act 3, Scene 2 where Lucio (believing, on account of the disguise, that he's talking to the Friar) says of the Duke: 'Ere he would have hanged a man for the generating a hundred bastards, he would have paid for the nursing a thousand. He had some feeling of the sport; he knew the service; and that instructed him to mercy.' This isn't fair and reliable comment on the Duke personal life, but it sheds a dim sidelong light on how 'mercy' tends to spring from a magistrate's sense of his own sinfulness and why it's so liable to be construed as a failure of authority. Even dedicated liars can be the vehicle of truth.

We wonder all along what sort of man this Duke really is. In the case of Bernadine he sticks firmly to his religious principles and is even prepared to put Claudio's life, which we know he's dedicated to saving, back into jeopardy rather risk sending an outrageous reprobate to his eternal doom. In the event, Providence – what else could it be? – is merciful and doesn't drive him to this extremity of choice. The Provost announces that the pirate Ragozine (who fortunately happens to look much more like Claudio than Barnadine does) has just died in his cell of a fever. Thank God! We can use **his** head!

This head-swapping business – which is at least as ludicrous and bizarre as the bed-trick business, which it 'echoes' - can cause amused titters in the audience, but the Duke's moral dilemma is far from a trivial one. OK, we're all grown-up people here, and we know that 'dodgy' means deceptive, even if used for worthy ends. But you can't say that **any** end justifies **any** means. There has to be a sense of 'measure'. Maybe it's out of proportion to send one man to eternal perdition to save another man's earthly life. But maybe it isn't. Maybe the Duke/Friar's taking it upon himself to decide what it's not for him to decide. On the other hand, maybe he can and should send a young woman into a dark garden as a sexual decoy in order to save the chastity of another young woman, and to entrap a hypocritical power-abuser. Who's to say? Well, there's an answer proposed to that question: the magistrate, or any man of responsibility who seeks to act justly, is the one who says that justice is more, and less, than precise law-enforcement. It depends on circumstances, and making a moral as well as a legal judgement of the balance of good and evil. And as it's a human being who has to make these decisions it's vital that he should be as good, wise and humble as fallen human nature allows. This is the central point of the Duke's definitive-sounding 'short-line' soliloquy at the end of Act 3.

He who the sword of heaven will bear,
Should be as holy as severe:
Pattern in himself to know,
Grace to stand, and virtue, go:
More nor less to others paying,
Than by self-offences weighing... (3.2.254-259)

In practice, of course, it isn't only Angelo that falls short of these steep moral requirements – to a lesser extent the Duke himself has. In the end justice, like injustice, is only what fallible people do to other fallible people, but it's important for them to know that the sword they bear is 'the sword of heaven'.

This message (the words of which may be Middleton's) is one that Shakespeare considers important enough to repeat in the next Act. The life of the law-enforcer needs to be:

..... paralleled
Even with the stroke and line of his great justice:
He doth with holy abstinence subdue
That in himself which he spurs on his power
To qualify in others: were he mealed *(i.e. stained)* with that
Which he corrects, then he were tyrannous;
But this being so, he's just. (4.2.77-82)

The play shows the process whereby the Duke makes amends for his previous failings and becomes more fit to rule. He has things to learn as well as to teach. The 'making amends' - this being a deeply Christian play - has to be through humility. It involves not only the abdication of worldly status but in a sense the abdication of **moral** status, too. When the Duke transfers his responsibilities to Angelo he also renounces the pride of being, doing and looking 'good'. Now he has to work in the world through devious and demeaning shifts; there's no more masking his personal faults and intrigues with the dignity of office. His edgy encounter with Lucio in Act 3, Scene 2 sheds a wonky light on this. The Duke gets the better of his impudent detractor, but not before Lucio says some interesting things. At one level the issue is how vulnerable people in power are to calumny. At another level it explains **why** they are. No rulers can be as good as they seem, or need, to be. It's only right that the position of those who judge their fellow men and women should be regarded as morally perilous. It **is** perilous. But the cynical Lucio, apart from lying about personal faults that the Duke never actually had, misses an essential point. The Duke's overall intention is to be just. True, no magistrate will be morally entirely up to the job, but the job has to be done and it can be done well enough. The difficulty of the task needs to be understood and honest attempts at tackling it need to be respected.

Some people take particular exception to the Duke's mendacity, which can seem to rival Lucio's, in inventiveness if not in malice. There are two points to make about that. One is simply to remember that this is a play, and that if you're watching a comedy of this sort lying and deceit are of the essence, and the more ingenious they are the better. If it all works out in the end – and it will, surely, however dark the material is at times - there's no need to take up a moral attitude about something that resides in the genre as much as in any of the specific dramatis personae. (If you think otherwise perhaps you should go and join the Puritans and campaign to ban play-acting.) The other point is that, as I've tried to explain, the Duke's reduction to dodgy methods is a part of his moral humbling, and we should charitably suppose that he feels much more uncomfortable about it than we do.

Other people get uptight about the bed-trick. My comment on this is the obvious one - that we need to apply a bit of cultural perspective. Shakespeare is drawing his plot from a mediaeval Italian popular story. 'Bed-trick' episodes, in which a man is tricked into making love to one woman when he thinks he's making love to another, occur fairly frequently in such stories, and this isn't even the only example in Shakespeare – there's another in 'All's Well that Ends Well'. Mediaeval Italians, and London playgoers, seem to have found it a bit spicy, though some fastidious modern folk, like the old-fashioned Puritans, regard it as a bit 'off'. Nowadays we like to think that both parties in a sexual act should at least know who the other one is. We don't need to deride this as modern sentimentality, but 400+ years ago what mattered more was whether they were married in the eyes of church and state. Angelo and Mariana **are** married – near as dammit, in much the same way that Claudio and Juliet are. Again, it's just a matter of a few legal details missing. Mariana's dowry has gone down, along with her brother, to the bottom of the sea, and that was Angelo's excuse dumping her; but their marriage contract remains valid. So a bit of jiggery-pokery is in order, if it forces Angelo to honour his obligation to Mariana, exposes him for what he is and saves Isabella's chastity. Yes, of course, it's fraudulent and (if you're that fussy) distasteful but there's no reason to doubt that the Duke/Friar's telling the truth when he tells Mariana:

> Fear you not at all;
> He *(Angelo)* is your husband on a pre-contract:
> To bring you thus together is no sin,
> Sith that the justice of your title to him
> Doth flourish the deceit. (4.1.70-74)

The Duke has forfeited the moral luxury of being able to pursue outright good ends by outright good means. This doesn't make him unusual but more like the rest of fallen humanity. In the business of justice keeping your hands clean can't always be the top priority. If you think it is you may end up doing nothing, which isn't right either. All you can do is to use your best judgement to prefer better purposes to worse, and choose the 'least-worse' means of achieving them. That's all the Duke/Friar's doing here. There are ludicrous as well as dodgy touches (why didn't Angelo bring a torch into the dark garden? and where's the bed then? - oh, there's a thought!) but morally speaking they're neither here nor there. Isabella, fiercely chaste but quite unprudish – a combination that Jacobeans may have understood better than we do today – wasn't too bothered. So why should we be?

There's one more aspect to the Duke's character that needs to be recognised. It's his determination to control events. It may seem an unlikely trait in one who regards himself as essentially a contemplative but it's there all right. He's a fixer when he's planning his withdrawal from Vienna, a fixer throughout, and a **supreme** fixer in the last Act with his brilliantly managed 'return' and his contrivance of the happy ending for all concerned.

The Duke has decided in advance how

> By cold gradation and well-balanced form,
> We shall proceed with Angelo. (4.3.99-100)

and this is how he brings the play to its conclusion.

Shakespeare clearly regarded this last act as an opportunity to enthral his audience with a virtuoso display of stage-craft in the winding up of a very complex plot. He wants all the surprises and suspense he can get into it. This means, of course, that the Duke (his 'plotter') will need to be on the top of his devious, manipulative form, managing the whole show. And so he is. He's the man in charge. He 'measures' everything right, making and then breaking the tit-for-tat formula for justice that the play's title suggests in masterly fashion. But in his well-timed entrances and exits, in his cleverly calculated absence during which he sheds his disguise, and even in his weighty moral pronouncements, we wonder what else there is in him than guile and a rather impersonal good intent. 'Cold gradation'. Yes, it **is** rather cold. He doesn't seem to show any love, even when at the end he tells Isabella that she's going to be his wife. His philosophy, spelt out at length in his spiritual advice to Claudio (3.1.5-41) boils down to something like this: life is hopeless and death much to be preferred. He also tends to overassociate the delivery of justice with the infliction and endurance of pain. As the play approaches its end he keeps Isabella in a prolonged torment of fear that her accusations against Angelo will be dismissed (he hasn't seen fit to tell her that he was the Friar) and we find ourselves asking the same question that we asked about his earlier treatment of Juliet - is it really **necessary** for him to put her through all that? Is he, after all, like Angelo, a bit of a devotee of severity for its own sake? Couldn't the denouement be managed more 'considerately'? But the point is that more considerately would mean less dramatically. The play's the thing, and it's a better play for all that complication and painful suspense at the end. 'Don't worry,' Shakespeare seems to be telling us. 'It's only a play. The Duke and I will work it all out in the end. The pain won't last forever, and in the meantime try to think of it as a spiritual learning experience, a purification, even. Everything, no matter how tricky, will be resolved, no matter by what trickery.'

And so it proves. The plot is brilliantly resolved, both dramatically and morally. But the characterisation of the Duke was always going to be a more difficult matter. The Duke has given us the necessary happy (i.e. just+merciful) outcome, but we're left with a sense of something incomplete or unresolved about him. It's not easy, in art or life, to blend wisdom with wiliness and moralism with manipulation to produce a credible, let alone good and lovable, character.

It's in the midst of the Duke's final flurry of machinations that the culminating 'moment of truth' occurs. He organises it, along with everything else. He sets up a test of Isabella's virtue much more formidable than any test that Angelo had ever set her.

The Duke has condemned Angelo to death, and tells Isabella why:

> ...as he adjudg'd your brother,
> Being criminal in double violation
> Of sacred chastity and of promise-breach
> Thereon dependent, for your brother's life,
> The very mercy of the law cries out
> Most audible, even from his proper tongue:
> An Angelo for Claudio; death for death. (5.1.401-407)

He builds a massive wall of words, with moral bricks cemented together by strict reason, leaving no aperture for Mariana or Isabella to insert a counter-argument. This is the 'measure for measure' (see Matthew 7.2.3 for the scriptural reference) that it's all supposed to be about, isn't it? He even co-opts the key word 'mercy' (5.1.405) into his side of the argument.

But even if it's hopeless Mariana doesn't back off in the teeth of the Duke's magisterial manner. 'We are definitive', he tells her,

> you do but lose your labour.
> Away with him to death. (5.1.425-426)

Then, addressing Lucio, he proceeds to 'next business': 'Now, sir, to you.'

And as if that isn't discouragement enough he virtually forbids Mariana to ask Isabella to join her in her plea for Angelo's life, warning:

> Her brother's ghost his paved bed would break,
> And take her hence in horror. (5.1.433-434)

We see the full rigour and (apparent?) cruelty of the Duke's nature, and we squirm. After all, we know, even if he's at pains to conceal it from the women, that Claudio's still alive and that all this anguish and suspense isn't strictly necessary. We're prepared to take Isabella on trust from what we've seen of her. Why isn't he?

But Mariana – and good on her! – won't be silenced. The argument she comes up with may be less than a clincher but it reveals her unconditional love for her deeply unlovable and unloving rediscovered husband.

> They say best men are moulded out of faults,
> And, for the most, become much more the better
> For being a little bad. So may my husband. (5.1.437-439)

The general idea is that love, no matter how helpless and anguished, can somehow or other come up with a response to evil.

We may well be touched by Mariana's words but if the Duke is touched too he isn't going to let it show. 'He *(Angelo)* dies for Claudio's death,' (5.1.441) is his (apparently) final pronouncement.

He's setting up the supreme test of Isabella's virtue, and he wants it to be as extreme as possible. He wants to see – well, don't we all, really? – if Isabella can bring herself to rally to Mariana's aid still believing, as he's careful to ensure that she does, that Angelo's responsible for her brother's death.

After standing silent for a while – actress! what will you/she be **thinking** in those moments? – Isabella falls to her knees in front of the implacable Duke. Mariana has begged her to

> kneel by me;
> Hold up your hands, say nothing: I'll speak all (5.1.435-436)

so the image we expect to see is of a 'plaster saint' but, if so, it's one that exceeds all our expectations of a plaster saint. She says:

> …Most bounteous sir:
> Look, if it please you, on this man condemn'd
> As if my brother liv'd. I partly think
> A due sincerity govern'd his deeds
> Till he did look on me. Since it is so,
> Let him not die. My brother had but justice,
> In that he did the thing for which he died:

251

For Angelo *(short line here: actress! supply three heartbeats-worth of something, and take your time about it)*
His act did not o'ertake his bad intent,
And must be buried but as an intent
That perish'd by the way. Thoughts are no subjects;
Intents, but merely thoughts. (5.1.441-452)

This is the moral and intellectual pinnacle of the play. Like Mariana (and Desdemona) she uses the word 'bad' and speaks of how 'badness' can be answered by patience and forgiveness. In ignorance of the facts of the case and at risk of appearing ridiculously overgenerous she focuses unerringly on the question of responsibility – what makes it grave and even where it truly lies. She offers in mitigation that she herself was the unintending but not altogether unconscious trigger of Angelo's fall from grace. (We spotted the element of truth in that, didn't we?) She associates herself in his blame to the extent that he behaved well 'till he did look on me,' (5.1.445) And after all his lust was thwarted, while Claudio's ran its course and had its consequences. There's a moral luck, or a moral mercy, that says you can't judge sinful intentions on the same basis as actual sins.

No, Isabella's not a plaster saint. Only a **true** saint, albeit misinformed and conscientiously hard-pressed, could have made that speech.

She's passed the test and the Duke – who, we note, has recently shown an admiring affection for her, calling her 'dear maid' (5.1.386) and 'most kind maid' (5.1.391) – must be inwardly rejoicing. But only inwardly. He's still a **dramatic** Duke and he doesn't want to ease the suffering, relax the tension or spoil the show by taking the stuffing out of his well-planned coup de theatre, i.e. when a thickly swathed figure will be led on stage and 'unmuffled' to general amazement as Claudio, good as new and no harm done.

Angelo, whether he's ready to acknowledge it or not and whatever the odds modern marriage counsellors might place on their chances of a happy marriage, needs Mariana. She'll provide the top-up of compassion and mercy that so far, he's lacked. And by a similar token the Duke needs Isabella. So let's let them have them, eh?

Modern directors, thank goodness, seem to have dropped the idea of Isabella as a pretty-as-a-picture, naïve virgin whom all decent blokes would like to protect from the wicked world if only she wasn't so set on disappearing into that awful convent. They're much more inclined now to see her as a courageous and formidably intelligent young woman entitled to our full admiration. Sometimes, though, in response to what they suppose to be contemporary values and attitudes, they go too far in this direction by turning her into a tough feminist miss tussling with her wayward, spineless brother, the semi-psychotically lecherous judge who unjustly condemns him and the sadistically-minded Duke with his impossible patriarchal attitudes. A typical expression of this kind of moral revisionism applied to her character is to delete or underplay the lines that convey her religious vocation and to have her end – this seems to have become the almost standard treatment - by having her reject the Duke's proposal of marriage. She makes no **scripted** response to the Duke's proposal, so it's an interpretive free house. Traditionally, and I'd argue, originally, her acceptance of the Duke was taken for granted, an integral part of the happy ending for all concerned (the exception being Lucio, for whom marriage is a curse). Alternatively, the director can duck the issue, and leave us wondering whether she accepts the proposal or follows her original vocation and returns to the convent.

In my view, though, the right ending is that she marries the Duke, with at least good grace. It's partly respect for the well-known dramatic conventions of Shakespeare's stage in which hero and heroine do couple up at the end, although admittedly in this case there hasn't been much 'romance' in the air until now. But I'm more persuaded by the consideration of what this play's centrally been **about.** There's been a searching analysis of the relationship of justice in the social sphere and underlying spiritual values, and the implication has always been that the two things should 'marry'. The union of the Duke and Isabella is surely meant to symbolise the resolution of the conflicts that we've watched in the course of the play.

So congratulations, Vincenzio and Isabella!

OTHELLO

In 1598 two merchant adventurer brothers from London, Robert and Anthony Sherley, visited Shah Abbasi (aka 'the Sophy' of Persia) in his new show city of Isfahan to discuss the expansion of the silk-for-silver trade. They found that he was planning a war against the Sunni Ottomans, so they also discussed a deal to supply his Shi'ite army with the latest European weapons. When the court received their report Queen Elizabeth chartered the East India Company to develop the trade. This was 'news' from an unfamiliar source.

Another well-known Muslim political player – this one a genuine North African Moor - was Abdul Guahid, ambassador of the King of Barbary, who came to London on a diplomatic visit a year or two later. He and his richly-robed retinue of dignitaries provided Londoners with an unusual spectacle during the autumn and winter months in 1600-1601 and the court asked Shakespeare's company to put on a show for them during the Christmas festivities. The ambassador had a portrait painted of himself which has survived and shows what an impressive figure he was.

Shakespeare had other triggers for his 'Moor' play of late mediaeval and Renaissance literary culture. They are, of course, racially and culturally alien – that goes without saying. They are challenged by European Christian values, especially the value of love and mercy. The Moor Aaron of Titus Andronicus is capable of immense cruelty and stoicism but doesn't forgive, or ask for forgiveness. The cultural hint that Shakespeare took for Othello is rather different; he is seized by an extreme jealousy which makes it emotionally impossible for him to offer any quarter to those who (he believes) have wronged him. When at last he realises his error he shows violent remorse and damns himself to Hell, but the Christian alternative - humble repentance and hope of forgiveness - doesn't seem to be in his spiritual repertoire.

The cast-list of Ariosto's 'Orlando Furioso' (1516), recently translated by Sir John Harrison (1591), includes Rodomonte, a North African Saracen king who wrought great destruction and killed many a Christian in the siege of Paris until Charlemagne, the first Holy Roman Emperor, eventually saw him off. Rodomonte finds himself distracted from his soldierly metier by the arrival of a messenger with the news that his intended, Doralice, has been abducted by a rival. The messenger is accompanied by a 'Vice' personification called Dame Jealousy who, together with her sisters Pride and Discord, determines his emotional reaction. The jealousy of the 'Sarcin bizzaro' (Ariosto: 18:36:1) is deliberately started with a spark and quickly fanned into an uncontrollable flame. He

Sospira e freme con si orribil faccia
Che gli elementi e tutto il ciel minaccia. (Ariosto: 18:34:7-8);

(He sighed and groaned in such a terrible fashion that it threatened all the earthly and heavenly spheres.)

This is a recognisable glimpse of Shakespeare's Moor - the formidable soldier infuriated by sexual jealousy.

Actually, although something of the character of Rodomonte comes through into the play none of his **narrative** does. Shakespeare gets his basic plot from his main source, the story of the jealous Venetian Moor in Cinthio's 'Hecatommithi' .(1565). He's a cultural import from Italy where Islam-jumpiness was understandably greater than in Northern Europe. As it happened, in the same year that 'Hecatommithi' appeared, Suleyman the Magnificent was laying siege to Malta as a step towards the invasion of Italy, and the picture of the Moor quite understandably expresses a Christian fear of the infidel. The propaganda effect is strengthened by making him more animal/sexual/irrational (i.e. less human), than 'we' are. When, for instance, his emotions rise to a certain level of intensity he'll express himself in shaking, groaning, sighing and grotesque facial expressions. As we see both in Rodomonte and in Cinthio's nameless 'typical' Moor, self-control and dignity tend to go out of the window. Obviously, extreme emotionality - and what can be more extreme than sexual jealousy? - is a weakness that **all** flesh is heir to, but Moors, so it's inferred, are more likely to have it, than European Christians.

Shakespeare invariably adds complications and qualifications. He makes Othello a Christian (convert) and a military defender of Christendom – which ought to (but actually doesn't) answer the question: is he one of 'us' or one of 'them'? He himself is awkwardly aware of his tendency to be taken over by 'passion' (or at least of his fear of being suspected of it), as is shown by his explicitly and unnecessary denial of it in his speech to the Duke when he asks him to allow him to take his lovely new bride off to the war with him – an unusual arrangement! – assuring him that there's no risk of him falling prey to unbusinesslike (i.e. amorous) distractions to the detriment of his military duties.

........................No, when light winged toys
Of feathered Cupid seel with wanton dullness
My speculative and officed instrument,
That my disports corrupt and taint my business,
Let housewives make a skillet of my helm

And all indign and base adversities
Make head against my estimation. (1.3.262-275)

The Duke buys the argument, or seems to, although the rest of us may detect Othello underlying insecurity and feel that he's protesting too much.

It's following the prompt of the stereo/archetype that Shakespeare repeatedly emphasises the dominance of excitable physicality in the Moor's nature. We may or may not have recognised an early sign of it when, stepping off the boat to greet Desdemona, he becomes breathless – almost as if a heart attack is coming on:

I cannot speak enough of this content,
It stops me here. It is too much of joy. (2.1.194-195)

But there's also the 'trance' (i.e. fainting or epileptic fit) which, preceded by the 'shakes', (4.1.41) he falls into when Iago has him visualising Cassio lying on Desdemona, 'topping' (or 'tupping' – cf 1.1.88) her.

And again, the Moor 'loses it' completely in Act 4, Scene1 when Desdemona's 'cousin' Lodovico (probably accompanied by Graziano, her uncle, too – though the text doesn't make his presence clear) brings him word from Venice that Cassio is replacing him as governor. Misconstruing her positive reaction to the news, he strikes and abuses her. We see brutal and civilised elements in the Moor's nature jostling for the upper hand. He alternates between shouting 'devil!' (4.1.239) and 'Get you away!' (4.1.258) at Desdemona while confirming to Lodovico that he will 'obey the mandate' (4.1.259) - and courteously inviting him to supper! Then he charges off-stage raving about 'goats and monkeys' (4.1.263) - the delusional sexual imagery that Iago has carefully prepared in advance for him. (3.3.406).

Few if any traces of civilised self-restraint remain in the murder scene (Act 5, Scene 2), where physical manifestations of emotional disturbance come thick and fast. The Moor makes inarticulate noises, like Hum! (5.2 36), rolls his eyes (5.2.38) - a stress symptom, by the way, that Desdemona seems to have observed in him before - and gnaws his nether lip. (5.2.43) He also trembles with 'bloody passion' (5.2.44) before the struggle in which he smothers her.

But let's step back at this point and look at the **dramatic,** rather than the **emotional/physical,** starting points of the play.

There are two men on stage, arguing. We've missed the opening exchanges. One of the men (whose name we won't pick up for some time yet) is reproaching the other, and the other (whose name, we learn at once, is Iago) is trying to placate him - albeit more along the lines of 'just trust me' than 'let me explain'.

But what are they arguing about? The aggrieved man's mention of purse strings (1.1.1-2) suggests that he's been paying Iago money for something that he hasn't got yet, but it isn't clear – and it won't be clear for some while - what it is.

'How is it,' the aggrieved man asks Iago, that you 'should know of this?' (1.1.3)

What's 'this'? we wonder.

Iago re-affirms his honesty of intent but sheds no further light.

The next thing the aggrieved man says, quite inconsequentially as far as we can tell, is:

Thou toldst me thou didst hold him in thy hate. (1.1.6)

Now who's this 'him', for goodness sake?

Too many pronouns, not enough nouns. We're not getting anywhere.

Although the men are at loggerheads they evidently share a general understanding of the situation, which makes it unnecessary for them to spell things out to each other. Shakespeare keeps us tantalizingly outside their knowledge zone. He doesn't seem to **want** us to know what the man who isn't Iago is complaining about and whether he has a case. And believe it or not, he'll keep us waiting for the full picture until **Act 4**, when he gives this opening conversation a more explicit re-run! (4.2.174-246)

So far it's been short exchanges, but now Iago, in a 27-line speech (1.1.7-32), lifts one corner of the covering sheet. He explains that the hated man is an important public figure in Venice, and that he hates him because he's kyboshed his hopes of promotion. He'd hoped to rise to the rank of lieutenant - ah! so he's a soldier! – but although 'three great ones in the city' supported his application this hated man rejected him in favour of another candidate. So he's stuck at the rank of 'ancient' (ensign), a sort of NCO, which he resents bitterly, particularly as the man who got the job, one Michael Cassio, is a man he loathes and despises. As a long-serving, battle-hardened soldier he has to give way to a callow military theoretician. 'Mere prattle without practice', he says, 'is all his soldiership.' (1.1.25-26) But that's how it is these days, apparently. Promotion's no longer a matter of Buggins' turn, as it used (and ought) to be. It

> ....goes by the letter and affection,
> And not by old gradation, where each second
> Stood heir to the first. (1.1.36-38)

All this is in the public domain. If the aggrieved man - his friend or whatever he is – doubts that Iago's grudge against this hated public figure is genuine all he has to do is ask around. But what's still unclear is how any harm that might befall the h.p.f. at the hands of Iago would benefit **him**. We don't even know the h.p.f's name yet, but our ears prick up when we hear Iago refer to him as 'His Moorship'. (1.1.32) Did we hear that aright? A Moor? Tell us more!

But no, Shakespeare's still in teasing vein. The talk moves on to other things.

On the stage, especially if we're seeing the play for the first time, all this flashes by too fast for us for us to clock. As readers, though, we have a chance to pause and turn our uncertainties into questions.

Who is 'His Moorship'? And does he really deserve Iago's enmity?

Is Cassio really just an over-promoted no-hoper?

Is Iago simply a **probus miles** with an understandable chip on his shoulder? Or is there more - or less - to him than that?

Is the other aggrieved man Iago's friend? client? side-kick? or dupe? What's he paying Iago to get for him? And why would the downfall of 'His Moorship' work to his advantage?

To these questions the other aggrieved man (this is getting silly: I might as well tell you his name - Roderigo) adds one more. Why, he asks, if 'His Moorship' has treated Iago so shabbily, does he remain in his service?

Just for once we get a clear and immediate answer. Iago declares: 'I follow him to serve my turn upon him.' (1.1.41)

So that's it. Iago's opportunity for revenge depends on his biding his time and staying 'in' with 'His Moorship'. He makes no bones about it: it will involve deep duplicity. 'I am not what I am,' (1.1.64) he declares, and this disclosure, we realise, gives us the key to his character. However he might appear, he's not a straightforward soldier – or not **just** a straightforward soldier.

OK, we've got our villain.

A more reflective client than Roderigo might wonder if such a self-declared intriguer can be relied upon to deal straight with him - or with anyone, for that matter. But he evidently needs to trust him. After all, if Iago's an unscrupulous operator that's what Roderigo's paying him to be. Sure, there's foul play afoot, but if 'His Moorship' is really the sort of man Iago says he is he's got it coming to him. Iago doesn't come cheap, but perhaps that's a guarantee that he'll get results.

We're following everything very closely and trying to guess whatever **can** be guessed but we're still floundering.

But Roderigo's next remark, a complete non sequitur, just adds one more to the stack of quandaries:

What a full fortune does the thicklips owe
If he can carry it thus. (1.1.65-66)

'Thicklips' = Moor, no problem. And 'carry it' evidently means 'get away with it'? But that doesn't get us very far. What's the 'it' is that he'll be trying to get away with?

Little do we know – how **could** we know? - that this 'it' is the same thing as the 'this' that we tripped up on in Roderigo's initial:

………………..'I take it most unkindly
That thou, Iago,….shouldst know of this'. (1.1.1-3)

- and a fat lot of help it would be if we **did** know, not having any purchase on 'it' **or** 'this'!

Confused? Aren't we all?

But now there's a sort of dream transition. We find, quite out of the blue, that the two men have been holding their conversation in front of 'her father's house' (1.1.73). In the absence of any explanation all we can do is stick with the action in hand and see what emerges. Evidently Iago and Roderigo have arranged this venue beforehand and what's more they have a plan, which they're now about to put into operation. Iago tells Roderigo to

Call up her father,
Rouse him. (1.1.66-67)

'Her father' and the rest of the household are rudely awakened with the sensational news that the daughter of the house – she's not named until the next scene but (unlike Shakespeare) I'm trying to be helpful so I'll tell you now that she's called Desdemona – has run off in the night with 'His Moorship' who, as Iago proclaims in bracingly non-euphemistic language, is at this very moment having his filthy way with her:

Even now, now, very now, an old black ram
Is tupping your white ewe. Arise, arise.
Awake the snorting citizens with the bell,
Or else the devil will make a grandsire of you. (1.1.87-90)

Ah! Of course! 'It' (1.1.66) and 'this' (1.1.3) both refer to the **elopement**! All you have to do to solve the problem is know the answer!

But how did Iago know about it in advance? It must have been a closely guarded secret, and the Moor – let alone the lady in question - would hardly have tipped him off. (Don't hold your breath for the explanation, though. It's is one of several things that's **never** explained.)

What will the consequences of the elopement be? Iago thinks that the Moor will probably manage to 'carry it off' because he's regarded as militarily indispensable, and that his marriage to this well-born Venetian heiress will open his way to further advancement in public life – although as an ill-wisher that's the last thing he wants to see. But it could go the other way. The Moor could be disgraced, even banished, and that's what he must work for. He'll try to bring down the wrath of society on the couple by applying all the negative spin he can to the elopement story as it breaks. Hauling the girl's father – his name's Brabantio, by the way, and he's a distinguished senator - and his whole sleepy household out of bed in the middle of the night helps to create the right sense of scandal. But of course the elopement is a total surprise to him. It's been plotted in secret – though Iago's caught wind of it – by Othello and Desdemona. For Iago the elopement's only a turn-up for the book, an unlooked-for publicity opportunity, but he sees at once how to make maximum use of it. Not only does it give him an opportunity to ruin Othello but maybe he can also use it to try to diddle the distinctly subanalytical Roderigo into believing that he's actually propelling events on his behalf and doing something to earn his fee. It doesn't hold water, of course. The whole of Venice would soon know all about it anyway, midnight hullabaloo or not, and just the same consequences would ensue, albeit a few hours later. But Roderigo might not twig that.

Which reminds us: we're still in the dark about what Roderigo stands to gain from Othello's ruin.

But now at last we get a clue. Brabantio spots Roderigo in the dark street and rebukes him angrily:

I have charged thee not to haunt about my doors:
In honest plainness thou hast heard me say
My daughter is not for thee. (1.1.95-97)

So that's it! Roderigo fancies Desdemona! And, ah yes! - maybe he's paying Iago to procure her for him! But hang on a minute: how's **that** supposed to work? and how on earth will her running away with the Moor improve his chances?

Mmm… Head-scratching time again.

Meanwhile, Iago's having a whale of a time. Yelling at the deeply discomfited Brabantio he lays the sexual stuff on thick.

'You'll have your daughter covered with a Barbary horse; you'll have your nephews neigh to you; you'll have coursers for cousins, and jennets for germans.' (1.1.109-112)

The line of thought is still 'the black ram tupping your white ewe', but with the imagery now switched to horses. This Iago, we realise, has an outlandish sort of wit and his mockery is merciless. He doesn't pull his punches. We're aware, too, that in his mind sexuality is an 'animal' thing which generates images heavily charged with contempt, disgust and fear. When he tells Brabantio: 'Your daughter and the Moor are now making the beast with two backs' (1.1.114-115) it's a very graphic image of monstrous miscegenation. And it's not 'just words'. Iago seems to virtually **see** what he describes, and he has an uncanny way of getting others to see it, too. He has the poor old Brabantio, in all his distress and indignation, visualising - and so virtually believing - what he describes. It's a power that we'll see Iago use again. It'll be an effective substitute for the 'ocular proof' of Desdemona's infidelity that he later on induces Othello to demand. (3.3.363)

It's Iago's filthy-mindedness and cruelty that Shakespeare chooses to bring home to us first. By comparison, he reveals his deviousness in a relatively oblique and eventual way. The nastiness is there for all to see in the Brabantio-baiting scene but he doesn't hit on an overall plan until the end of the first act. Then, soliloquising, he lets us know that he intends

..............to abuse Othello's ear
That he *(Cassio)* is too familiar with his wife. (1.3.394-395)

266

It's quite simple really, like most brilliant ideas. And it'll work, he calculates, weaving daylight realism and dark intention seamlessly together, because Cassio's the way he is – a ladies' man – and Othello's the way he is – an ass. He celebrates his inspiration, typically, in sexual-reproductive imagery:

I have't, it is engendered! Hell and the night
Must bring this monstrous birth to the world's light.
(1.3.402-403)

As the hullabaloo subsides Iago, still more the impromptu deviser of odd tricks than the grand strategic schemer, tells Roderigo that he's going to make himself scarce when Othello and Desdemona are brought face to face with Brabantio and the other bigwigs to account for themselves. He doesn't want to be

     …...produced, as, if I stay, I shall,
Against the Moor. (1.1.144-145)

His worry is that if he's present at the showdown Brabantio will point him out as the one who woke everyone up to break the news of the elopement. And where would that leave him? He still needs Othello to trust him. But slinking away now won't necessarily save him from being caught out, will it? It doesn't cover all the angles. When the time comes for Brabantio to bring his grievance before the Duke and the other Venetian senators there'll be nothing to stop him naming Iago, whether he's present or not, as one of the two midnight alarm-raisers.

Unless, of course…

Unless Brabantio (or his retainers) didn't get a clear view of him, or recognise his voice, during the hullabaloo. It's a possibility. Did Iago have the foresight to stay incognito, lurking in the shadows or around the corner as he yelled out the news of the elopement? The text doesn't rule it out, or in.

Iago's wish to make himself scarce at this stage may or may not be a red herring, but he has another consideration in mind. He wants to be with Othello when the word reaches him about the events outside Brabantio's house so that he can put a spin on his master's understanding of what's been going on. In the next scene (Act 1, Scene 2) we find him telling his master, with superb aplomb, that it was Roderigo, off his own bat, who raised the alarm. He professes to be so outraged by hearing Roderigo speaking in 'such scurvy and provoking terms' (1.2.7) about him that

…nine or ten times
I had thought t'have yerked him here, under the ribs.
(1.2.4/5)

It all helps to divert suspicion but it won't get him off the hook if he's later identified as one of the alarm–raisers himself, will it? He'll need more than quick-wittedness to get out of **that**. He'll need the luck of the devil.

Well, he **has** the luck of the devil.

The outstanding example of his luck occurs in Act 4, Scene 1. It's the sort of scene (like the disputation episode in Act 2 and the handkerchief episode in Act 3) that you'd expect to find in a comedy. Of course there's a rather nasty taste to it, but you could say that of quite a few scenes in plays like 'The Merchant of Venice', 'Twelfth Night', 'All's Well that Ends Well' and 'Measure for Measure', too, couldn't you? One of the features, apart from its highly contrived 'business', that makes the scene seem 'comic' is the extent to which the villain's luck oversteps the bounds of realistic credibility. He stages a conversation with Cassio, who has no idea it's a set-up, for the benefit of Othello hiding nearby. The two men talk disrespectfully about Cassio's mistress Bianca, but Iago's idea is to have the Moor believe that they're discussing Desdemona. It's hair-raisingly risky because its success depends not only upon Iago's own prompts and questions (which he can control) but also upon Cassio's 'easy-arrogant' body language and his bursts of scornful laughter (which he can't control). There's absolutely nothing to prevent Cassio mentioning Bianca by name at any time, which would bring the whole precarious pack of cards tumbling down and expose him in mid-trick. As it happens, everything works perfectly, and there's even an unlooked-for extra success when Bianca herself turns up, by chance and at exactly the right moment, talking about the handkerchief that Cassio's given her.

There's a nice question for the actors and the director to decide on here. How much of the Iago-Cassio exchange is Othello supposed actually to **hear**, and how much are his jealous inferences steered merely by the postures and laughter of the two men? Othello starts out of earshot and may need to move stealthily closer as the conversation proceeds, but it's reasonable to assume that he's catching everything by the time Cassio says 'I never knew woman love man so' (4.1.110) and Iago says 'She gives it out that you shall marry her'. (4.1.116) However it's staged, though, the scene is one in which the Moor is in danger of becoming a figure of fun in his eagerness to drink in all the farcical poison that Iago is concocting for him.

But it would be a mistake to believe that Iago's pulling all the strings and that his plots are tantamount to the plot of the play. His control is always incomplete, and what he manages to arrange is only ever a relatively small part of what happens overall. The decisions of other characters still matter. Iago's powers of deception are only one side of the coin; the other side is Othello's capacity for **self**-deception. Iago comes up with the evidence of Desdemona's infidelity, such as it is, but then has to rely on Othello drawing the (wrong) conclusion. For example, after telling him about Cassio's dream of being in bed with Desdemona – a pure, or rather impure, invention of his own - he maintains the pose of an objective man who still isn't convinced that her guilt's beyond reasonable doubt. He goes no further than to say:

…This may help to thicken other proofs
That do demonstrate thinly. (3.3.432-433)   .

But like a Napoleonic general Iago needs to be lucky as well as smart. As P.G. Wodehouse says about one of his own plotters in 'Something Fresh' (1915): 'He was full of methods. But they never led him anywhere without a coincidence.'

Those who are familiar with Cinthio's jealous Moor tale in 'Hecatommithi' will be aware how closely Shakespeare follows it for most of the play, but also how his first act owes nothing to it. It's a virtually independent work of creation, apparently detachable from the rest of the action – as Verdi and Boito ('Otello' 1887) demonstrated in eliminating it from their operatic version of the story. But we can see why Shakespeare made the extra creative effort, though: several juicy theatrical ideas had occurred to him for which there was no cue in Cinthio: the slow teasing start, leading to the explosion of shouting in the dark outside Brabantio's house; the revelation of what an extremely nasty piece of work Iago is **before** we see how 'honest' he manages to appear in the eyes of (nearly) all and sundry; and the highly dramatic 'quasi-courtroom drama' in which Othello and Desdemona, arraigned before the elders, are given the chance to tell the story of their courtship, are let off and sent post-haste to Cyprus by the Duke.

There's another point to make about this first act. Shakespeare always has something interesting to say about fathers and daughters and he spots an opportunity here that's too good to miss. Cinthio briefly mentions Desdemona's headstrong disregard of her relatives' objection to her match with the Moor, but in his version of the story (as in the Boito/Verdi version) there's no **father** to be opposed or betrayed. Shakespeare creates one for her, though, and he's no mere cipher. The emotional texture is interestingly complicated by the fact that although he figures only as an angry old man – not, usually, the most attractive sort of character - he seems entitled to a fair share of our sympathy. He certainly loves his daughter – in his fashion - and she certainly pulls a fast one on him. After the action moves to Cyprus we won't see him again but he continues as a point of reference for a number of issues that are developed later on in the play.

The daughter that Brabantio loves is

......a maiden never bold,
Of spirit so still and quiet that her motion
Blushed at herself, (1.3.95-97)

but we soon realise that this maiden's a figment of his patriarchal imagination. The Desdemona that we're looking at is a very different kettle of fish. She's been quite a naughty girl, secretly eloping with a black man and though caught in the glare of scandal not in the least repentant. Her father still insists on angelicising her, though, attributing her fall from grace to some sort of heathen enchantment that the Moor must have cast upon her. There's a painful contrast awaiting our attention when we see the way that the next male authority figure in her life, the Moor himself, will get her hopelessly wrong too, but in the opposite way, by grossly be-whoring her – 'O thou public commoner', (4.2.74), 'Impudent strumpet' (4.2.82), etc, etc. In fact Desdemona isn't 'recognised' by either of them for anything like what she actually is. It seems to be the story of her life.

Desdemona's deception of Brabantio is what mainly interests Iago in her. Early on, he draws it to Othello's attention:

Look to her, Moor, if thou hast eyes to see:
She has deceived her father, and may thee (1.3.293-294)

and he doesn't miss the chance to pick it up, and put it to good (i.e. bad) use later on in Act 3, Scene 3.

Iago: She did deceive her father, marrying you.
And when she seemed to shake, and fear your looks, she loved them most.
Othello: And so she did.
Iago: Why, go to then:
She that so young could give out such a seeming
To seel her father's eyes up, close as oak –
He thought was witchcraft… (3.3.209-214)

After the first act Brabantio's not seen again but Desdemona hasn't forgotten him. In Act 4, Scene 1 the Moor is falling to pieces before our eyes. He's been sent word that HQ in Venice is making Cassio governor in his place, and he's not taken the news well. Desdemona's attitude is understandable: her relationship with Othello is going inexplicably wrong in Cyprus and her instinct, one might reasonably surmise, is to get back to Venice – and sanity. But her reaction when she learns that her husband has been recalled – 'By my troth, I am glad on't' (4.1.237) - makes us gasp with alarm. The Moor unhesitatingly interprets it as a confession that she's been intriguing against him on behalf of her lover and, to everyone's horror, he hits her, slags her off in the crudest terms and dismisses her with: 'Hence, avaunt!' (4.1.260). 'Are his wits safe?' (4.1.269) asks the shocked Lodovico, on behalf of us all. When, in the next scene, alone with Othello, she comes under direct accusation of infidelity she innocently thinks that it's **political** infidelity that he means. She doesn't know what's been going on back in Venice (nor do we) but naturally her father comes to mind:

If haply you my father do suspect
An instrument of this your calling back,
Lay not your blame on me; if you have lost him
Why, I have lost him, too. (4.2.45-48)

We catch the note of guilt and regret. In fact, it seems that the old man's innocent, too. We learn later from Graziano (5.2.202-207) that he died of a broken heart.

There's one other 'marker' that Brabantio leaves behind. With him Shakespeare puts in the initial strokes of what will become a pattern: the plight of a man who loses, or believes he's losing, a woman he thinks of as his. It's something of an understatement to point out that this is the central pattern of the play.

In Act 2, Scene 1 is a long, multipurpose scene. It's the first scene set across the sea in Cyprus but it marks the point where the wide-sweep drama of love, war and politics which initially we might have been expecting – something along the lines of the (still unwritten) 'Antony and Cleopatra' perhaps – condenses into the shape of a rather claustrophobic 'domestic tragedy'. It shows the main cast of characters arriving safely on the island, where it turns out that there's no Turkish enemy to fight after all. The enemies, it will prove, are within. And for good measure it contains no fewer than three more very diverse 'moments' in the characterisation of Iago: his debate with Desdemona, his handling of Roderigo and his concluding soliloquy.

The scene begins with the good news that the Turkish fleet has been destroyed by storms. The (potentially) bad news is that the three ships travelling from Venice to Cyprus (carrying, respectively, i) Cassio, ii) Iago accompanied by Desdemona, Emilia and Roderigo, and iii) Othello), are still out there in the same perilous weather. Montano and his two gentlemen scan the sea anxiously. Then Cassio's ship arrives and he comes ashore. But he's hardly found his land legs when there are excited cries off-stage as another sail is sighted. Soon a gentleman comes to report that this second ship brings

….. one Iago, ancient to the general. (2.1.66)

The gentleman doesn't seem to have heard of Iago before, and he doesn't know about anyone else on board. There may even be a note of disappointment in his voice. It's **only** Iago, not Othello, the big shot. But Cassio's better informed than the gentleman and sees things in a different light. If Iago's safe, so is Desdemona, and that means a lot to him. In his joy and relief he rather extravagantly suggests that it was her presence on board that saved the ship from disaster. He speaks of her as a goddess (Venus comes to mind, of course, this being Cyprus) whom even the unruly sea elements have too much reverence to harm.

Tempests themselves, high seas, and howling winds,
The guttered rocks and congregated sands,
Traitors ensteeped to clog the guiltless keel,
As having sense of beauty, do omit
Their mortal natures, letting go safely by
The divine Desdemona. (2.1.68-73)

However, Othello's still out there amongst the menacing winds and waves, his fate unknown. Cassio prays that great Jove will swell Othello's sail with his powerful breath

That he may bless this bay with his tall ship,
Make love's quick pants in Desdemona's arms,
Give new fire to our extincted spirits
And bring all Cyprus comfort! (2.1.79-82)

We get the point. Cassio's genuinely devoted to his master as well as to his mistress. His motives are honourable. His joy isn't that Desdemona, saved, will be united in love with **him**, but with Othello. We may feel that the way he expresses it is a bit surprising, though. The imagery is oddly 'Freudian', with a pronounced tilt towards the orgasmic. We have to resist the temptation – although the temptation's certainly there - to link it to the sort of voyeurism that Iago's so given to, and which he's so effective in imparting to Othello.

In his own way Cassio's as much on the sexual 'qui vive' as Iago. His gallantry expresses a high level of erotic as well as social alertness. It's very much 'ladies first' with him, which pleases the women but naturally risks antagonising the men, especially if they're as touchy as Iago or as gullible as Othello.

The travellers come ashore: Desdemona, Emilia and Iago (and Roderigo: we mustn't overlook him – though Cassio, for all his 'manners', does). Cassio greets 'our captain's captain' (see 2.3.309-310) first. For no less than fourteen fulsome lines the others are left standing by while he delivers his welcome speech:

...............................O, behold,
The riches of the ship is come on shore:
You men of Cyprus, let her have your knees! (2.1.82-84)

Desdemona thanks him, but at the moment she's less interested in compliments than in news of Othello. And immediately – as if her wish is fate's command – a third ship is sighted and Cassio sends one of the attendant gentlemen to 'see for the news'. (2.1.95) As far as Cassio's concerned it's been a case of first things first: give Desdemona the big hello, and then do what he can to abbreviate her anxiety – hopefully - by sending someone to find out whether this latest ship to arrive is Othello's. This done, he turns to the ancient and his wife Emilia. He thinks he's following the correct etiquette, but it doesn't take much to offend anyone with a social/sexual chip on his shoulder the size of Iago's. 'Good ancient,' he says, 'you are welcome.' (2.1.96) Nothing wrong with that, you'd think, but it hits Iago on a tender spot. Is this fancypants Cassio, now he's finally got round to noticing him, calling him 'ancient' to rub in his inferior rank? In any case - who does he think he's fooling? - Cassio isn't interested in him at all; he just wants to flirt with Emilia.

The lieutenant says:

Let it not gall thy patience, good Iago,
That I extend my manners; 'tis my breeding
That gives me this bold show of courtesy (2.1.97-99)

– and he kisses her on the lips.

For Iago this is no innocent gaffe. But what is it for
Cassio? He'd deny that he meant to rile Iago by addressing
him as 'ancient'. Soldiers **do** address each other by rank.
But kissing Emilia is another matter. It looks perfectly
designed to annoy. His mention of 'manners' and
'breeding' looks very much like red-rag-to-bull, pointing
directly to what Iago's short of and why he hasn't risen
higher in the world. And it won't come as a surprise to
anyone if, when a handsome, sexually 'lit-up' Alpha-male
lieutenant kisses the wife of an 'other rank' whom he's
recently beaten in a competition for promotion, the 'other
rank' bridles at it. And all the more so if the wife seems to
rather enjoy it. Cassio's behaviour may be innocent in the
sense that it's **socially** 'passable' but surely he realises,
whether or not he gives a damn about it, that it's
humiliating for Iago. Perhaps he wants to take the
opportunity to pull rank over a man who recently
presumed to put himself up as a professional rival; perhaps
he just fancies kissing Emilia and knows that in the
circumstances Iago will just have to like it or lump it.
Later on we may reflect that this isn't the only occasion
when the 'gentlemanly' Cassio humiliates a person of
lower rank who can do nothing about it. Obviously there's
no love lost between him and Iago so he may feel it's fair
enough. But his mistress Bianca **does** love him, and he
doesn't treat her particularly nicely either, does he?

A 'structural' description of the incident would run
something like this: a man experiences a moment of
existential insignificance when he enters a situation in

which more important business is going on than his arrival: he feels that the manner in which he's greeted is a put-down, but he can't do much about it and it stokes up his already-negative feelings.

Now where, earlier in the play, have we had another incident which fits this description? The answer, of course, is in the previous scene when Brabantio goes to the Duke to seek redress for the elopement of Othello and Desdemona. The outraged senator has, as he thinks, hauled the Moor across the city to receive the Duke's condemnation. But the Duke, in war cabinet, is preoccupied with the Turkish emergency. He looks straight past - or through! - Brabantio and greets Othello first:

Valiant Othello, we must straight employ you
Against the general enemy Ottoman. (1.3.49-50)

Only then does he acknowledge the senator. The gaffe is all the more hurtful for being unintended. Brabantio's a proud and powerful man, a 'magnifico' who

..........hath in his effect a voice potential
As double as the duke's (1.2.12-14)

so protocol requires that he be greeted first, but by the time the Duke gets round to addressing him at all his 'I did not see you' (1.3.51) has rendered all his subsequent courtesies unavailing. The damage has been done. When, having put Othello and Desdemona in the clear, the Duke tries to placate Brabantio with a string of vapidly sententious couplets -

When remedies are past the griefs are ended
By seeing the worst which late on hopes depended. (1.3.203-204) etc -

the senator is far too angry to try to conceal his feelings. He replies to the Duke in five well-chiselled and scathing couplets of his own, ending with:

These sentences to sugar or to gall,
Being strong on both sides, are equivocal.
But words are words: I never yet did hear
That the bruised heart was pierced through the ear.
(1.3.217-220)

Brabantio goes off, never to return, although he casts his shadow over what's to come and he remains a point of dramatic reference through the play.

Brabantio and Iago are both humiliated not only by social slights but by being, or feeling, dispossessed of a woman. In Brabantio's case it really happens; he loses his only daughter, in the full glare of publicity, to the Moor. The case of Iago is somewhat different, but there's an underlying emotional parallel. Convinced in any case that he's being cuckolded right, left and centre, he has to stand there trying to look amused as Cassio practically charms the pants off his wife Emilia in front of his eyes. And of course Brabantio's and Iago's 'woman-losing' experiences match up not only with each other but with Othello's conviction that Cassio has 'taken' Desdemona from him. All three men feel 'unmanned' by the notion that the woman in question has sexual inclinations beyond their control and that she's a willing participant in her own seduction/abduction. Othello will put his finger on it when, though still only half-persuaded of Desdemona's treachery, he says:

O curse of marriage
That we can call these delicate creatures ours
And not their appetites! (3.3.272-274)

But to return to Act 2, Scene 1. The third ship has shown up but there's an interlude of anxious suspense for Desdemona, Emilia, Cassio and Iago before they find out whether Othello's on it. All they can do is wait and worry - and make conversation. But what is there to talk about? Iago takes the initiative. He's just seen what liberties Cassio can get away with, masking – as he sees it – his lecherous intent behind silver-tongued flattery. So now he wants to see what he can get away with himself, in the same company, as an 'honest' teller of unvarnished truths about women. He reckons that he can make a good case for misogyny provided it's contained within the frame of light badinage.

As daylight reappears between Cassio's mouth and Emilia's, he says:

> …. would she give you so much of her lips
> As of her tongue she oft bestows on me
> You'd have enough. (2.1.100-102)

It's a man-to-man comment. I'm her husband and I'm telling you, she's not as desirable as you seem to think. You feel the smoothness of her lips; I feel the roughness of her tongue. But we chaps don't want too much of either, do we?

It's an odd as well as a very ungallant remark. We wonder exactly what Iago's getting at, or inadvertently revealing about himself. Lips and tongues are sexually suggestive. But what are they suggestive **of**? Well, it's hard to be definite, but how about this? As well as nagging her unappreciative husband (which is one kind of tongue-work) Emilia may once have tried to signal her sexual hunger to him with a spot of French kissing – or he **thinks** she has, or that she might **want** to, or he wants to **pretend** she has, or..........whatever.

But in any case he thinks it's disgusting!

'Lips', like 'tongue', is a hot word in the play, a trigger for sexual rage. Remember 'thicklips'? (1.1.65) Later on, the Moor, on the brink of a 'trance' or fit brought on by his Iago-prompted visualisation of Desdemona and Cassio making love, says: 'Pish! Noses, ears, and lips. Is't possible?' (4.1.42)

Desdemona may not pick up such connotations but what she certainly **does** see is that Emilia's under attack and she leaps to her defence. 'Alas!' she protests, 'she has no speech.' (2.1.102) OK, one can quibble about whether this means that Emilia is **never** an assertive talker (unlikely) or that her husband's offensive remark has left her bereft of speech just for the moment (more likely), but it makes no difference either way. Shakespeare sees no need to clarify. He's done what he meant to do. He's dropped the hint about Iago's mouth-focussed aversion to, and fear of, his wife's sexuality, before revealing his more general hostility to women.

For such a disingenuous man Iago can be very unguarded about his private life. Emilia, he complains, gives him no peace. Even when he's trying to get to sleep she keeps him awake. A familiar picture comes up on the screen – a chap comes home all knocked up after a hard day at the office running around after the Moor and she pesters him for sex. She's a nymphomaniac! This uncomfortable picture of Emilia trying and failing to seduce her own husband will reappear in Act 3, Scene 3 when she has the handkerchief he's been asking her to get hold of and says, perhaps a little flirtatiously:

'I have a thing for you,' (3.3.305), only to get a crude, insulting rejection:

'You have a thing for me? It is a common thing....' (3.3.306)

At risk of putdowns like that we can see why Emilia might be inclined to stick to low-level nagging – which, according to Iago, she's learned to do without even opening her mouth.

She puts her tongue a little in her heart
And chides **with thinking.** (2.1.106-107)

Even when Emilia's tongue isn't wagging – in his mouth, or Cassio's, or just 'in her heart' – he feels that she's always getting at him. That French kissing speculation may not have been so wide of the mark after all.

Emilia can't win, can she? She knows that her 'you have little cause to say so' (2.1.108) will be water off a duck's back. Iago will believe what Iago needs to believe, and say what it suits him to say. It's what holds him together.

And he's holding together remarkably well at the moment, thoroughly enjoying his control of the situation – as he did outside Brabantio's house. He senses that the moment has come to switch from the Max Miller-ish putting-down of the missus - 'Take my wife - **please**!' – to a broad attack on the entire female sex. We notice that the switch coincides with a change of pronouns. So far he's been referring to Emilia, in her presence, as 'she'; he now refers to women in general (though absent, of course, apart from their representatives Emilia and Desdemona) as 'you'. The inclusion of Desdemona in 'you' helps him to draw her further into the discussion.

'Come on, come on,' he cries in his frank, let's-face-it manner, as if summarising all that's been learned from bitter experience over the years (but which only hypocrites - and women - try to deny) and then reels off this folklorish catalogue of female faults and vices:

.......you are pictures out of doors,
Bells in your parlours, wild-cats in your kitchens,
Saints in your injuries, devils being offended,
Players in your housewifery, and housewives in...
Your beds! (1.2.109-1113)

Desdemona cries: 'O, fie upon thee, slanderer!' (1.2.113) But she's not quite sure how to take him. Is this just a playful wind-up, to pass the time, or is he serious? Of course the best way to wind people up is to **pretend** to be serious even if you aren't, but when people start getting hurt – as poor Emilia has been! - it **becomes** serious.

Iago's got the bit between his teeth now.

Nay, it is true, or else I am a Turk:
You rise to play, and go to bed to work. (2.1.114-115)

Beds again! Desdemona thinks. Here he goes again, harping on female sexuality. Does the man have a problem? He may be 'honest Iago', but someone's going to have to stand up to him if he carries on like this.

Meanwhile **we** think: Turk – work; that was a rhyming couplet, wasn't it? What's he up to now?

The answer, as will be apparent in a moment, is that Iago's manoeuvring the discussion, before it gets too edgy, into a safe-seeming mode of social discourse - a contest of wits in a formal disputation under the equivalent of the

Marquess of Queensberry rules. Understandably enough, Emilia's in no mood at the moment for vivacious repartee with her husband, and Cassio, less understandably, has fallen silent and fails to come to the aid of the fair sex, so it falls to Desdemona to take on this unexpectedly intelligent non-commissioned officer in verbal combat, though her heart isn't really in it either. 'I am not merry,' she says – and how could she be, on tenterhooks awaiting news of Othello? – but she'll take up the cudgels if no-one else will. It'll pass the time, as Didi says in Samuel Beckett's 'Waiting for Godot' - although she'd probably also agree with Gogo's rejoinder that it would pass anyway.

She didn't invite the gallant Cassio's compliments, but got them anyway. Now she gives the disputation a kick-start by asking outright what the very ungallant Iago would say about her.

Come, how wouldst thou praise me? (2.1.124)

Iago flounders, or pretends to flounder, for a moment before coming up with:

If she be fair and wise, fairness and wit,
The one's for use, the other uses it. (2.1.129-130)

Unpacked, this is: a woman's beauty is for sexual use, and if she's smart she'll know how to profit from it.

A sort of stage routine is being established. Desdemona, with a little help from Emilia, will be asking the questions in prose and Iago will give his rather Delphic replies in rhyming couplets, a verse form often associated with the witty praise of ladies in cultivated society. But we already know enough about him to suspect that he'll subvert it to quite contrary ends. And that's exactly what he does.

The two women, Desdemona taking the lead, proceed to work through a permutation of conventional terms balancing beauty/ugliness with/against intelligence/folly. Their questions will test Iago on what he has to say in praise of women who are i) fair and wise, ii) 'black' (i.e. ugly) and 'witty', iii) fair and foolish and iv) 'foul' (i.e. ugly again) and 'foolish'?

We've already heard Iago's reply to the question about the woman who's 'fair' and 'wise'. It's liable to slide past us unchecked in performance but if, as readers, we pause to ask what 'use' and 'uses' mean we'll realise that Iago's conjuring up the image of a glamorous gold-digger. Desdemona innocently – or is she smarter than that? – simply says, 'Well praised.' (2.1.131) But Iago's started with a 'miss' – Desdemona's certainly no gold-digger! - and she passes on to the next question. What would Iago say about a woman who's 'black' and 'witty'? (Desdemona, the leading lady, is probably a blonde, and Emilia a brunette.)

Iago buys time by versifying Desdemona's question in his first line:

If she be black and thereto have a wit, (2.1.132)

while he thinks up his second – punch? – line; and then he hesitates, either because he needs to or for effect, before coming out with:

She'll find a white that shall her blackness fit. (2.1.133)

Yes, we get the rhyme but where's the reason? Perhaps psychoanalysis rather than verbal analysis is what's called for here. It seems to have sprung from a level of the mind where irrational associations lie beyond the reach of conscious scrutiny. 'White' seems to be a pun on 'wight' – a person, usually male but, as we'll see in a moment, sometimes female. The general drift seems to be that the 'black' (Emilia-like?) woman will find and unite ('fit') with a white (therefore better-looking) sexual opposite (Iago?). There seem to be two references entwined: i) one to his own marriage, and ii) an 'inside-out' one to the black-white union of Othello and Desdemona. But all this is hopelessly obscure, not worth puzzling over, and we're glad when Emilia moves things on with the next question. 'How if fair and foolish?' (2.1.135)

To this Iago comes up with another cryptic couplet, almost as obscure as the previous one.

She never yet was foolish that was fair,
For even her folly helped her to an heir. (2.1.136-137)

That is to say: a beautiful woman has it made, one way or another. Through her 'folly' - sexual looseness - she'll either capture an heir (i.e. a rich man) in marriage, or at least get pregnant and give birth to an heir. (Or both, maybe.)

Top marks for swift verbal facility, of course, but what he actually says isn't particularly clever or convincing, is it? We're inclined to agree with Desdemona: 'These are old fond paradoxes to make fools laugh i' th' alehouse.' (2.1.138-139)

There's one more question left in the permutation box. Desdemona asks: 'What miserable praise hast thou for her that's foul and foolish?' (2.1.139-140).

Iago's reply is an insult to all women, present company **not** excepted.

There's none so foul, and foolish thereunto,
But does foul pranks which fair and wise ones do. (2.1.141-142)

Desdemona isn't going to leave it there. She insists that present company, at the very least, **must** be excepted. She comes up with an extra, unpermed, question to try to force him either to say something positive about womankind or reveal how indiscriminate his malice is. What would he say about 'one that in the authority of her merit did justly put on the vouch of very malice itself', (2.1.145-147) i.e. a woman so virtuous as to provoke the malicious to say their worst about her but who had nothing to fear from anything they might say?

That should have him cornered. Ears prick up as we hear him strike a note of praise for the first time. He produces a string of five fluent couplets eloquently describing the female virtues of modesty, attractive discourse, financial good sense, forbearance, chastity and tact. Is this a last-minute volte face? Was he just teasing after all?

He begins his sixth couplet with:

She was a wight, if ever such wights were, (2.1.158)

and then pauses. Desdemona can't wait for the clinch-line. 'To do what?' (2.1.159), she asks, and then it comes:

To suckle fools, and chronicle small beer. (2.1.160)

'O, most lame and impotent conclusion!' (2.1.161) Desdemona cries. She's got him! She's made him admit that he despises good women as much as the assorted hypothetical trollops that he's been slagging off. He's not a moral critic; he's a total misogynist and 'a most profane and liberal counsellor'. (2.1.163-164) He repudiates the very virtues that the deserving women aim to live by. Interestingly, though, Desdemona doesn't subsequently talk as if she's seen through Iago and wants to discredit him at every opportunity. She doesn't splutter when, later in the play, she hears him described as 'honest'. Is this because she naively continues to believe that the banter was just a game to pass the time? Or is it a sign of her willingness to give everyone the benefit of the doubt?

If Desdemona expected Cassio to support her against Iago she must feel disappointed. The suave lieutenant who so easily upstaged Iago a little while ago has been upstaged himself. Yes, the man may have gone a bit too far, but for some reason he doesn't feel able to reprimand him. He can do no better that trot out the standard deluded view of Iago, that he 'speaks home' (2.1.165) with rough soldierly bluntness, and that being low-born and not 'a scholar' (2.1.166) he isn't able to trade in elegant compliments. This may rub a bit more salt into the wound of Iago's social inferiority, but it hardly repudiates the insults to Desdemona and Emilia. So as if to make up for his failure as a champion of the ladies he turns on the charm again and takes Desdemona by the hand -

Let's stop there, for a moment. We need a bit of background on the hand-holding.

With Shakespeare - early, middle and late - the question regularly arises whether hand-holding is 'courtesy' or a form of sexual foreplay. In 'Romeo and Juliet' (1595-6), the hero, alone with Juliet for the first time, diffidently takes her hand and breaks into a 14-line sonnet, by line 11 of which he's saying:

O then, dear saint, let lips do what hands do

and three lines further on he's kissing her full on the mouth! (RJ: 1.5.92-105)

The sequence is hands (here 'palms') to lips, and then…..? Well, we all know the natural sexual progression, don't we? It's this thought that grips Leontes's imagination in 'The Winter's Tale' (1611?) when he sees his wife Hermione take the hand of his best friend Polixenes. She's trying – at his request! - to persuade him to extend his visit. But he doesn't like the way she's going about it.

> This entertainment
> May a free face put on, derive a liberty
> From heartiness….'t may, I grant:
> But to be paddling palms, and pinching fingers,
> As now they are, and making practised smiles
> As in a looking glass…..O, that is entertainment
> My bosom likes not. (WT: 1.2.11-117)

And the next thing you know Leontes has jumped to the conclusion that wife and his best friend are about to make a cuckold of him – if they haven't already.

Iago, watching Cassio take Desdemona 'by the palm', (2.1.167) whisper to her, put his fingers to his lips and blow her a few kisses, is prompted to visualise a very similar hands-fingers-lips-sex sequence. He spells it out in an aside to the audience. (2.1.167-177) No doubt remembering the lieutenant's earlier gallantry towards Emilia he's fuming with rage to see him repeating the trick all over again with Desdemona. Gentlemanly courtesy? Dream on! Filthy lust! I'll have him for this! etc; and sure enough, he follows the 'natural' direction of the sequence to its culmination – sex – with an obscene reference to clyster-pipes. (2.1.176) Obviously this isn't just one of Iago's cynical insights; it's more of a sexual obsession – as we'll see about eighty lines further on when he runs through the same sequence **again**, for Roderigo's benefit. (2.1.251-261)

But now the bright notes of a trumpet confirm that the latest-arrived ship has indeed brought the new governor general, Othello. And suddenly there he is before our eyes! Magnificent! – but so **foreign**. Looks just like that Abdul Guahid chap, doesn't he?

This moment, we are to understand, is the high water mark of the couple's happiness. Even in his extreme joy Othello seems to understand that nothing that happens afterwards will come up to it again.

If it were now to die

'Twere now to be most happy.... (2.1.187-188)

Iago, listening to this rapture, concurs. No, it won't last - he'll see to it personally that it doesn't!

O, you are well tuned now; but I'll set down
The pegs that make this music, as honest
As I am. (2.1.198-200)

Soon Othello and Desdemona go off to take up residence in the citadel, leaving Iago to convince Roderigo that in spite of all appearances to the contrary the **real** sex story is the **Cassio**/Desdemona one!

It's a tall order, but we've learned by now not to underestimate Iago's powers of persuasion. We've seen what ingenuity he was capable of in the 'poet/philosopher/moral critic' role he adopted in his disputation with Desdemona. The rhyming couplets he used then maintained a certain 'distance' between speaker and hearer and confined what was communicated to what were (at least apparently) impersonal generalities. What it didn't do, and wasn't meant to do, was draw his listeners into confidential nearness. But now it's different. With his co-conspirator Roderigo his verbal performance takes quite a different form – fluent informal prose delivered from close range.

Later on, with Othello, he'll use a quite different 'roundabout' approach – passing off preposterous lies as unwilling admissions – but with Roderigo he generates credibility in the opposite way, by coming straight out with what he wants him to believe, as if its truth is so obvious that it only needs saying. 'First, I must tell thee this: Desdemona is directly in love with him *(Cassio)*'. (2.1.216-217) And just in case Roderigo doesn't swallow it in one gulp he proceeds without pause to unroll his proofs. Desdemona's 'violent' love for the Moor was only a passing infatuation triggered by his 'bragging' (2.1.221) about his adventurous life. But if ever there was a mismatch this was it. It can't last. Sex pulled then; now it palls. She's bound to be on the lookout for someone younger, handsomer, more culturally and socially compatible – **white**, for goodness sake! And that's where **you** come in, Roderigo, my friend!

No doubt Roderigo agrees with Iago's unfavourable picture of Othello, but he jibs at Iago's cynical view of Desdemona. 'She's of most blest condition,' (2.1.247-248) he protests. But Iago knows what to say to that. She's just a woman like all the rest. If you doubt it just use the evidence of your eyes. Did you see her 'paddling with the palm of his (Cassio's) hand?' (2.1.252)

Yes, but surely....

It's here that Iago re-runs the hands-lips-sex routine for Roderigo's benefit. 'Lechery, by this hand,' Iago asserts (bringing his **own** hand into it!). That hand-clasp was 'an **index** (think index finger as well as contents list) and obscure prologue to the history of lust and foul thoughts'. (2.1.255-256) Which brings us, bang on associative cue, to full-out sex. 'Hard at hand comes the master and main exercise, th' incorporate conclusion.' (2.1.259-261)

We caught the whiff of psycho-sexual derangement in Iago's rhyming couplet answers to Desdemona's questions earlier in the scene but it was difficult to pin it down because they might have been nothing more than examples of argumentative hyperbole – 'speaking for effect'. There are similar peculiarities in his (prose) conversation with Roderigo, although here the problem is where to draw the line between his personal delusions and his intention to deceive others. Now, in the soliloquy that concludes the scene (2.1.284-310) he has nobody apart from himself to deceive, so we're on the lookout for clearer signs.

Iago considers that he has a special, 'privileged' understanding of sex. The cruder your interpretation of what's going on, he believes, the less deceived you'll be. He's quite sure that Cassio's gallantries conceal plain lust -

He hath a person and a smooth dispose
To be suspected, framed to make women false (1.3.396-397)

- and it's perfectly possible that Emilia finds Cassio fanciable. (You could hardly blame her, in the circumstances, could you?) But his next assertion, that Desdemona has got Cassio in **her** sexual sights, takes us aback:

That she loves him, 'tis apt and of great credit. (2.1.285)

'Apt and of great credit' doesn't **quite** say that he believes it himself, does it? And he may not be very interested in whether she does or not. It's more a question of whether he can get **others** - Othello in particular, of course – to believe it, and he thinks he can.

But now, proceeding from the implausible to the preposterous, he says:

Now I do love her, too. (2.1.289)

Even Iago thinks he owes himself an explanation for this. No, he hasn't 'fallen in love' with her – if you can imagine such a thing! – and he doesn't just fancy her in the way that he alleges Cassio does, 'out of absolute lust'. (2.1.290) It's just that he believes that 'the lusty Moor', as per stereotype, has cuckolded him with Emilia and he wants to get even with him, 'wife for wife'! (2.1.297) What are we supposed to make of all this? Even if – against all likelihood – Othello has bedded Emilia his own chances of getting even by seducing Desdemona are plainly nil, for reasons that are too obvious to need stating. On reflection even Iago can see that. 'Failing so', (2.1.298) he continues, he has another idea. He'll just work the Moor up into a jealous frenzy by getting him to believe that Cassio, not content with having it off with Emilia, (and others he might mention – Bianca, for example) is having it off with Desdemona as well. Then the Moor will kill Cassio, and he'll apply for the vacancy.

'Tis here, but yet confused.' (2.1.309) These musings are indeed **psychologically** confused, but we can see a perfectly lucid **practical** idea for revenge is emerging.

We've learned a lot about Iago in this scene. We knew about his thwarted career before. Now we realise that there's a lot more to it than that. He's a slick operator with an eye for the main chance, but he's also a psychopath, which explains why, in his determination to destroy his twin targets, Cassio and the Moor, he doesn't give two hoots about destroying Desdemona in the process. She'll just be collateral damage.

Act 3, Scene 3 is the hinge of the play. In the course of its 484 lines Iago manipulates Othello into a 180-degree turn from infatuated husband to demented wife-killer.

Shakespeare ups the ante at the outset by making it look like game over before Iago even arrives on the scene. Desdemona, joyfully assured of her power over her husband, promises Cassio, now sacked and disgraced, that she'll give Othello no peace until he reinstates him. And she's as good as her word. As soon as the Moor comes on stage (and before Cassio has quite gone off) she pitches straight in.   Othello says: 'Not now, sweet Desdemona, some other time', (3.3.55) but she takes this as only token resistance and tries to clinch the matter then and there. It seems to work. Iago was right when he said earlier on that 'our general's wife is now the general'. (2.3.310) The

Moor caves in. 'I will deny thee nothing,' he tells her – twice. (3.3.76 and 3.3.83). This is a very different Othello from the imposing and decisive public personage that we saw imposing law and order on the city streets. The sight of Cassio slinking away from Desdemona's side and Iago's 'Ha, I like not that' (3.3.34) has flustered him. He suspects that she's bounced him into a commitment that, as a soldier, he shouldn't have made, although he can scarcely take back his promise now. He asks her to leave him for a while so that he can get his thoughts in order, and when she's gone we see what internal disarray he's in.

Excellent wretch! Perdition catch my soul
But I do love thee! And when I love thee not
Chaos is come again. (3.3.90-92)

We're getting our first clear glimpse of the Moor's inner contradictions. 'Excellent' and 'I do love thee' express his infatuation, but otherwise we notice that his language is full of what turn out to be **prophetic** negativities: 'wretch', 'perdition', 'when I love thee not' and 'chaos'.

We've just seen Desdemona twist her husband round her finger by feminine charm. Now we're about to see what Iago, her rival for the possession of his soul, can do by very different means. It'll be an uphill task but he's already scored one important point. His successful engineering of the fracas in the street (Act 2, Scene 3) has destroyed Cassio's reputation and got him sacked. Othello has seen for himself how, with a drink or two inside him, the debonair lieutenant can turn into a night-brawler, and it will have made him more open to the suggestion that there may be also be a sly lecher just under the skin of the courteous gallant. Trust has been dented. Cassio fancies Desdemona? – well perhaps with a few crafty nudges and winks Iago should yet be able to persuade the Moor of that. But Desdemona fancies Cassio? - that's a much longer shot.

In the series of Act 3 exchanges Shakespeare's virtuosity in dialogue-writing is shown. Nobody paying proper attention to what Iago and the Moor say to each other will need the kind of point-by-point commentary I gave on the more opaque Angelo-Isabella exchanges in 'Measure for Measure', but I think the comparison between the two scenes can be developed in another way.

If we analyse the scene in structural terms we see that it contains **two** conversations between Othello and Iago, embedded in a sequence of four episodes, as follows:

Episode 1 (3.3.1-89) shows Desdemona assuring Cassio that she will plead his cause with Othello. As Othello and Iago enter Cassio is glimpsed making himself scarce. Desdemona begins her persuasion of Othello, and she goes off happy that she's got her way.

Episode 2 (3.3.90-281) starts with Iago (who was silently present throughout Episode 1) hinting to the Moor that Cassio's scuttling away like that might be seen as a suspicious circumstance. Iago feigns unease about what's been going on between Desdemona and Cassio but pretends to be reluctant to divulge more. Othello swallows the bait.

Episode 3 (3.3.282-332) shows us Desdemona losing her handkerchief. Emilia picks it up and hands it to Iago, who intends to use it later as circumstantial evidence to 'prove' the suspicions that he's been sowing in Othello's mind.

Episode 4 (3.3.333-482) is the second conversation between the two men, in which Iago converts Othello's suspicions into (virtual) certainty. The two men vow together to kill Desdemona and Cassio.

If we ignore the (non-Shakespearean) scene divisions provided in modern editions, and a few minor deviations from strict parallel we'll find that Isabella's tussles with Angelo in 'Measure for Measure' follow a very similar four-episode design.

We find:

Episode 1 (2.2.6-25) Angelo insists to the Provost that he has no intention of commuting Claudio's death sentence.

Episode 2 (2.2.26-187) Isabella pleads with Angelo for her brother Claudio's life but in so doing unintentionally becomes an object of sexual temptation for him.

Episode 3 (2.3.10-42) Juliet, Claudio's lover, repents her own sexual fault but is left in anguish when her 'confessor', the Duke/Friar, tells her not to hope that Claudio will be reprieved.

Episode 4 (2,4,31-186) In the second encounter between Angelo and Isabella he offers to spare Claudio in exchange for her chastity. She's seen the offer coming and tried to forestall it, but all she can do now is indignantly refuse it.

In each play the 'argument' itself is divided into two phases (Episodes 2 and 4) with a 'prelude' (Episode 1) to the first phase and an 'interlude' (Episode 3) dividing the first phase from the second. The 'preludes' set things up for what is to follow. The 'interludes' introduce other characters and provide a curious combination of suspense and relief from the tension of the main argument. They also create an illusion of the stretching of time between the start and the finish of the arguments.

Needless to say, this four-episode 'persuasive' structure triumphantly proves its dramatic fitness in both plays.

Well, that's one way of looking at the U-turn scene in 'Othello'. Another way is to take a look at the **drift** and **direction** of the central exchanges as indicated by the incidence of certain key terms and concepts.

The first exchange (Episode 2 - 2.2.90-281) is thickly strewn with 'cognitive' verbs such as 'think', 'thought' and 'know', as well as a number of other variants and equivalents. We find 'think' (or 'thinks' or 'think'st') no less than twelve times; Othello uses it seven times (107,109,120,129,146,180,229) and Iago uses it five times. (99,108,128,132,230) We also find three other verbs more or less akin in meaning to 'think': 'fear(s)' is used three times by Iago (176,239,258) and once by Othello (260), who also uses the words 'mean' (111) and 'ruminate' (134). The related noun, 'thought(s)', occurs even more frequently; Iago uses it seven times, (97,139, 157,214,227,237,257) and Othello uses it six times. (98,110,119,135,147,164) No less than thirteen other nouns referring to mental acts or states also occur – 'thinkings', (134) 'apprehensions'. (142) 'meditations', (144) 'guess', (148) 'conceits', (152) 'doubts' and 'suspects', (172) 'surmises', (185) 'fear' and 'doubt', (191) 'doubt' (bis 193) and 'suspicion'. (224) Another 'cognitive' word, 'know', also has a high rate of occurrence in Episode 2. If we include variants such as 'knows' and 'unknown', it occurs nine times, Iago using it five times (94,106,119, 204, 207) and Othello four times. (121, 243, 247, 263)

So what? Good question.

Shakespeare's taking every opportunity to underscore the idea that it's not what's objectively true but what's in the characters' minds that we need to concentrate on. States of mind trump matters of fact. My excuse for labouring the point like this is that Shakespeare was labouring it himself.

In the **second** conversation (Episode 4 – 3.3.333-482) the 'think'/'know' terms are replaced by a different set of key terms. They don't altogether disappear but they thin out as 'see'/'sight'/'proof'/'satisfaction' words crowd in. When Othello uses the word 'think' four times in the space of two lines -

I think my wife be honest, and think she is not,
I think that thou *(Iago)* art honest, and think thou art not
(3.3.387-388)

- he uses it in a self-cancelling sense, and he follows it immediately with

I'll have some **proof**. (3.3.389)

This switch from 'think' to 'proof' is carrying Othello from uncertainty to conviction. By then the 'see'/'sight'/ 'proof'/'satisfaction' words have done their psychological job.

'See'/'sight' is used seven times, once by Othello (3.3.367) and six times by Iago, (394,402,405,435,437,492) upon whom the onus of providing 'ocular proof' (3.3.363), or an effective substitute for it, has fallen. Indeed, Iago dramatically intensifies the 'see'/'sight' motif with 'grossly gape on' (3.3.398) and 'behold her topped' (3.3.399), as well as 'prospect'. (3.3.401) Othello harps on the 'proof'/ 'prove'/'probation' motif, too, (362,368,389) and Iago, who had previously feigned a certain caution about circumstantial evidence, now refers to 'other proofs' (3.3.444) with the confident air of a prosecuting counsel finally placing guilt beyond all reasonable doubt.

What 'proof' provides is 'satisfaction', not in the sense of contentment, of course – on the contrary in Othello's case! – but in the sense of certainty succeeding uncertainty. Iago, whose task it is to give Othello 'satisfaction', uses 'satisfied' twice (3.3.396,397) and 'satisfaction' twice. (3.3.404,411) Othello uses 'satisfied' once. (3.3.393)

The charting of key words in order to trace Othello's transition from unease to murderous rage gives us an idea of how Shakespeare manages the process verbally, but it hardly yields an overview of Othello as a dramatic character, does it? We're still left asking, after all this analysis of structure and word-counting, what we're supposed to make of our 'hero'?

Well then, let's start with a consideration of his ruling passion – jealousy.

Fortunately, or unfortunately, jealousy doesn't seem to have altered much in the four hundred years since 'Othello' was first staged, and modern psychology still fits the case. It may be summarised as:

The child is born in the belief that he controls his mother and that she has no desires of her own other than those that fix on him. When he eventually learns otherwise he feels that it is a threat to his personal existence, which obliterates his love for her. He meets her threat to his existence with a threat to hers. Sexual jealousy in later life is a replay of that infantile experience. How can I avenge it when the illusion of security is lost?

So when Othello, the imperfectly grown-up child, realises (or, as here, is deceived into believing) that he can't control Desdemona's love he feels he's fighting for his very survival - and losing. He says:

She's gone, I am abused, and my relief
Must be to loathe her. O curse of marriage
That we can call these delicate creatures ours
And not their appetites. I had rather be a toad
And live upon the vapour of a dungeon
Than keep a corner in the thing I love
For others' uses. (3.3.271-277)

In other words, he'll kill her rather than share her. He can't relent in his anger and just let her go, or allow her any pity. When, later, he says: 'But yet the pity of it, Iago – O Iago, the pity of it, Iago' (4.1.192/3) he's reached the point of bidding pity (though not desire or regret) goodbye forever. He's chosen the murder option.

Although Shakespeare had no formal theory of infantile sexuality he obviously had a pretty good feel for the subject. He has the Moor's mother put in a fleeting remembered appearance in his play. It was she who gave him the handkerchief that he gave to Desdemona and which she's now lost. Othello says:

…. That's a fault. That handkerchief
Did an Egyptian to my mother give,
She was a charmer and could almost read
The thoughts of people. She told her, while she kept it
'Twould make her amiable and subdue my father

Entirely to her love; but if she lost it
Or made a gift of it, my father's eye
Should hold her loathed and his spirits should hunt
After new fancies. (3.4.56-65)

This passage is usually noted for the glimpse it gives of Othello's North African childhood. But, more pertinently here, the story attached to the handkerchief is about jealousy, the attempt to **control the loved one's love**.

Twice, describing how jealousy kills pity and kindness, Othello speaks of his heart being turned to stone. Convinced of Desdemona's infidelity he says,

…let her rot and perish and be damned tonight, for she shall not live. No, my heart is turned to stone: I strike it and it hurts my hand. (4.1.178-180)

Exactly! He'll strike his heart (i.e. Desdemona) but hurt himself.

His second 'stone' remark is:

Thou perjured woman, thou dost stone my heart
And makest me call what I intend to do
A murder, which I thought a sacrifice. (5.2.63-65)

Othello doesn't always talk sense, especially when he talks about himself. But he does here. His gist is: forget about 'sacrifice'; it's **murder** I'm talking about.

Othello's rage is usually expressed in terms of damage to his prestige – cuckold **me**! (4.1.197), for example - but there's one moment when he finds words to express the deep existential damage that Desdemona's (supposed) infidelity has done him. He could put up with more or less

anything – ill repute, poverty, career failure, even the
shame of being a cuckold – but not the loss of her love.

… There where I have garnered up my heart,
Where either I must live or bear no life,
The fountain from the which my current runs
Or else dries up – to be discarded thence! (4.2.58-61)

'No life'. 'Discarded'. These words fit in with the standard
view of jealousy pretty closely, don't they?

Our view of the Moor changes from stage to stage and
never really settles, even at the end. In the first Act he has
a personal and public grandeur that there's little hint of in
the Cinthio source story. The accounts we've had of him
hitherto, especially Iago's bad-mouthing, fade like
morning mists when he actually appears on stage –
imposing, handsome, eloquent, exotically dressed and
resplendently weaponed. We're impressed by his calm and
dignified address to the 'grave and worthy signiors' and
his masterful quelling of the street disorder. But once the
action moves to Cyprus and Shakespeare locks on to the
Cinthio 'jealousy' narrative, shifting the focus from public
to private life, we find ourselves watching Othello blueing
the 'capital' of honour and esteem that was heaped on him
at the start. We never **quite** forget the spectacular initial
impression he made on us, or the fact that Desdemona's
love and loyalty never waver – although maybe that tells
us more about her than him – but by the end it's difficult
not to share Emilia's scorn for him. From Act 2 onwards
he does and says little to offset the accumulating
misgivings we have about him. We're appalled by the
violence that he intends towards Desdemona - 'I'll tear her
all to pieces' (3.3.434) and 'I'll chop her into messes!'
(4.1.197) And later, after he's suffocated her, it's difficult

to feel, even allowing for the Iago factor, that he's entitled to very much of the 'extenuation' that he asks for. He speaks of himself as being wronged as much as wronging, of remorse but not repentance. He'll be damned – literally - before he asks for forgiveness. He despairs of himself, so we despair of him.

More than once Othello's called a fool. When he finds out how Iago has misled him he calls himself a fool three times over. (5.2.322) But there's more to it than just being made a fool of: he makes some remarkably silly unprompted remarks in the course of the play. Consider, for example, what he says about cuckoldry in Act 3, Scene 3. By now virtually convinced of Desdemona's infidelity he makes an attempt to pull himself together. All right, he tells himself, let's face it, I'm a cuckold. But let's think positive:

..........'tis the plague of great ones,
Prerogatived are they less than the base;
'Tis destiny unshunnable, like death. (3.3.277-279)

Proud words! – 'plague of great ones', 'destiny unshunnable, like death'. He doesn't – can't bear to - dwell too much on the collapse of his relationship with his wife, preferring to think in terms of his own social stature. Not a privileged Venetian insider but a foreign, black career soldier who's got on by making himself useful to the powers that be, he's acquired an authoritative manner and a respected position in public life. But he's not, and never will be, entirely secure. He is and isn't accepted. He's vulnerable to mistrust and underestimation, and his self-esteem and prestige need constant topping up. So, he tries to argue, cuckoldry is no humiliation if it admits one to the company of the 'great ones'. It's practically a mark of social distinction.

Others will never praise him enough, so he resorts to boasting. When Iago describes him as

loving his own pride and purposes
… with a bombast circumstance
Horribly stuffed with epithets of war (1.1.11-13)

he's laying it on rather thick, but he's got a point. The Moor **does** tend to blow his own trumpet. For example, when he's just won everybody's sympathy with his account of how he wooed Desdemona with his 'travailous history' (1.3.140) his speech accepting the commission to lead the defence of Cyprus jars badly:

The tyrant custom, most grave senators,
Hath made the flinty and steel couch of war
My thrice-driven bed of down. I do agnise
A natural and prompt alacrity
I find in hardness, and do undertake
This present war against the Ottomites. (1.3.230-235)

If that isn't pompous and bombastic what is it? I'm a tough-as-teak soldier, so please don't think I'll get distracted from my military duties by sex - as, for example, Antony was by Cleopatra, or the eponymous hero in 'Orlando Furioso'. 'Couch of war' and 'bed of down' express the contradiction which runs, Brighton-rock-like, through his understandable suspicion that the Venetian signiors only accept his bedding of one of their white women because he makes himself so useful slaying their Turkish enemies. But the boasting cuts less and less ice, until at the end he has a yawning credibility gap. He humiliates, abuses and then kills his blameless wife – and we have to listen to him worrying about the adverse effects on his personal prestige and trying to claw back a bit of credit by reminding us of his war record!

...............Behold, I have a weapon,
A better never did itself sustain
Upon a soldier's thigh. I have seen the day
That with this little arm and this good sword
I have made my way through more impediments
Than twenty times your stop... (5.2.257-262)

He briefly admits that playing soldiers now is a 'vain boast' (5.2.262) but then he just carries on boasting, in the next line blaming 'fate' for his crime. He doesn't learn, and he won't change. He's going to bluster his way right through to the end. One last bit of positive spin – a bit more self-promotion - might do the trick. He's thrown away his soul (5.2.270-278) but he still wants to polish his reputation.

To be fair, Lodovico gives him his cue. He wonders how Othello - once so 'good' - can have 'fallen to the practice of a cursed slave *(i.e. Iago)* '. (5.2.289) He asks: 'What shall be said to thee?' (5.2.290) and the Moor characteristically replies as if the question is: 'What can be said **about** me – not said **to** me?' He's got nothing remotely convincing to say, though. His two-and-a-bit-line answer – studded with the words 'honourable' and 'honour' -

........................why anything;
An honourable murderer, if you will,
For nought I did in hate, but all in honour (5.2.290-292)

is an embarrassing prevarication.

Honour? The trouble is he **means** it.

Let's go back to the moment when Othello has stifled Desdemona. Thinking she must be dead, he draws the bed-curtains to conceal her body and lets Emilia come into the room. Desdemona however, briefly regains consciousness and uses her dying breath to claim that she's killed **herself!** She wants to spare Othello the blame! It's a lie that would be laughable in any other situation. A moment before Othello had been saying: 'My wife! My wife! What wife? I have no wife' (5.2.96) but now he hears her voice again! The text doesn't give him any words to express his shock, so the actor has to do it by body language. It doesn't need to be overdone; no doubt a part of his mind still thinks of her as alive. His scripted reaction, though, is quite extraordinary. He pretends not to understand what's happened. 'Why, how should she be murdered,' (5.2.124) he asks, as if it's the first he knows of it, and the dazed Emilia, considering only the literal 'why' and the 'how' of his question but not the obvious '**who**', replies: 'Alas, who knows.' Then Othello, pouncing on the chance to use Desdemona's dying words in his defence, says:

You heard her say herself it was not I. (5.2.125)

It's a ludicrous but deeply unfunny remark - I've never known it to raise a titter in the audience and I've certainly never felt inclined to laugh myself. Chilled, we wonder what's happened to Othello, morally, that he can come out with such a thing. Plainly, he's fallen very low indeed. 'Noble Othello'? Forget it!

Until he makes his final bid for a damage-limiting posthumous reputation Othello's self-possession continues to be precarious, to put it mildly. He cuts an abject figure, threatening to kill Emilia as she prepares to speak out, shouting 'O, O, O', (5.2.195) and 'O fool, fool, fool', (5.2.322) and repeatedly cursing Iago. After all this it's a moot point just how much reputation he can hope to retrieve, if any. There's nothing he can actually **do** to redeem himself now it's come down to a public relations exercise. He has no-one other than himself to plead his case. Harking back to his 'pre-marriage' persona, the famous soldier and important public man, he launches into his last great speech.

Soft you, a word or two before you go.
I have done the state some service, and they know't:
No more of that. I pray you, in your letters,
When you shall these unlucky deeds relate,
Speak of me as I am. Nothing extenuate
Nor set down aught in malice. Then must you speak
Of one that loved not wisely, but too well:
Of one not easily jealous, but, being wrought.
Perplexed in the extreme; of one whose hand,
Like the base Indian, threw a pearl away
Richer than all his tribe; of one whose subdued eyes,
Albeit unused to the melting mood,
Drops tears as fast as the Arabian trees
Their medicinable gums. Set you down this,
And say besides that in Aleppo once,
Where a malignant and turbaned Turk
Beat a Venetian and traduced the state,
I took him by th' throat the circumcised dog
And smote him – thus! *(He stabs himself.)* (5.2.336-354)

The metre conveys an impressive sense of self-possession regained that compares very favourably with his previous incoherent exclamations and gesticulations. But impressive isn't the same thing as convincing. Of course, nobody wants to 'set down aught in malice' or deny the Moor the balanced and impartial justice that he is appealing for, but we aren't really being asked make up our own minds at all: we're being told what verdict to return, and it's a pretty lenient one at that. Only the all-forgiving Desdemona, looking down from Heaven, would be prepared to overlook or minimise all the cruel and shameful things he's done. So he has to do his own overlooking and minimising. 'Unlucky deeds' – even if 'unlucky' in 1601 wasn't as close in meaning to 'blame-free' as it is today - is patently euphemistic. As to his claim that he loved Desdemona 'not wisely but too well', (5.2.342) 'not wisely' strikes us as the understatement of all time and 'too well' conceals the truth that he loved her 'too jealously' or 'too possessively', and not 'well' at all in the sense that love is meant to confer some benefit on the beloved. Othello's picturesque image of the Indian throwing away the precious pearl casts a pretty questionable poetic lustre over the sheer brutality of his treatment of her. Likewise, 'subdued eyes' weeping 'medicinable gums' is a very sanitised image of the frantic and despairing remorse with which he embraces his damnation.

And what about 'not easily jealous'? (5.2.343)

Jealousy, we realise, isn't just a failing that Iago happens to select from others as the most handy to bring about the Moor's downfall. No, he's sniffed out jealousy as the deep, dangerous rage that Othello's very soul is steeped in. It's the rage of the infant screaming: 'It's all about **me**!' and the Iago-devil knows all too well how to work with that sort of egotism! It's what prevents the Moor ever really recognising Desdemona as a person in her own right. For him she's just a 'delicate creature' (3.3.273) that he could call his, were it not for his worry about the waywardness of her 'appetites'. As far as he's concerned, it's gone from attraction to shared sexual passion, to suspicion, to rage – and then he kills her. He'd have been better off with a bit less of all that 'passion', which is much more about him than her, and a bit more readiness to recognise her as a separate person, and accept her love and readiness to forgive. But no. Right up to the bitter end he's entirely wrapped up in himself or - more precisely - in his self-idealising image of himself. Desdemona dead, he fastens on to 'the (other!) immediate jewel of his soul', (3.3.159) his reputation. It's little more than an adjustment of his narcissistic posture. His self-regard allows nothing for human relativism or irony. What chance could Desdemona, for all her goodness, courage and intelligence, ever have had against him?

Make no mistake, though, the Moor does do **remorse** - in magniloquent spades:

Whip me, ye devils,
From the possession of this heavenly sight!
Blow me about in winds, roast me in sulphur,
Wash me in deep-down gulfs of liquid fire! (5.2.275-278)

We've had the special pleading. Now we get the showbiz-style doom-and-disaster hype.

Lodovico, shocked to see him clouting and bellowing abuse at Desdemona, has already expressed the disillusionment that we all feel:

Is this the noble Moor whom our full senate
Call all in all sufficient? This the nature
Whom passion could not shake? Whose solid virtue
The shot of accident nor dart of chance
Could neither graze nor pierce? (4.1.264-268)

As with Emilia's 'ignorant as dirt', (5.2.160) we find it difficult to disagree.

Desdemona has offered Othello forgiveness but that isn't what he's after. He goes from crazy self-righteousness –

'justice!' (5.2.17) to furious despair – 'roast me in sulphur' (5.2.277) with no thought of a stop anywhere in between. He always gets Desdemona wrong – and he always **does** her wrong. Finally, it's 'this look of thine' – which he decides is an **un**forgiving look - that will 'hurl my soul from heaven.' (5.2.272)

So that's his story now: **she** damns **him** to hell.

The fact is that Othello's life - apart from his public successes, which are behind him now - has turned out to be a story of weakness and crime which he's now trying to screen off from public view by erecting an elegant verbal monument around it. You do that by dictating your own obituary. In his very last words he asks to be remembered as a soldier in the service of Venice, killing a hostile Turk. The message is: I'm one of you! I'm a Christian! But the final image is deeply ambivalent. The 'infidel' he stabbed then seems to be the same man that he's stabbing now – himself.

Cassio's last brief comment on Othello - 'he was great of heart' (5.2.359) - seems to be a bit of a formality, said in the dutiful spirit of 'de mortuis nil sine bonum'. Emilia's 'O gull, O dolt,' (5.2.159-160) seems nearer the mark.

The Moor's moral degradation can't be ignored or minimised - it's as plain, and as painful, as a pikestaff - but it has to be held in balance with the diabolical power of temptation. This is a subtle and complex **Christian** play about goodness (grace) and evil (the workings of the devil), and about the choice between salvation and damnation. What is there to say when the devil succeeds in luring a soul down to hell? 'Devil's fault' doesn't quite cover it: it seems to exonerate the victim without rescuing him. The victim (if that's the right word) must surely have given some kind of self-incriminating assent. On the other hand if the temptation amounted to **possession** could there really have been any such assent? It's a tricky one, unless you believe, as Shakespeare apparently did, that grace was fully available to the Moor in the form of Desdemona's wifely patience and forgivingness. All he had to do was love and believe her, and repudiate Iago. But he got it wrong and his soul is forfeit.

Oddly enough, Othello **does** finally come across as some sort of Christian. He tells Desdemona to pray before he kills her -

If you bethink yourself of any crime
Unreconciled as yet to heaven and grace,
Solicit for it straight (5.2.26 – 28) -

but it doesn't occur to **him** to pray (as other bad hats like Claudius and Angelo do). He recommends repentance for her but puts up a terrific resistance to anything like that for himself. As we've seen, his first impulse is to make use of Desdemona's lying attempt to put him in the clear. Then, realising that this won't wash, he comes up with these truly despicable lines:

She's like a liar gone to burning hell:
'Twas I that killed her. (5.2.127 – 128)

In the end, I think, what we have here is less a classical tragedy about the downfall of a hero than a Christian morality about the contest for the soul of the Moor, between extreme Evil (personified by Iago) and extreme Goodness (personified by Desdemona).

But even saying that doesn't entirely settle the picture. You can never be entirely certain about who's damned and who isn't. Othello lives long enough after stabbing himself to drag himself across to the bed where Desdemona's body lies, and he has breath enough to speak two more lines:

I kissed thee ere I killed thee; no way but this,
Killing myself, to die upon a kiss. (5.2.356-357)

Is the Moor, against all recent form, here accepting Desdemona's offer of forgiveness, even though - she being dead - it may no longer be available? The balancing of 'kiss' and 'kill', and the rhyme, seem to suggest some sense of 'quits'. In every production somebody's got to decide how to stage this moment, and if the actress playing Desdemona lies with her arms apart as if ready to accept him into her embrace I wouldn't necessarily quarrel with the suggestion that in falling dead onto her body he might **not,** after all, be falling into the perdition that a few moments ago he was clamouring for.

After Desdemona's death the impetus of the action pushes us along without giving us time to grieve. At the time we weren't sure exactly what she was signalling to us, and then the signals ceased, so it feels like something we've promised ourselves to come back to later in reflection, to try to 'get her meaning', which at the moment has eluded us.

Our first impression of her was of the unabashed, father-fooling young Venetian girl who's recklessly run away with a black man. There's a hint that her sexual appetite for him was no less than his for her, and that it was she who gave him the come-on. We see her boldly facing down the disapproving elders of the city, saying:

That I did love the Moor to live with him,
My downright violence and scorn of fortunes

May trumpet to the world. (1.3.249-251)

But the next time we see her she's like one of Shakespeare's comedy heroines. In the rather hairy disputation scene with Iago (Act 2, Scene 1) she comes off the clear winner; we learn to admire her confidence, her quick wits, her good humour - and her innocence. But that was just an edgy game, wasn't it? We wonder how she'll do when she's up against his malice in full spate and her sufferings really begin.

Desdemona's straightforward in one sense of the word but not in another. People get her wrong. Apart from Emilia only Iago sees her pretty straight and clear, without any particular admiration or malice. He can assure Cassio in (for once) good faith that she's not just willing but **able** to help him back into the Moor's favour. Then, soliloquising - so with no motive to lie - he says:

> She's framed as fruitful
> As the free elements: and then for her
> To win the Moor, were't to renounce his baptism,
> All seals and symbols of redeemed sin,
> His soul is so enfettered to his love
> That she may make, unmake, do what she list,
> Even as her appetites shall play the god
> With his weak function. (2.3.334-343)

Unlike Iago she's a peacemaker; she wants to bring about the reconciliation of two friends, Othello and Cassio, who find themselves at odds. Typically, she doesn't reflect whether Cassio deserves to be reinstated, or bother with roundabout tactics. It's 'ask and you shall receive' as far as she's concerned.

Iago is her competitor and he envies her power. If she

chose, she could dechristianise and unman the Moor. She won't do it, of course, but it makes you think, doesn't it? We know what **he'd** like to do - not just bring him down in this world but damn him in the next.

Emilia recognises Desdemona's rather 'non-standard' innate goodness, and loves her for it, but she sees her folly, too. She doesn't bother to conceal her feeling that the Moor's a bad lot and that Desdemona is 'too fond of her most filthy bargain.' (5.2.153) She also knows that under pressure, like herself, her mistress will tell the odd fib, as she does, for example, about the lost handkerchief. Emilia's a moral realist. She doesn't expect too much of people. Allowances have to be made. She admits that she needs a few allowances to be made for herself and quite likes the idea that Desdemona might need some, too.

Although Desdemona isn't perfect she never ceases to surprise and impress us. In the death scene she's absolutely terrified of the unhinged Moor – and who wouldn't be? – but somehow she manages to love and honour him to the very last. And what an extraordinary idea it was of Shakespeare's to have her die gasping out that last pathetic lie: Othello didn't suffocate me, **I** did it myself!

Finally, I'd like to make a few additional points about the symmetries, affinities and contradictions that the play gives rise to, some of which are immediately obvious and others apparent only after analysis and reflection.

Shakespeare likes to do things in twos. As we saw, he gives the big Iago-Othello scene (Act 3, Scene 3) a two-part 'hinge' structure. But he also has a 'two-strike' technique for Iago's 'fingers-lips-and-whatever-next' speeches, writes a (belated) reprise of the opening Iago-Roderigo plotting session and has Othello submitting twice over to Desdemona's plea for Cassio.

There are other examples of a similar sort of 'doubleness', too. He has Iago's and Othello's life-lines running closely parallel. They're both soldiers who've had a tough life. They're both conscious of social disadvantage; in Othello's case it's to do with being black and foreign, but in Iago's case it's to do with class inferiority and thwarted ambition. The two men develop a hand-and-glove intimacy, the glove being Iago's 'proofs' and the hand being Othello's readiness to accept them. Both men abuse and kill their wives. Simply on the verbal level, Iago's 'prime as goats, as hot as monkeys' (3.3.406), echoed by Othello later at 4.1.263, has a double-message for both men.

Othello and Desdemona are another complementary 'duo'. She's his 'anima', his 'better half' and his exact **opposite** – young, white, beautiful and, of course, female. Her love promises to make good the implicit social-cultural-spiritual deficit of his non-European origins, and later takes the form of an implicit offer of redemption from sin and error - which he spurns. In her eyes the Moor's love will give her a vicarious part in his adventurous lifestyle and public glamour. Through it she hopes to expand her own humanity across the divides of gender and race. Just for once Othello gets it right when he says:

……… she wished
That Heaven had made her such a man. *(i.e. as him)*
(1.3.163-164)

These things represent the hopeful possibilities of a match which the Venetians (Cinthio stresses this point much more than Shakespeare does) regard as a hopeless **mis**match - and in the end, of course, they have the satisfaction of being proved right.

Rivalry provides another sort of symmetry. There's the unreal (but much spoken of) rivalry between Othello and Cassio for Desdemona and the all-too-real (but 'silent') rivalry between Iago and Desdemona for the Moor's very soul. In this latter case the opposition is shaped by the frequency with which the epithet 'honest' is used of them. The count of 'cognitive' and 'evidential' words in Act 3, Scene 3 can be matched by an equally impressive count of 'honest' and 'honesty', used indiscriminately between them. If you doubt it, do your own counting – and don't stop till you get to 40!

There's another pair of 'subliminal co-ordinates', as Nabokov calls them, to be investigated in Shakespeare's handling of stereotypes. We've noted the important 'Moor' stereotype, but there's also a latent 'Venetian woman' stereotype haunting the play. In a nutshell, the 'Venetian woman' lived in a prosperous but decadent city where women, married and unmarried, enjoyed a Europe-wide reputation for being beautiful, independent, sophisticated and sexually liberated. So the question arises: is Desdemona a 'Venetian woman'? Shakespeare clearly wanted the possibility to flit through our minds. First, he gives us the feisty Desdemona who's run away with a black man – that makes you wonder, doesn't it? And what about the smart cookie we see next who puts down Iago in formal disputation? And is there more than meets the eye in that very assured young wife nagging her husband to do her (male) friend a favour? But no, we realise with ever-growing certainty, Desdemona's as straight as a die - in **our** eyes at least, if not in the eyes of her husband's when he calls her

> ……………..that cunning whore of Venice
> That married with Othello. (4.2.91-92)

As the play develops we see more and more of the Moor stereotype emerging in Othello, while Desdemona increasingly figures as the **anti**-stereotype of the 'Venetian woman'.

Another contrast-pairing can be pointed out between Desdemona and Iago. For most of the play we in the audience can be appalled by the Moor but we can't be expected to identify with him; his delusions and rages keep him at spiritual and emotional arm's length from us. His reality and ours don't tally. At the end, though, Shakespeare adds a 'theological' quality to the spiritual contradiction between Desdemona and Iago, making her, in the despairing Othello's eyes, an emblematic angel (or saint) and him an emblematic devil. It's at this point that Othello's reality and ours start to converge. We can now allow ourselves to be drawn into his understanding of the pair who've been competing for his soul. Desdemona is the 'good angel' that he's just destroyed, and Iago is the devil destroying him and drawing him down to hell.

We've seen Desdemona as fallible, forceful, even in some ways a bit odd. The actress playing her shouldn't make her too uniformly noble or 'spiritual' than the text, read straightforwardly, requires. She's very much a 'developing' character but towards the end there's a touch of something else about her – a certain saintliness (heavily emphasised by Boito and Verdi, for Romantic/sentimental rather than Christian reasons), which suggests that she somehow 'stands for' Othello's opportunity for salvation.

Climbing into the fatal marital bed, full of foreboding about her husband's violence, Desdemona bids Emilia 'Good night, good night' and completes the rhyming couplet with the prayer:

God me such usage send
Not to pick bad from bad but by badness mend. (4.3.103-104)

These simple words are a 'signature' of Christianity. The hope of salvation lies not in evil being simply vanquished by good, but in a painful 'mending' of good from the midst of evil. The Moor, of course, is deceived by Iago almost to the end, but even the audience, although convinced early that Iago's a nasty and dangerous piece of work, may not quite grasp his essentially diabolical nature, as we watch him moving from denunciation of Iago as a particularly toxic villain to the conviction that he's the devil incarnate. Othello, staring downwards to see if Iago's feet are cloven – the sure sign of the devil - sees that they aren't but knows that it proves nothing because 'that's a fable'. (5.2.283) A better test, he thinks, would be to run him through with his sword because

If that thou be'st a devil, I cannot kill thee. (5.2.284)

- which he does, and his dreadful suspicion is confirmed by Iago, saying, 'I bleed, sir, but not killed.' (5.2.285) He hasn't killed Iago, so he must be the devil!

There are only sixteen words in their exchange, and it needs careful directing and acting to get the horror of the moment across to an audience. Modern people – directors, actors and audiences - may be inclined to jib at this direct and literal interpretation as too 'internal' to the Moor's subjectivity. They may ask why, if so much of his consciousness is deluded, we should join him in his final 'theological' – or perhaps they'd say superstitious – recognition of Iago's diabolical nature. On the other hand, they should also consider whether an attempt to understand the scene in the way that Shakespeare quite likely intended his audience to understand it might not repay the imaginative effort and sacrifice of scepticism required.

When Iago's wickedness is finally and fully exposed he refuses to explain anything he's done, let alone why he's done it. He takes a vow of silence.

Demand me nothing. What you know, you know.
From this time forth I never will speak word. (5.2.300-301)

He means it: he's not waiting for his lawyer to arrive. Lodovico's sure that he'll have to speak again, if only to pray for mercy when he's being tortured. Silence. Graziano agrees: 'torments will ope your lips'. (5.2.302) Silence. (Those silences need to be prolonged!) Then Othello says:

Well, thou dost best. (5.2.303).

His thought is that if a devil 'opes his lips' to pray it will be an appalling prayer. Silence is preferable, whatever it conceals.

The silencing of Iago is a stroke of dramatic genius. He's faithfully followed his theological vocation – doing evil for its own sake and for the damnation of souls. He's done his honest worst and he has no further use for speech with human beings.

THE TEMPEST

We look down from above to see what the trouble is. There's an island, surrounded by churning seas and threatening storm clouds. Huge waves crash over a ship as it reels towards the rocky shore.

Looking closer, we see that this is taking place on a wooden platform, which is both a foam-washed foredeck and a playhouse stage.

Sailors are staggering about, shouting at each other through the shrieking wind.

Master: Boatswain!
Boatswain: Here master. What cheer?
Master: Good. Speak to the mariners. Fall to't yarely or we'll run ourselves aground. Bestir, bestir!
Boatswain: Heigh, my hearts; cheerly, cheerly, my hearts! Yare! Yare! Take in the topsail. Tend to the master's whistle! (1.1.1-7)

It's a desperate emergency, but at least there appears to be a clear chain of command. The master gives his orders to the boatswain, who passes them on to the mariners, who strain every nerve and sinew to save the ship. But it's not as simple as that. There are other men standing around on the deck. They don't look like sailors. Too well-dressed. Passengers. The boatswain gets quite shirty with them, telling them to get down into their cabins below deck, out of the way of the crew. But they don't like being spoken to like that. One elderly gentleman tells him to keep a civil tongue in his head when he's addressing his betters, but the boatswain doesn't see this as a place or time for social deference. 'You are a councillor', he yells at him, and 'if you can command these elements to silence and work the peace of the present, we will not hand a rope more. Use your authority! If you cannot, give thanks you have lived so long and make yourself ready in your cabin for the mischance of the hour, if it so hap... - Out of our way, I say!' (1.1.20-26)

The boatswain starts unceremoniously clearing the passengers off the deck, but the arguments go on amidst the uproar, until the ship goes down with all aboard.

In the next scene the wooden platform has shifted to dry land where a tall man in strange robes is talking to a teenage girl. She saw the shipwreck and it's left her in tears. There can't have been any survivors. But the man seems quite unmoved, even pleased. It's as if he's seen something quite different. He tells her that 'there's no harm done', (1.2.15) then he launches into his narrative.

(£5 for a theatre synopsis. Here it's free of charge.)

In a violent tempest, raised by Ariel on Prospero's orders, the ship is wrecked with King Alonso of Naples and his retinue aboard.

About a dozen years ago, Prospero, the rightful duke of Milan became immersed in the study of magic and neglected his duties as a ruler. His envious younger brother Antonio, in cahoots with King Alonso of Naples, seized the chance to usurp him. Prospero and Miranda, still a toddler at the time, were set adrift at sea in a small boat. Their chances of survival were slim, but a kindly Neapolitan courtier, Gonzalo, saw to it that they had some food and drink – as well as Prospero's magic books - on board. Providence was kind to them. They were washed up on this unknown Mediterranean island.

Since then Prospero has ruled the island with his daughter Miranda and acquired two slaves. One is Ariel, a 'natural' spirit whom he rescued from the power of the witch, Sycorax, who lived on the island. The other is Caliban, the island's only native son and the offspring of that same Sycorax and a passing devil. Ariel is beautiful, possessing the ability to fly and other magical powers. Caliban by contrast is an ugly monster, greedy, lazy and rebellious, and he's already tried to rape Miranda. He regards himself as the ancestral ruler of the island and has resisted all his master's and mistress's attempts to civilise him into European ways. The only way to keep him in check is by incessant intimidation and punishment.

But what is the royal party doing so far from Naples? They've been sailing home from North Africa where King's Alonso's daughter Claribel has just married the Prince of Tunis.

King Alonso, with his younger brother Sebastian, Antonio and other nobles and servants in his retinue, have survived the shipwreck in spite of all appearances to the contrary and come ashore on the island. They're shaken, though physically unharmed. They don't know that Prospero's awaiting them. Alonso's son and heir Ferdinand isn't with them and they fear he's drowned.

But no, Ferdinand isn't drowned. Ariel makes an air-search, spots him alone in a deserted bay, casts a spell on him and brings him to his master's cave. Miranda and Ferdinand fall in love with each other at first sight. Actually, the romance fits in with Prospero's plan for making a Milan-Naples dynastic match when he's regained his dukedom, but for the time being he chooses to test Ferdinand's character by enslaving him as an enemy spy. He gives him one of the menial jobs that Caliban especially hates doing - humping logs for firewood.

Meanwhile two of the royal party launch a new plot. Antonio, the usurper of Prospero's dukedom in Milan, urges Sebastian to assassinate his elder brother King Alonso and seize the throne of Naples. In the nick of time the murder is prevented by Ariel's magical intervention.

This isn't the only murder plot afoot. Caliban falls in with two of the humbler members of the royal retinue, the clown Trinculo and the drunken butler Stephano, and tells them about the tyrannical Prospero and his beautiful daughter Miranda. Over a drink (or two, or three) they agree to assassinate Prospero. Stephano will be king of the island and make Miranda his queen. Again, it needs the ever-vigilant and resourceful Ariel to thwart their plans with another magic spell.

In Act Four there's a masque. Prospero feels that Ferdinand has passed his test and he gets Ariel to stage a 'prophecy' with the classical goddesses Iris, Ceres and Juno playing starring roles. It foretells the prosperous order of things that will come about through the dynastic union of Miranda, of the house of Milan, with him, the heir of the royal house of Naples.

Ariel now rounds up the full company for the final scene in front of Prospero's cave. The royals and nobles are still in the guilty trance that he's cast upon them and the Caliban-Stephano-Trinculo revolutionists are exhausted after having been chased across country by a pack of dogs. But Prospero, now that he has them in his power, renounces his magic powers, pardoning them all and reclaiming his own dukedom. He will keep Caliban in his charge – 'this thing of darkness I acknowledge mine' but he will give Ariel his long-promised freedom, before the rest of the party sail home together in their miraculously repaired ship.

The play, we note, takes place on an island, and within a very limited time-scale. It may seem an absurd question to ask, knowing Shakespeare, but is he by any chance proposing to observe the 'classical unities' of place and time in this play?

Well, of course not. But he toys with the idea.

The unity of place that the island setting provides turns out to be more apparent than real. The action takes us to several different locations – various bays, inland venues, including Prospero's cell, not to mention the off-shore scene of the shipwreck, and the effect is to disperse rather than concentrate the action and cause confusion about the whereabouts and doings of others. Everyone (pace Donne) here seems to have his own island. It's described with contradictory features and details. Adrian, one of the minor lords in the royal party, argues in a self-contradictory way that although the island's a 'desert', (2.1.34) and 'uninhabitable and almost inaccessible', (2.1.37) it's also 'of subtle, tender and delicate temperance' (2.1.41-42) where the air 'breathes upon us here most sweetly'. (2.1.45) And Gonzalo – yes, the kindly Neapolitan courtier who equipped Prospero and Miranda for their voyage into exile – agrees with Adrian's more positive comments; for him it's a providential place - 'Here is everything advantageous to life.' (2.1.52) The Machiavellian Antonio and Sebastian, though, see it as a rotten, stinking and pestilential place without any natural beauty or saving grace. The characters are telling us more about themselves than about the island.

The island is nameless, and you won't find it on any map, but we can deduce that it lies in the Mediterranean Sea not too far to the east or west of the north-south line that the royal flotilla was aiming to follow on its return journey from Tunis to Naples. It's not clear how big it is, and it's a moot point whether it has an indigenous population or not. Only Caliban figures as a 'native'.

If we try to assemble all the observations and topographical details that are mentioned we end up with a sort of kaleidoscopic picture.

Inland, Prospero tells us, there are

……… fresh brook mussels, wither'd roots, and husks
Wherein the acorn cradled. (1.2.466-467)

But these details, no doubt, are examples of the meagre prison fare that Prospero's means to feed Ferdinand on when he has him in captivity. A bit of starvation will take the edge off his sex-drive, build up his character and make him a more worthy husband for Miranda. But they hardly capture the overall conditions on the island.

Maybe we get a better idea when Caliban curses his master with:

All the infections that the sun sucks up
From bogs, fens, flats, on Prospero fall … (2.2.1-2)

He conjures up the picture of a steamy, disease-ridden landscape offering little relief either in terms of hills or eye-interest. But the context here is Caliban's malediction:

'bogs, fens and flats' have to be seen as cuss-words as much as hard-and-fast general descriptions.

We get yet another 'landscape' in Act 2, Scene 2, when Trinculo scans it in vain for somewhere to shelter from an oncoming storm.

Here's neither bush nor shrub, to bear off any weather at all, and another storm brewing. (2.2.18-19)

Bleak and exposed then, but it's the current weather that we're looking at, not the general climate. And it hardly tallies with the more luxuriant picture in the next scene when Caliban offers to show Trinculo and Stephano round 'his' island, which he (unlike Prospero) clearly knows every inch of. I prithee, he says,

Let me bring thee where crabs grow,
And I with my long fingernails will dig thee pignuts;
Show thee a jay's nest, and I'll instruct thee how
To snare the nimble marmoset; I'll bring thee
To clustering filberts, and sometimes I'll get thee
Young scamels from the rock. (2.2.166-171)

Caliban is talking eatables, listing some of the delicacies to be found on the island if you know where to look – and he certainly **does** know where to look. 'Crabs' (crab-apples or crustaceans? – nobody seems to know which), pignuts, jays (though Caliban may be thinking of their eggs rather than the birds themselves) and filberts are things that Shakespeare may have seen - and perhaps even eaten - in his native Warwickshire. 'Scamels' are less familiar - they're sea-side creatures of some kind but there's no agreement about whether they're fish or fowl. But those **marmosets** - small and rather fetching Brazilian monkeys sometimes brought to Jacobean England as pets. Goodness knows how they got onto the island! - and onto Caliban's menu of local specialities, no doubt.

Elsewhere Caliban mentions a variety of wild creatures, which we assume are non-edible - although he's a very belly-minded beast and may draw the line less fussily than we would. Some, like 'urchins' (2.2.5) (i.e. hedgehogs), 'adders' (2.2.13), and 'the blind mole' (4.1.194), are native to the English and European countryside, while 'apes' (2.2.8), like marmosets, are distinctly exotic.

The island has no coherent 'unity' as a place. It's a heterocosm designed as a dramatic backdrop.

Antonio and Gonzalo don't agree about much but they seem to see pretty much eye to eye on one thing. The island is a place of suffering and punishment. Antonio simply resents it, but it's also a place where, as Gonzalo realises, good can emerge from harm. It is a version of Purgatory. The tempest/shipwreck was a kind of death for the voyagers, which Miranda thought she had witnessed, but their time on the island since then has been a 'between-time' period of confusion and contrition between death and the final placement of their souls in the life to come. The key sign that this is a Purgatorial place is that although the courtiers are 'men of sin' they now find that they're unable to commit any **new** sins. Swords get drawn – by Ferdinand (1.2.465-466), by Antonio and Sebastian (2.1.295-297) and by Alonso, Antonio and Sebastian, (3.3.60-65) - but no new blows fall.

We need to remember that belief in Purgatory, like belief in ghosts and praying for the dead, was officially condemned by Reformation theologians as a Papist superstition. Purgatory allowed a gap between the moment of death and the final enactment of God's eternal judgement, but there was no basis for it in Scripture. You had to atone for your sins in **this** world, the Reformers insisted; there was no last minute chance to settle things right with God after death. His judgement was instant and irreversible. You were either damned or saved.

But 'The Tempest' isn't a particularly 'reformed' play. Whatever kind of faith (if any) Shakespeare may have professed at various stages of his life mediaeval Christian ideas had clearly soaked deep into his mind and imagination in his earliest years, and stayed there. So we shouldn't be too surprised if, when he came to write his 'farewell' play with its 'last things' themes of sin, repentance and forgiveness, the notion of Purgatory floated up from the bottom of his oceanic imagination in the form of this mysterious island. Prospero may not describe the island objectively but he clearly sees it as a place of judgement, with himself, at least for the time being, as the judge. But in the end it can also provide 'blessings'. When Miranda, hearing how she and her father fetched up there, asks him:

What foul play had we that came from thence *(i.e. Milan)*? Or blessed wast we did? (1.2.60-61)

he replies:

        Both, both, my girl,
By foul play, as thou sayst, we were heaved thence,
But blessedly holp hither. (1.2.61-63)

Unity of place brings us to Purgatory, then. But what about unity of time?

The passage of time covered by the action on stage in 'The Tempest' is something like 6 hours. That's shorter than the passage of time covered in distinctively classical plays like Euripides's 'Medea' or Racine's 'Phèdre', and the sense of tautness is further emphasised – especially at first, anyway – by the impression that Prospero in his impatience gives of driving events. I say 'at first' because that's what he intends but not quite how it works out.

Act 1, Scene 2, which is no less than 502 lines long, includes Prospero's long-pent-up and occasionally ranting back-story to Miranda and the first appearances of three other important characters: Ariel, Caliban and Ferdinand. When Miranda - who's been oscillating between rapt attention and sleep - finally drops off he suddenly switches from narrative to executive mode. He summons up his servant-spirit Ariel and runs through the agenda. He'll be running the show, making **this** happen, in **that** order, and with not a moment to lose.

Now that the tempest's died down Item 1 on Prospero's business plan can be ticked off. Ariel's carried out his first instructions to the letter. He's scared the living daylights out of the shipwrecked courtiers without doing them any physical harm. They're now wandering about distractedly on the island, their feelings divided between gratitude for their survival, misgivings about where they've fetched up, and grief for the supposed loss of the king's son. 'We're celebrities,' they seem to be thinking. 'Get us out of here!'

Prospero's appreciates Ariel's efforts so far but 'there's more work', he tells him. 'What is the time o' th' day?' (1.2.239) Ariel, who also counts the time (and who may be hoping he's at least earned the afternoon off) replies, 'Past the mid season' (1.2.239) - i.e. noon and he's not inclined to do anything more.

Prospero bristles: 'At least two glasses', i.e. it's 2.00 p.m. (But if he knew, why did he have to ask?) Then he adds: 'The time between six and now must by us both be spent most preciously.' (1.2.240-241) His long-awaited opportunity has finally come. Two o'clock already – how time flies! – and he's intent on getting everything done and dusted by six. Hurry! Hurry! There's not a moment to lose. Let's get on with it!

'Is there more toil?' (1.2.242) Ariel asks, and Prospero instantly flares up at the signs of resistance in his face. 'How now? Moody?' he demands,

What is't thou canst demand? (1.2.244-245)

Ariel knows that he's in no position to demand anything, but it is freedom that he's really after. And freedom **now!** He was remitted a year off the original sentence for good conduct, but the reminder of that promise brings his boss, so grateful a moment before, down on him like a ton of bricks. 'Before the time be out? No more!' he says (1.2.246) and gives him a prolonged tongue-lashing. He's a liar, a 'malignant thing', (1.2.257) a 'slave' (1.2.270) and a 'dull thing' (1.2.285), and he ends with a dire threat: if he doesn't buckle down and stop whingeing, he'll imprison him in some sort of Ovidian oak tree for twelve years, which will make this slavery seem like freedom!

Prospero's certainly not an easy boss to work for! And Ariel's reply:

Pardon, master,
I will be correspondent to command
And do my spriting gently. (1.2.296-298) –

is that of an intimidated spirit.

His submission immediately softens Prospero's rage and he undertakes to free Ariel in two days. Before long he'll repeat this promise - even improving it to '**within** two days' (1.2.422) - although the repetition still seems to be that of a man who'll honour it only when it suits him, and not before. Ariel may well be wondering, 'Why two days, if we're going to have all this business wrapped up, bar the shouting, in the next few hours? Is the old man stringing me along again? Has he got something else in mind for me after that?' But with the prospect, for what it's worth, of only two days of his sentence left, and his boss being such a touchy old so-and-so, he drops the subject for the time being.

Prospero's clash with Ariel prompts him to unburden himself of two more bits of back-narrative - about how he came to attach to his staff first his brilliant spirit-servant Ariel, and then his repulsive slave Caliban. It's interesting and relevant information, but it deflects him from the implementation of his action plan. 'Unity of time', whatever it may theoretically promise in the way of strengthening dramatic coherence, seems to be going a bit haywire. Need-to-know narratives, staff disciplinary issues and displays of temper keep cutting across his action plan.

Ariel's next instruction, which Prospero whispers in his ear so that the audience will catch it, is to go and impersonate an invisible water-nymph. For decency's sake, presumably, he has to go off-stage for a moment, but when he duly 'reappears', with attendant spirits, (if 'reappears' is the exact word here) he is, as ordered -

subject to no sight but thine and mine, invisible
To every eyeball else (1.2 303 -304)

except, of course, that we can see the 'invisible' water-nymphs perfectly well, too.

Where are we here? we wonder. Inside Prospero's mind, or outside, simply watching its effects on things?

But by now the don't-waste-a-minute Prospero is dragging his poor cringing daughter to go and see Caliban!

After what we've heard about Caliban we're naturally quite curious to get our first eyeful of him. What exactly we find ourselves looking at it's hard to say but he doesn't disappoint. He's quite as loathsome as we were led to expect. And, like Ariel, he wants freedom, too, which doesn't exactly bring out the best in his master either. In the jarring encounter that follows we see the harsher side of Prospero's character again, as he subjects him to the same kind of threats and abuse, though raised to the power of ten, that just now we saw him dishing out to Ariel.

Miranda heartily joins in with her father's condemnation, but with other business afoot at the moment Caliban can only be a brief distraction. When he's driven away with 'So, slave, hence,' (1.2.375) there's a lifting of the atmosphere as water-nymph Ariel, and his spirits, 'reappear', leading in a handsome but spellbound young man (yes, it's Ferdinand, the king's 'lost' son – no prizes for guessing that).

Ariel breaks into enchanting song:

Come unto these yellow sands,
And then take hands;
Curtsied when you have, and kissed
The wild waves whist;
Foot it featly here and there,

And sweet sprites bear.

To which his spirits sing the burden:

Hark, hark! Bow-wow,
The watch dogs bark, bow-wow.
Hark hark, I hear,
The strain of strutting chanticleer
Cry cock a diddle dow. (1.2.376-387)

We notice that time, the 'unity' which we have in mind at the moment, here does an eccentric thing. It splits itself into a simultaneous 'now' and 'then'. If Prospero were to glance at his real-world Rolex it would say something like 2.30 p.m. but in the world conjured up by Ariel's captivating aubade the clocks have gone backwards and it's glorious morning again – yes, **this** morning, i.e. eight hours ago! The 'bow, wow' of the watchdogs and 'cock a diddle dow' of the strutting chanticleer, sung as a refrain by spirits scattered around the stage, tell us that the terrors of the stormy night are being dispelled by the arrival of dawn.

Whatever it says on anyone's clock this is an enchanting moment, especially as it's also the moment when Miranda and Ferdinand fall in love with each other.

> At the first sight
> They have changed eyes, (1.2.441-442)

as Prospero puts it.

But the mood quickly sours. Although he has dynastic plans for Ferdinand he doesn't trust Miranda with him yet. He puts him under arrest and when the dazed but still spirited prince tries to resist he magically disarms him. He needs a dose of enslavement before things go any further. He'll treat him like Caliban. The love-smitten Miranda is dismayed, but he roughly rebukes her with:

> ....Foolish wench,
> To th' most of men, this is a Caliban,
> And they to him are angels. (1.2.480-482)

You're never quite sure where you stand with Prospero, are you?

Ariel's stunts are fascinating entertainments and by no means mere showbiz distractions from more serious matters. They go to the heart of the action. In wrong-doers they prevent further crimes and create necessary states of disorientation and fear. Prospero can work with all this.

Let's look at what's in Ariel's box of tricks.

i) In Act 1, Scene 1 it's Ariel, acting as Prospero's agent, who whips up the tempest. It's a **meteorological** stunt.

ii) In Act 1, Scene 2, in his 'invisible' guise of a water nymph, Ariel captivates Ferdinand with his song and brings him to Prospero's cave. The magic combines **self-transformative, musical** and **hypnotic** elements. In the same scene he casts the **erotic** spell that makes Miranda and Ferdinand fall in love. We see only the effect of the spell, not Ariel working it, and we only realise that he's done it to further his master's plan when Prospero says,

> Delicate Ariel,
> I'll set thee free for this. (1.2.442-443)

iii) In Act 2, Scene 1 Ariel sets up the opportunity for, and then foils, Antonio's and Sebastian's attempt on King Alonso's life. It's a **psychological-hypnotic** stunt in which he manipulates the mysterious boundaries of sleep and waking.

iv) In Act 3, Scene 2 he sows discord amongst the three low-life conspirators by mimicking Trinculo's voice: a **ventriloquistic - echo** stunt. Soon afterwards he pulls off a **'Pied Piper'** stunt to dance them away from the scene of their intended mischief.

v) In Act 3, Scene 3 he lays on a banquet, with dance entertainment, for the hungry courtiers, before suddenly 'vanishing' it just as they're about to tuck in. It's a now-you-see-it-now-you-don't **conjuring** trick. After which he makes a terrifying appearance as a harpy warning the courtiers of retribution if they don't repent and reform: an impressive display of **classical mythological impersonation.**

vi) In Act 4, Scene 1 he stages a masque, casting (and dressing) his under-spirits as divine and mythological personages. It's an all-singing-all-dancing **theatrical** stunt. Following this (and following the power-dressing scene that he apparently sets up without resorting to magic), he organises a cross-country manhunt of the would-be revolutionaries with his own under-spirits morphed into a baying, snapping pack of hounds, accompanied by Prospero and his troupe of 'goblins'. (4.1.258) It's a **spirit-raising** and (Ovidian) **spirit-transforming** stunt.

vii) In Act 5, Scene 1 he brings the courtiers, whom he's put in a frenzy, to Prospero's cave for judgement. It's another **hypnotic-spell** stunt. He then repairs the damaged royal ship: a feat of what we might call **marine**

engineering. Finally he arranges good weather for the royal party's voyage back to Naples: his second and final **meteorological** stunt - this time using his powers to calm rather than infuriate the sea.

A very busy and ingenious spirit, this Ariel. Mr Fixer, in fact. His repertoire of stunts covers the course of the action surprisingly fully, but he's only the shadow to Prospero's substance and it's Prospero who, however erratic his business-plan may seem at times, comes over as the architect and protagonist of the play, and the one whose moral values determine the final outcome.

It's worth thinking about how they work as a duo.

Officially, Prospero is in overall charge at the strategic level but he allows Ariel ample scope to deploy his own magical skills at the tactical level. He's the master and Ariel is just his 'hey you!' But sometimes we're tempted to ask if things are really as straightforward as that. We can get the impression that it's not always the great magus, robes and all, but his lovely assistant Ariel who is actually waving the effective wand. He can't carry through his plan on his own. Ariel isn't just useful: he may actually be indispensable. Slaves are there to spare him the indignity of having to go 'hands on' himself, but when Ariel shows signs of defiance he has the uncomfortable thought that he may be on the flip-side of a dependency that he hadn't bargained for. His brutal humiliation of Ariel in Act 1, Scene 2 comes from Prospero's insecurity about this. Yes, he works **through** Ariel, and Ariel works **for** him, but it's not exactly clear **how** it all works.

For example, in the case of the tempest, Miranda assumes that it's her father, in his 'magic garment', (1.2.24) who's in direct control of events. Shocked by the violence of the storm she pleads:

If by your art, my dearest father, you have
Put the wild waters in this roar, allay them. (1.2.1-3)

But we note that tell-tale 'if' – she doesn't really know it was him, does she? She raises a good question: where **was** he at the time? He delegated the job to Ariel and wasn't an eye-witness, even as a clairvoyant, otherwise why would he have to rely on Ariel's report? And when Ariel delivers his report he talks, un-contradicted, as if he did it all off his own bat.

I boarded the King's ship: now on the beak,
Now in the waist, the deck, in every cabin
I flamed amazement. (1.2.196-198)

Likewise, Prospero expects Ariel to use his own magic when he orders him to 'Go make thyself like a nymph o' th' sea'. (1.2.302) It's 'make thyself', not 'I'll make thee'.

On the other hand, in Act 1, Scene 2 Prospero clearly calls on his own magic to sap Ferdinand's strength when he tries to resist arrest. 'It works,' (1.2.494) he says in an aside, almost as if he felt he was rather out of practice and wasn't sure it **would** work.

Although Prospero has renounced his magical powers by the end of the play it doesn't stop him promising the royal party a calm sea and a prosperous voyage on their return journey back to Italy. 'Ariel, my chick,' he says,

That is thy charge. Then to the elements
Be free, and fare thou well. (5.1.315-317)

'Chick' drops a big hint. Prospero's not the formal boss any more. He's asking for one last favour, which Ariel grants, although he's certainly not obliged to.

A few more examples.

i) In Act 1, Scene 2 Miranda, with her very own eyes, sees the king's ship 'dash'd all to pieces', (1.2.8) and that is what the mariners, who were right in the thick of it, believe they experienced. But now it turns out that Ariel has not sunk the ship but hidden it. It's 'safely in harbour,' he informs Prospero,

…………… in the deep nook, where once
Thou call'dst me up at midnight to fetch dew
From the still-vex'd Bahamas, there she's hid. (1.2.226-229)

Ariel has left the mariners comatose and 'all under hatches stowed' (1.2.230) until everything's finally sorted out and everybody can safely sail back home to Naples in a perfectly sea-worthy ship. But neither Miranda nor the mariners will be able to give the police a very coherent account of what happened in the shipwreck.

ii) In Act 2, Scene 1 Ariel drops in (invisibly) on the courtiers and lulls them asleep with 'solemn music', which they hardly notice hearing. Antonio and Sebastian remain awake, but in a very peculiar state of consciousness. Antonio begins to tempt Sebastian to murder his elder brother King Alonso and usurp his throne, as if inviting him to imitate his own crime against Prospero. He starts with:

My strong imagination sees a crown
Dropping on thy head (2.1.207-208)

but in the conversation that ensues 'strong imagination' turns into a metaphor for talking in one's sleep.

Sebastian: What, art thou waking?
Antonio: Do you not hear me speak?
Sebastian: I do, and surely
It is a sleepy language, and thou speak'st
Out of thy sleep. What is it thou didst say?
This is a strange repose, to be asleep
With eyes wide open – standing, speaking, moving,
And yet so fast asleep.
Antonio: Noble Sebastian,
Thou let'st thy fortune sleep – die rather; wink'st
Whiles thou art waking.
Sebastian: Thou dost snore distinctly.
There's meaning in thy snores. (2.1.208-218)

This isn't just a psycho-poetic conceit. It's a crime plot being hatched.

iii) In Act 3, Scene 2 the revolutionary gang of three agree to assassinate Prospero and seize control of the island. The prospect makes Caliban 'jocund' (3.2.117) and he suggests that they sing a catch to celebrate the bright future opening up before them. Stephano starts - 'Scout 'em and flout 'em', etc (3.2.121-123) - and Trinculo is about to join in when Caliban, who's learned the tune from them earlier, stops them with: 'That's not the tune' (3.2.124) just as Ariel – invisibly present again – joins in by taking over the tune on his tabor and pipe! Where on earth, or elsewhere, is this strange new instrumentation coming from? It must be the devil's work. Who is 'scouting' and 'flouting' whom? Perhaps their plots have been overheard.

iv) In Act 3, Scene 3 the royal party have been 'all knit up in their distractions' (3.3.89-90) following Ariel's terrifying harpy speech, but now the voice of conscience and remorse is beginning to return to King Alonso's mind. Gonzalo, too, is already *compos mentis* enough to ask the king: 'Sir, why stand you in this strange stare?' (3.3.94-95) Alonso replies,

> O, it is monstrous, monstrous!
> Methought the billows spoke and told me of it;
> The winds did sing it to me, and the thunder –
> That deep and dreadful organpipe – pronounced
> The name of Prospero. (3.3.95-99)

The word 'methought' catches him with one foot still in the nightmare and the other in the returning consciousness that enables him to report it. (The nightmare-ridden Clarence's 'methought' in Richard III (1.4.9) has exactly the same effect.)

v) We might add that in Act 4, Scene 1 drunkenness works in the same direction. It's another 'spell' that subdues sanity and conscience, the difference being that it's self-administered. This is how 'delicate Ariel' describes Caliban, Stephano and Trinculo stoking themselves up for a bit of wicked violence:

> they were red-hot with drinking,
> So full of valour that they smote the air
> For breathing in their faces, beat the ground
> For kissing of their feet, yet always bending
> Towards their project. (4.1.171-175)

No, drink isn't 'official' magic, but if it helps to add to the guilty confusion of the gang of 'varlets'. (4.1.170) It makes its own contribution, too.

Now let's have a look at the 'sources' of the play.

All plays are assumed to have sources, or references, of one kind or another, and if they can be traced they can often shed light on themes in the play. We can define a 'source' as an earlier text or reference from which the playwright has borrowed at least some of his plot-line and characters. He has a free hand to follow it as closely or loosely as he likes, selecting, telescoping and altering things that he has a use for and sometimes even lifting identifying words, phrases and details.

In 'The Tempest' no obvious sources for the main plot have been identified, or are ever likely to be. It's very much Shakespeare's own concoction although – as is to be expected - particular incidents 'recall' various items of classical and Renaissance literary culture, with bits of folklore and 'current affairs' thrown in for good measure. This independence from anything like a main or 'substantive' plot source is unusual with him, but not unique. In one of his earliest plays, 'Titus Andronicus', he pieces together his plot entirely out of generalised 'Roman' associations and historical hints, weaving in Ovidian and Virgilian poetic references and ideas plucked from the recesses of his own imagination.

But although these two plays lack 'substantive' sources they do provide us with a range of 'associative' ones to consider. They can be dropped knowingly or casually, providing particular insights or what are no more than incidental side-lights. To categorise them all as 'sources' is a matter of discretion. We can easily find ourselves chasing shadows which actually tell us little or nothing of significance about the play itself.

Let's assume, though, that Shakespeare's classical references promise 'insights'. The expensively educated members of Shakespeare's original audience would have twigged that the courtiers' references to 'the widow Dido' in Act 2, Scene 1 recall the Dido who figures in Virgil's Aeneid (Book 1, lines 343-352, and in Book 4), and that Ariel's vanishing banquet in Act 3, Scene 3 invites comparison (though it turns out to be a rather oblique one) with the 'harpy feast' in the Aeneid (Book 3, lines 209-260) where another bunch of hungry diners have their meal spoiled by supernatural mischief. Prospero's renunciation of magic (5.1.33-57) would also have put them in mind of Medea's invocation to the witch Hecate in Ovid's Metamorphoses (Book 7, lines 263-289). These are all clearly deliberate borrowings. Highly interesting for the classically-educated connoisseurs in the audience, but if they float past the notice of the non-classical majority would they miss anything essential to the understanding of the play? I suppose the answer depends on what you mean by essential.

Montaigne's often-cited essay 'Of the Caniballes', translated by John Florio and published in London in 1603, is another recognised source. It's from here that Gonzalo draws his speculations (2.1.148-169) about living in harmony with Nature in the imaginary commonwealth that he fancies himself setting up. The unmistakable verbal and descriptive echoes of Florio's translation establish the connection for those familiar with it, but Gonzalo's utopian sentiments were presumably *au courant* in the public discourse of the time for people who hadn't read Montaigne and/or Florio as well as for those who had. It's a point of characterisation, rather than political philosophy, that's really at issue here. Gonzalo's utopian sentiments make him look like a 'good guy' in the liberal-minded public opinion of the day, and scorn for them classifies the two courtiers as 'bad guys'.

But what are we to make of the phrases about 'still-vexed Bermudas', (1.2.229) 'men of Ind', (2.2.57) and 'nimble marmoset' (2.2.167) - that we can pick out of this mystery-basket of 'sources'? Some people see them as evidence that Shakespeare meant his play to be a serious commentary on New World explorations, while others regard them as little more than current affairs 'floaters' in the flux of his creative mind. Some of the most intriguing of these references stem from William Strachey's 'True Reportary...' which was written and privately circulated in MS in London in 1610 and which Shakespeare may well have discussed with friends in the Earl of Southampton's circle who had a financial interest in the new Virginian colony. Storm, shipwreck and rescue loom large in the 'True Reportary', but the details don't match up with the play, and there's no sign that Strachey's story or characters exerted a recognisable shaping influence on it. Shakespeare had a powerful and original vision of his own to communicate, and the 'New World' references which leave their marks on the text, however intriguing, are few - and arguable.

The characters are 'old world', too. Yes, that applies even to Caliban and Ariel. The Mediterranean has its own monsters and spirits; Shakespeare didn't have to go to the New World to find them. As with plots and episodes, they can be thought of, up to a point, as having traceable 'sources', but we shouldn't overestimate their explanatory value. It might be more helpful, in trying to see what the play's really about, to see them as emerging from a generalised European cultural background, and in particular as creations of Shakespeare's free imagination, rather than as borrowings from specific literary examples.

The characters range from fairly stock examples to the 'outlandish'. Amongst the stock ones are Italian royals and courtiers of the kind found in Renaissance tales of political rivalries. We also get, in outline if not in detail, a pretty standard pair of lovers who run into a snag or two, but whose eventual union in marriage helps to shed a warm glow over the final outcome. Then there's the lynch-pin character at the centre of the play, Prospero, who combines 'stock' with extremely unusual features. He's partly the readily recognisable Duke of Milan type, with political scores to settle and personal wrongs to right, but also a high-powered magician, operating with the aid of Ariel, his extraordinary spirit-slave. There are also two fairly standard clowns, Stephano and Trinculo, who join up with Caliban in a plot to overthrow Prospero's rule of the island. It's a very motley crew.

'The Tempest' isn't only very incidentally about the encounter of the 'New' and 'Old' worlds. Centrally, it's about the conflicts between those who stand for the established social and moral order and others who challenge their authority with plots and rebellions. It's the same old story of the conflicts of 'masters and men'. But it goes beyond that. A 'State of Man' scenario is also shadowed in. There's been a fall from grace and a happier previous state has been forfeited. The rightfully ordained order of things has been damaged, and corrections have to be made before the *status quo ante* can be restored. The clock needs to be turned back and old wrongs, half-forgotten except by the victims, need to be remembered and righted. Repentance and forgiveness are called for. Only then can the true future – a faithful continuation of the past and the present – begin.

And that's why the key figure – Prospero – has to be a reactionary. He's both the victim of wrongs and the judge with the power to correct them. Socio-politically he's partly ready-made but he also has a very particular and relevant 'source' in one of Shakespeare's own plays of four or five years before - Duke Vincenzio in 'Measure for Measure'. The parallels are striking. Both dukes have been reclusive bookworms whose neglect of public duty, as they themselves admit, has led others into the ways of temptation. Both believe that it's now down to them to repair moral harms that they, albeit unintentionally, helped to cause. In spite of (or could it be because of?) this feeling of personal responsibility for the wrong-doing of others they now take a pretty rigorous and punitive line. They are both prepared to shelve their duke-roles for the time being and resort to questionable methods – disguise, magic – in their pursuit of justice and moral reform. Both have a bit of a thing about sexual irregularity. Both put characters that they have power over through trials that are more painful and prolonged than they strictly need to be.

The quasi-dukes share a taste for increasing and prolonging suffering. There are dramatic advantages in this. It offers extra opportunities to complicate dramatic situations and to generate greater suspense and emotional engagement in the audience. And there's an important moral element, too. Trials, tests of patience and deferral of gratification are all 'good for the soul'. But it's not altogether clear where Prospero's – like Vincenzio's - mistrust of human nature ends and his moral wisdom begins. Although Ferdinand seems to us to be an exemplary young man Prospero arbitrarily decides to impose a sort of pre-emptive purifying punishment on him. Prospero later admits to the harshness of this when he says: 'If I have too austerely punished you…' (4.1.1) But he's not **too** apologetic; he feels entitled to test his prospective son-in-law's moral mettle. After all, this handsome young prince is Alonso's treacherous son -

which puts him into the territory of 'sins of the fathers' - and his love for Miranda presumably has a sexual element in it – well, it would, wouldn't it? So the arduous log-heaving that he assigns to Ferdinand suggests that he doesn't trust him with Miranda any more than he would trust her to Caliban. In his view they both need their flesh well and truly chastened.

Halfway through this essay it may be as good a moment as any to pause and take our bearings. You can be excused for not keeping a tally of the topics we've dealt with so far. Just to remind you, though, they were: the **tempest**, the outline of the **'story-so-far'**, Shakespeare's ironic obeisance to the **classical 'unities' of place and time**, the **magic** that Prospero and Ariel use and the **'sources'** of plot and character that are drawn on. So what still remains? Analyses of several **scenes and characters,** involving Gonzales, Stephano, Trinculo, Caliban and Ariel, and the **bitter-sweet conclusion** that finally emerges.

A strong vein of cynicism runs through the play. We see it, for example, when Prospero tears a strip off Ariel in Act 1, Scene 2 and rebukes his daughter Miranda with his cutting 'Tis new to thee' when she exclaims: 'How beauteous mankind is!' (5.1.183-184) But Prospero hasn't got a monopoly of cynicism. Antonio's and Sebastian's scorn for Gonzalo is pretty wounding, too. The old counsellor is a kindly man, full of faith and optimism. He's also a political idealist, arguing in favour of the possibilities for human happiness in his speech about the 'Golden Age' commonwealth, in which everyone was (and will again be!) equal. He repeats the assertion that there's no need for distinctions to be made between masters and men, and no call for 'sovereignty'. (2.1.144-169) His idealism has a wide-eyed appeal, but it doesn't convince, does it? We have to admit that Sebastian's on the mark when he says: 'Yet he *(Gonzalo)* would be king on't' and that Antonio also scores when he points out that 'the latter end of his commonwealth forgets the beginning.' (2.1.157-159) Prospero isn't there to overhear the discussion, but we wouldn't expect him to come out in support of the dear old fellow's egalitarian opinions. Gonzalo's a good man - no denying it - but a bit silly.

But Prospero is on the spot there when Gonzalo delivers his opinion on the supposed 'islanders' who attend the banquet to feed the famished courtiers.

> If in Naples
> I should report this now, would they believe me?
> If I should say I saw such islanders
> (For certes, these are people of the island),
> Who, though they are monstrous shape, yet note
> Their manners are more gentle, kind, than of
> Our human generation you shall find
> Many – nay, almost any. (3.3.27-34)

Gonzalo willingly recognises them as fellow humans who, though of 'monstrous shape', are kindly disposed to them. But he's talking through his hat. They're actually the sub – Virgilian figments that Ariel has provided to crowd round the feast. Gonzalo has never seen any such 'islanders', any more than Trinculo has, and disbelieving Neapolitans may well scoff at such garbled travellers' tales but Prospero, standing unseen nearby, spots a truth in the latter part of the old man's misguided comments. Looking at Antonio, on hand and ready to mock, he agrees that Gonzalo's islanders, whoever they are, **must** be 'more gentle, kind' than his brother. Gonzalo's facts may be awry, but there's nothing wrong with his comparisons. Prospero says to Gonzalo,

> Honest lord,
> Thou hast said well, for some of you there present
> Are worse than devils. (3.3.34-36)

It's having the right attitude, not the right opinions, that really matters. It's the attitude – forgive me, I extrapolate for a moment now! - that you look for in an audience when you ask it to 'suspend its disbelief' in a play full of monstrous and confusing things in its search for a happy conclusion. Lies can tell truths in the right ears; not only the audience but the characters in the play need to be 'believers' to get things right. Soon Alonso, about to repent, or kill himself in despair, will hear the name of Prospero 'pronounced', as if he's about to appear in person, by the waves and winds of a troubled sea.

> O, it is monstrous, monstrous!
> Methought the billows spoke and told me of it;
> The winds did sing it to me, and the thunder –
> That deep and dreadful organpipe – pronounced
> The name of Prosper. It did base my trespass. (3.3.95-99)

Gonzalo, always a believer, represents Prospero's positive side, the 'self' that he'd like to have fuller possession of when he gets all his business worries off his hands. Finding Gonzalo weeping in Act 5 he weeps in sympathy. There's an affinity in their thoughts and feelings that's far more brotherly than any thoughts he shares with his 'dark side' brother Antonio. When his better side eventually wins and his project is completed he'll release all the culprits from the delusions that he and Ariel have inflicted upon them:

Their senses I'll restore
And they shall be themselves. (5.1.31-32)

It's an idea confirmed by Gonzalo, who in nine lines summarises the whole story of the island adventure, where so many blessings have been found, including – especially - the regaining of that kind of 'true-self' by all.

Was Milan thrust from Milan that his issue
Should become kings of Naples? O, rejoice
Beyond a common joy, and set it down
With gold on lasting pillars: in one voyage
Did Claribel her husband find in Tunis;
And Ferdinand, her brother, found a wife
Where he himself was lost; Prospero his dukedom
In a poor isle; and all of us ourselves,
When no man was his own. *(i.e. knew himself properly)*
(5.1.205-213)

The affinity between Gonzalo and the more positive side of Prospero accelerates us towards the end of the play, but we're not there yet. Let's step back to Act 2, Scene 2. Another storm is brewing. It's not a supernatural storm this time but a fairly standard sample of the island weather. The clown Trinculo, alone and lost, looks around for somewhere to shelter. Not a tree in sight, but what's that over there? - a bit of ground covered with a gabardine. Perhaps he can hide under that from the oncoming downpour? But there seems to be somebody else already there. He lifts a corner of the sheet.

'What have we here,' Trinculo asks, reeling back, 'a man or a fish? Dead or alive? A fish: he smells like a fish, a very ancient and fish-like smell, a kind of – not of the newest – poor-John. A strange fish! … Legged like a man and his fins like arms! Warm, o' my troth! I do now let loose my opinion, hold it no longer: this is no fish but an islander that hath lately suffered by a thunderbolt.' (2.2.24-36)

Long uncomprehending stares and exclamations occur frequently in this play. This is evidently another gobsmacking sight, but our view of it is restricted and we have to depend on how Trinculo does his shock-and-horror reaction to it. Whatever it is, it's something utterly repulsive and it stinks, and it seems to have been struck dead by a thunderbolt. A 'fish' shape morphs into a 'man' shape, but definite description is defeated by its monstrosity. Trinculo does his best. He uses no less than four of his five senses in his effort to confirm its material reality. He **sees** it (yuk!), **smells** it (pooh!) and **feels** it – and finds it's 'warm, by my troth!' (2.2.33). Soon he'll **hear** it, but he'll never find out (we hope) what it **tastes** like!

The rain's belting down now and it's freezing cold but shivering wretches can't afford to be too fussy about the company they keep, so Trinculo joins this 'strange bedfellow' (2.2.39) under the gabardine. He's in need of a body-heat supplement, though he's not sure whether what he's getting is the residual glow of a thunderstruck corpse or the warmth of a living fellow creature.

There's a lot of undignified wriggling and thrashing about under the gabardine, before Stephano, the alcoholic court butler, staggers onstage, bottle at lips, roaring bawdy sailors' songs. He hears a voice, 'Do not torment me! O!' (2.2.55) coming from under the gabardine. He sees four human legs poking out. It doesn't occur to him in his boozy daze to do the sensible thing and divide the number of legs by two and conclude that there are two men in there. No, he takes the easier arithmetical option, dividing by one and concluding that 'this is some monster of the isle, with four legs, who has got, as I take it, an ague.' (2.2.64-65)

Actually, Stephano isn't only interested in the ratio of legs to bodies but in the fact that the monster can speak 'our language'. (2.2.68) It's a point of human contact. He will 'give him some relief, if it be but for that.' (2.2.68-69) He's not being sentimental, though. He's spotted a chance to make a few bob for himself. 'If I can recover him and keep him tame, and get to Naples with him, he's a present for an emperor', (2.2.67-69) he says, echoing Trinculo's earlier remark: 'In England...when they will not give a doit to relieve a lame beggar, they will lay out ten to see a dead Indian.' (2.2.31-32) Monsters can be nice little earners.

Stephano hasn't twigged it yet but there are two separate but entangled 'monsters' under the gabardine, with two minds about the sort of 'relief' they want. One simply wants to get out of the freezing rain. The other wants relief by eluding the spirits sent by his master Prospero, and who have just jumped under the gabardine, as he believes, to pinch him to death. He tells them that 'thou dost me yet but little hurt. Thou wilt anon, I know it by thy trembling. Now Prosper works upon thee.' (2.2.78-80)

Too confused to care about anybody else's confusions, Stephano splashes a slug of his cure-all medicine into a mouth he can see. Then he hears **another** voice, also coming from under the gabardine! He can't place it, but it seems to have placed him. It's Trinculo saying, 'I should know that voice. Surely it can't be...' (2.2.86) Stephano has a problem. Is this one monster with two mouths or two monsters with one mouth each?

Four legs and two voices – a most delicate monster!
(2.2.88-89)

Stephano's nothing if not an egalitarian. If there are two
mouths there must be two slugs, so he splashes some
booze into the other mouth. Hearing his voice, Trinculo
calls out, 'Stephano!' He thought his ship-mate had been
lost in the shipwreck.

When the writhing mass of limbs gets untangled and
Caliban realises that he's no longer being tormented by
Prospero's spirits but has fallen into human company (it
takes over 40 lines for this to happen) he has some
interesting things to say. He makes it clear that he's a
native and that he knows where to find food on the island.
(2.2.157-161 and 2.2.164-169)

Later on, when Trinculo and Stephano get over their first
impressions of Caliban, they still can't account for him in
anything like rational terms. He remains easier to insult
than to describe. Their abuse ranges from 'deboshed *(i.e.
drunken and debauched)* fish' (3.2.25) to 'half a fish and
half a monster'. (3.2.28) No fewer than fifteen times they
call him 'monster' to his face-
(3.2. 2,3,4,7,10,11,17,24,30,34,68,78,104,117 and 148) but
nevertheless, they accept him as a revolutionary comrade.

With him they will liberate themselves from tyranny and
oppression by bumping off Prospero during his afternoon
nap. (3.2.87-91) Interestingly, Caliban, though the self-
proclaimed natural heir of the island, doesn't aspire to the
top job after the revolution. Sebastian will be the new king
and have Miranda as his queen; he'll settle for the humbler
rank of 'viceroy'. (3.2.108) Caliban is more interested in

revenge than in personal power, and he remains incurably servile. 'Let me lick thy shoe,' he tells Sebastian, 'I'll not serve him *(i.e. Prospero)*'. (3.2.22-23) His innate slavishness can't be cured by political success. It's just that he prefers to lick the boots of a servant to those of a duke.

It's not that he lacks intelligence. The fifteen-year-old Miranda has known him most of her life and can vouch for that. He was twelve when she and her father came to the island, which makes him about twenty-four now. For a few years, and although she was considerably younger than her pupil, Miranda was his teacher. He made good progress as a second language speaker. His first language was 'gabble' (1.2.358) but he picked up Italian (i.e. - for our purposes - English) very quickly. Nevertheless, he now feels that Euro-talk alienates him from his authentic (i.e. malignant) self, except when he uses it to curse his master and mistress.

You taught me language, and my profit on't
Is I know how to curse. The red plague rid you
For learning me your language. (1.2.364-366)

He showed no such aptitude for moral education, though, where he averaged 0 out of 10, both for theory and practice. His attempt to rape Miranda, and his regret only that he didn't succeed, has put him profoundly at odds with his master and mistress, who're still struggling to understand why their efforts to instil any sense of decency into him have failed so completely. It's as if he just hasn't got the usual ethical 'wherewithal'. It isn't simply that the primitive life he lived for his first twelve years has left him beyond the claim of civilisation. Cases have been reported (by Montaigne, for example) of natural virtues in primitive men which put civilised but decadent Europeans to shame.

The problem seems to be that Caliban isn't merely primitive but that he's not fully human. His family background, son of a devil and a witch, is worse than unpromising. He doesn't belong to any anthropological 'type', race or nation or family. He's a one-off; there don't seem to be any other 'Calibans' – though, as we'll see, that's not the unanimous opinion.

In inventing Caliban did Shakespeare's 'make a man' (2.2.30), or some kind of biological-humanoid freak?

Scholars have pointed to 'monsters' and other kinds of barbaric creatures from which Shakespeare may have taken hints for Caliban, such as the 'salvage men' who put in an appearance in Edmund Spenser's 'The Fairie Queene' (1596), or the ferocious and remote-dwelling Bremo, in the anonymous play 'Mucedorus' which had made 'wild men' a topic for discussion when it was revived in London by Shakespeare's own company a year or so before 'The Tempest' in 1611. There are other possibilities, but none of them gives us anything like a recognisable 'model' for Caliban. Outside the field of earlier and other literature and drama, but still within Shakespeare's cultural ken, there were European folk-tales about primitives living in faraway lands, not to mention accounts of 'Indian' natives brought to London by New World adventurers. No doubt some of these materials – but goodness knows which! – must have found their way into the melting-pot of Shakespeare's creative imagination, to emerge as this fantastical character who, for all his outlandishness, turns out to be perfectly 'fit for use' in the complex argument of a play about civilisation and barbarism.

Trinculo and Stephano aren't capable of speculating intelligently about Caliban's precise ontological status vis-à-vis *homo sapiens.* Miranda's better qualified. Protected and carefully nurtured by her father she can see him from a more privileged and educated standpoint. Too ladylike to mention his repulsive physical appearance, she focuses on his ethical deficiencies. After the terrible shock of that attempted rape she's convinced that there's something terribly 'wrong' about him which can't be corrected by education. In her mind he's an

Abhorred slave,
Which any print of goodness will not take,
Being capable of all ill. (1.2.352-354)

A young woman of her time, Miranda uses the word 'slave' as a term of straightforward contempt, not – as we do today - to acknowledge a victim of social oppression entitled to our moral sympathy. Well, this is a Jacobean not a contemporary play so we have to take her as she comes. If we insist on trying to bring the 'abhorred slave' within the pale of modern moral approval we have to do it in the teeth of the values that she and others express very clearly. Keeping Caliban in abject servitude - if you can manage it! - is the best you can do with him. What would the alternative be? Let him loose? Perish the thought! Of course he feels terribly unjustly treated, but 'European civilisation' had no alternative but to 'keep him down'.

As we've already noted, Miranda and her father didn't start with a preconception of Caliban as an 'abhorred slave'. They took him in to live with them in their cell (see 1.2.348) and only then lost their illusions about what he was like. Not only did he try to rape her but he refused to show any regret.

O ho, O ho! Would't had been done;
Thou didst prevent me, I had peopled else

This isle with Calibans. (1.2.350-352)

The graft of civilisation simply didn't 'take' on him. He had symptoms which today we might describe as psychotic: either he was **incapable** of moral training or, being innately evil, he **refused** to apply it to himself. Their educational project for him was a complete failure. He understood perfectly well what he would and wouldn't be punished for, but he never developed a conscience which distinguished inwardly between 'right' and 'wrong'. He remains a creature 'whom stripes may move, not kindness.' (1.2.346)

Well then, is he a 'man' or not? Miranda's not sure. Sometimes she counts him as a man, sometimes she doesn't. Once, gazing enraptured at her first sight of Ferdinand she gasped:

This
Is the third man that e're I saw, the first
That e're I sighed for. (1.2.446-447)

The other two men could only have been her father and Caliban, couldn't they? - so here she's definitely including the 'monster' as one of her own species. But a recount later on produces a different answer. Speaking to Ferdinand she says:

Nor have I seen
More than I may call men than you, good friend,
And my dear father. (3.1.50-52)

She's free to call Caliban a 'man' or not - and here, comparing him with her father and her lover, she'd rather not.

In the 'Great Chain of Being' hierarchy, which structured ideas about life-forms in Shakespeare's day, mankind was the link that came between God and the beasts. At the upper end of the chain, God, the angels and mankind share language, which suggests that Caliban belongs with mankind, looking upwards towards the divine rather than downwards towards the animal kingdom. Physical appearance is another factor. Beauty fittingly tallies with higher existential status. Mankind is beautiful – remember Miranda's

> O brave new world.
> That has such people in't (5.1.183-4) -

although less beautiful than the angels, being further down the Chain from God. Caliban, diabolical on the paternal side, is at least one link even further down. He looks so repulsive that it's very difficult to think of him as 'made in the image of God' at all.

There's another, even more important, test of humanity that he fails – his lack of a conscience. On this score, though, one can ask if he comes out any lower than Prospero's brother Antonio, who boasts:

> I feel not
> This deity *(i.e. conscience)* in my bosom. (2.1.278-279).

In Antonio's case it's only his virtue, not his very humanity, that's called into question. But the comparison suggests that Caliban may be able to claim that he's the victim of discrimination built into the Chain of Being model.

The benefits of civilisation, it was assumed, could be accessed only by beings who, whatever their faults and oddities, could be unequivocally classed as human. That was what civilisation was for – to express and enhance 'humanity'. Dogs, apes, horses, not to mention ants and fleas, need not apply. On this count Caliban seems to do quite well. He's not a dog or an ape and although there's something distinctly fishy about him he's certainly not **just** a fish. He has human language; he understands what he's told and his powers of speech range from bloodcurdling curses (2.2.1-3) to exquisite poetry. (3.3.125-143) He's picked up a rudimentary knowledge of astronomy and he hears music **as** music, which isn't what you'd expect to find – certainly not to any marked degree – in an animal.

His existence is 'biological' - which of course is true of human beings, too - but as with human beings that's not the whole story. Human beings have 'other bits' apart from the biological that define them as human. And so up to a point does Caliban, except that he doesn't have the full range. The verdict on Caliban's humanity or otherwise seems to end in a two-all draw. He scores two points **for**, for language and culture, and two points **against**, for hideousness and lack of conscience. But there are still confusing factors. One is that, in spite of his name (Caliban seems to suggest an anagram on 'cannibal') and however greedy and omnivorous he is, he's not actually a cannibal. And anyway who says that cannibals are not human? Another is that he remains anthropologically unclassifiable. We have difficulty recognising Caliban as 'like us' because we can't readily identify him in terms of race, nation, tribe or family. When the 'something-like-a-fish' under the gabardine morphs into 'something-like-a-man' Trinculo's first thought is that he must be 'an islander', an individual representative of a findable human group. We need to fit him in somewhere. He's got to be 'one of them', if not actually 'one of us'. So Trinculo just

invents relatives for him. 'They say there's but five upon this isle.' (3.2.5-6) Pull the other one, we say. Trinculo's using a statistical empty 'five', plucked out of thin air, to make it sound as if some research has been done.

Miranda ought to know better, but does she? She seems to 'multiply' Caliban (as he wanted to multiply himself by raping her!) into a full-scale tribe. She gives us a glimpse of other Calibans in the offing when she says to him:

> thy vile race
> ………………….had that in it which good natures
> Could not abide to be with. (1.2.359-361)

'Vile race' seems to transform Caliban from the freakish loner that we see on stage before us into a member, possibly even the representative, of a people who for some reason have not yet been sighted. Political antennae start twitching. The phrase 'vile race' has been seized on by those who want to use the play to set Miranda and her father up in the Great Dock of History as white colonialist oppressors. Steady on, though. The meaning of the word 'race' 400 years ago hardly supports that reading. The OED gives a range of meanings, including one - 'natural or inherited disposition' – which appears close to Miranda's use of the word here. It's a definition which tends to point to Caliban's progenitors, the devil and the witch, rather than suggest his membership of any larger ethno-political group. It steers us away from thinking of 'race' with its modern political connotations. If Shakespeare had wanted to add political interest of that kind by encouraging us think of Caliban as the representative of a 'race' he'd have given more signals. As it is, Caliban casts no such social shadow of that kind because there's scarcely any group that we can conceive of him as a member of. If Shakespeare had wanted us to think of the island as home to Caliban's brothers and sisters, uncles and aunts, cousins, ex-wives, nephews and nieces, etc, there was nothing to stop him writing them into the script. He didn't. He could have had Caliban bringing some of them along with him to a Prospero Out meeting with Sebastian and Trinculo and he could even have added a 'slaves uprising' episode to the play. He didn't. He could have written a terrific racist rant for Prospero about the fecklessness of 'the natives'. He didn't. He could have worded Caliban's drunken freedom song at the end of Act 2, Scene 2 a bit differently, to suggest that he had the plight of others at heart as well as his own. He didn't. And as for Caliban's offspring there's nothing there either, and not likely to be. When Caliban speaks of 'peopling this isle with Calibans' (1.2.351-352) he's already lamenting the childlessness that Prospero has condemned him to by forestalling his rape of Miranda. After all, she's the only woman on the island.

Ariel tends to know what he's talking about. He tells the 'three men of sin', that they have been 'belched up'

> … on this island
Where man does not inhabit. (3.3.53-58)

That's it then, surely. Except in the present quite exceptional circumstances 'man' does **not** inhabit this island, either in the singular or in the plural.

Question: So how did Caliban get there, then?

Answer: Caliban's not a man.

Got it!

Nevertheless, whatever Caliban is and however he got there this is now 'Prospero's island'. Actual possession and control is at least nine tenths of the law. But if you insist on your feeling that 'native rights' deserve political respect you might want to argue that point. After all, if Prospero is entitled to get his dukedom in Milan back because was wrongly ousted from it, you have to admit that Caliban (provided you regard him as fully human, which we've just been taught to doubt) is equally entitled to get 'his' island back. He had it first - until Prospero arrived out of the blue, took it over and enslaved him. Well, it's a good argument, which no doubt Caliban believes himself, but it's not conclusive. How can a monster and a slave have property rights? In the *dramatis personae* in the first Folio he's billed as 'a salvage and deformed slave', a thumbnail description which we have no reason to doubt that Shakespeare penned himself. Monsters and slaves can't even be trusted to choose whose slave they'd prefer to be – as Caliban tries to do when he signs up with Stephano and Trinculo. So Caliban's 'natural' claim to the island looks very far-fetched. Nevertheless, we'd be missing something important if we didn't recognise that he innately **belongs** to, even if he can't **own**, the island. He has a close ecological affinity, as animals as well as men do, to the landscape and everything that grows and lives on it. His 'salvageness' consists, in part, in his scavenging mode of life; he's always on the lookout for something to eat, whether disgusting or delicious to the human palate. Early on, rebuked by Prospero for neglecting his chores, he makes no bones about the fact that the voice of hunger speaks louder to him than the voice of duty. He snarls, 'I must eat my dinner'. (1.2.332) For him, that's Rule No 1 in life.

In Act 3, Scene 2, after Ariel's unnerved the revolutionary gang with his magical-musical 'take-over' of their song of premature triumph, it's Caliban - to our surprise perhaps - who takes it upon himself to reassure his colleagues. Picking up on the 'strange music' theme he tells Stephano and Trinculo to:

Be not afeard. The isle is full of noises,
Sounds and sweet airs that give delight and hurt not.
Sometimes a thousand twangling instruments
Will hum about my ears; and sometimes voices,
That if I then had waked after a long sleep,
Will make me sleep again: and then in dreaming,
The clouds, methought, would open and show riches
Ready to drop upon me, that when I waked
I cried to dream again. (3.2.135-143)

This isn't at all how Caliban usually speaks, but here he reveals his spiritual (no, that can't be the right word; what about 'quasi-spiritual'?) affinity with the island. It's more than just his 'natural habitat'. He's intimately in touch with this place of sleep-defended music, dreams and delights, even though Prospero, Miranda and the new arrivals have taken it over. We feel the poetic power of his speech, but we misconstrue it if we see it as evidence that after all we've seen and heard about him we now find that he possesses a 'human' soul with aesthetic and imaginative qualities. Yes, he certainly has an ear, which others lack, for the secret harmonies and rhythms of 'his' island, but his gift has a biological origin. He remains in tune with it and can still re-enter the innocence and promise of the dreams that weave and wander through his island, but this doesn't make good his other deficiencies. It's an entrancing speech but it does nothing to raise his existential status.

Fast forward now to the end of Act 5, Scene 1, line 254, where the topic is clothes and dressing up.

We find Prospero, a familiar-unfamiliar figure, standing outside his cave looking every inch the rightful Duke of Milan. He's swapped his magical robes for his official magisterial outfit and as the courtiers gradually regain their senses he sets about meting out justice, tempered with characteristically reluctant mercy. But that's not all the business in hand. He tells Alonso that

There are yet missing of your company
Some few odd lads that you remember not. (5.1.254-255)

Ah, here they come! Ariel drives them in – Stephano, Trinculo and Caliban. They're a sorry-looking crew, in tatters, exhausted and still hung over. Ariel has been leading them a not-very-merry dance 'up to their chins' through a 'filthy-mantled pool' stinking of horse-piss, (4.1.181-184) and then, for good measure, chasing them with a pack of hounds, Conquistador-style, across difficult country, as a punishment for trying to steal posh clothes that they thought would become their new rank when they'd seized power. They stand before a very formidable-looking Prospero.

Caliban has understandable misgivings.

I am afraid
He will chastise me. (5.1.262-263)

Stephano and Trinculo stare at the courtiers. They've been assuming that they'd all been drowned, and they aren't especially glad to find that they haven't been.

Prospero begins to pick up the dropped stitches in the fabric of the social hierarchy. He inspects the prisoners' stinking rags and finds the tell-tale 'badges', or liveries, which show whose service they're in.

Mark but the badges of these men, my lords,
Then say if they be true. (5.1.267-268)

The badges on the otherwise almost unrecognisably bedraggled Stephano and Trinculo tell him who their rightful master is – King Alonso. The odd lads' political aspirations suddenly appear to have been nothing but a silly bit of play-acting. Now the 'insubstantial pageant' is over and all the actors will soon be shedding their clobber, rags and finery alike, in the tiring-house. Prospero, fantasy-maker turned fantasy-shredder, is sending everyone back to his true social position. 'These two fellows' *(i.e. Stephano and Trinculo)*, Prospero tells King Alonso,

                              ...you
Must know and own; this thing of darkness *(i.e. Caliban)* I
Acknowledge mine. (5.1.274-276)

Caliban's well aware that treason's punishable by death and that the method of execution – pinching – is slow and inhumane. 'I shall be pinched to death,' (5.1.277) he quavers. But then he hears his master's voice again, not sentencing him but telling to get back to work.

                    Go, sirrah, to my cell;
Take with you your companions. As you look
To have my pardon, trim it handsomely. (5.1.292-294)

Do his ears deceive him? 'Have my pardon'?

It's a let-off!

A let-off, but not a let-out. Let's face it, Caliban reflects, Prospero's got me bang to rights. Freedom? No chance now. Getting my island back? Forget it. When I agreed to Stephano being my king instead of Prospero I abdicated my own claim. Prospero, curse him, has a point when he says that slavery's all I'm fit for. Kissing Sebastian's shoes – I ask you! Was that my highest ambition? Alright then, I'm pardoned, but Prospero's pardon feels like another punishment! Half an hour ago he and Ariel were hunting us down with hounds, and suddenly he's talking about pardon! I get the message: be a nice obedient little slavey from now on and he might – just **might** - ease up a bit on the torments, except that he's going to try to make me like it by talking about 'grace', 'repentance', 'forgiveness', 'reform', reconciliation', etc. as if he's doing me a favour. Thank you very much! how kind! – and in return I promise never to mention freedom again, which is all I really want. But beggars can't be choosers. If he offers pardon I must accept it.

> ...I'll be wise hereafter
> And seek for grace. What a thrice-double ass
> Was I to take this drunkard *(i.e. Stephano)* for a god
> And worship this dull fool! *(i.e. Trinculo)* (5.1.295-298)

So I must learn to be a liar and a hypocrite. So I'll learn then.

Well, that's one take on what's going on in Caliban's mind, although there are others. Is it possible, after all, that Prospero's gruff pardon has produced a response from Caliban that isn't altogether hypocritical? Prospero doesn't expect a reformation of character in his slave. He still insists that

He is disproportionate in his manners

As in his shape. (5.1.291-292)

Nevertheless, could 'wise hereafter' mean that he'll 'seek for grace' by annoying his master less? He's certainly wise enough to regret the consequences of the failure of his rebellion – his ongoing servitude – in the same breath as he acknowledges the folly of his seeking freedom in that way. In any case he needs to find a way of living more painlessly under his master's power. Can he learn to be wiser without trying to be morally better?

Prospero's response to Caliban's *mea culpa* – 'Go to, away' - (5.1.298) is worth thinking about, too. For example:

i) it may mean **'all's well'**. Everything's going Prospero's way. His troubles are over. He smiles and relaxes into brusque geniality, slaps 'this thing of darkness' on the back and pushes him playfully off stage in the direction of his cell;

ii) it may mean **'we'll see'**. Prospero hopes (but doubts) that Caliban's change of heart is sincere. 'All right then,' he's saying, 'but I'll still be keeping an eye on you';

iii) or it may mean **'nothing's changed'**. Prospero hears only hypocrisy and impudence in Caliban's words and he hustles him out of sight, containing his rage just well enough to invite his countrymen to join him in the hospitality of his cell.

If you ask me, I personally would let the decision swing in the wind for a moment. Prospero, say, could start with a bit of iii), then allow Caliban time, through body language, to express surprise, relief or whatever, until he switches to ii) or even i).

Prospero owns Caliban and can do anything he likes with him, but there's a further option we haven't mentioned yet. Provided it involves no danger or loss to others he can always just let him go. When he sails back to Italy he can just leave him behind on the island, all on his own-some, digging up pignuts with his dirty overgrown fingernails. Why not? This is how he found him and this is where he really belongs. He'll still be a slave, of course, but only to himself.

Finally let's consider how the play reaches its end.

Prospero's pleased with the progress of his master-plan and Ariel's in his good books again. 'My charms crack not, and my spirits obey.' (5.1.2) But it hasn't always been like this. We remember the clash with Ariel in Act 1, Scene 2, when it came home to him that his wonderful servant-spirit, just as much as Caliban, was dedicated to his own freedom, not to him. His anger masked a kind of lovelorn disappointment that all he could expect of Ariel was obedience under compulsion, not personal loyalty or affection. Ariel will give 'service' if he has to, but the first chance he gets he'll be off and away without so much as a backward glance.

In Act 1 it was Prospero who was looking at his watch all the time and wanting to press on with the business in hand. Now it's Ariel who's doing the time-checks. He reminds his master that 6.00 p.m. was the time by which everything was supposed to be done and dusted – hinting, so to speak, that he's now he's on (unpaid) overtime. It's

… the sixth hour, at which time, my lord,
You said our work should cease. (5.1.4-5)

Prospero doesn't flare up this time. He asks: 'How fares the King and his followers?' (5.1.7) Ariel replies that he's got them just where he wants them, 'confined together'. The 'three men of sin', Alonso, Sebastian and Antonio, are having full-blown mental breakdowns following his blood-and-thunder 'harpy' sermon, and the others are 'brimful of sorrow and dismay'. (5.1.14) 'Him that you termed, sir, good old Lord Gonzalo' (5.1.15) is sobbing his heart out.

Good, thinks Prospero. Resistance broken.

Prospero seems to be a bit more laid back than he was before. Chasing the rebels across country with a pack of dogs has helped to work off the hyper-tension that seized him as he broke up the masque, and since then we've had glimpses of the Mr Nice Guy that he really wants to be. He's called Ferdinand 'my son' (4.1.146) and apologised to him for giving him such a hard time. He's even admitted that he's inwardly 'vexed', and asked him to

Bear with my weakness; my old brain is troubled.
Be not disturbed with my infirmity. (4.1.158 -160)

To be fair, Prospero's fully entitled to be angry. He's been seriously wronged and naturally his project of redress is bound to run on the fuel of anger to some extent. But he's angry with himself, as well as with others. For example, he sees that it was silly of him to take his eye off the ball by putting on an elaborate masque in anticipation of his daughter's marriage to the heir to the throne of Naples while Caliban & Co were still running about on the island plotting against his life. First things first, for goodness sake! He also realises that now his project is coming to an end he'll have the opportunity to let go of all the punitive emotions that he's been pumped up on for years; and this in turn means renouncing all the supernatural powers that

369

he's had at his command. As the actors and the scenery of the masque vanish he says,

Our revels now are ended. These our actors,
As I foretold you, were all spirits and
Are melted into air, into thin air;
And – like the baseless fabric of this vision –
The cloud-capped towers, the gorgeous palaces,
The solemn temples, the great globe itself,
Yea, all which it inherit, shall dissolve,
And like this insubstantial pageant faded,
Leave not a rack behind. (4.1. 148 -156)

'Ended', 'melted', 'baseless', 'dissolve', 'faded' and 'leave'; they're all 'loss' words, and the idea of the 'great globe itself' disappearing gains a valedictory poignancy from our knowledge that in 1611 the playwright was about to bring his career on the South Bank to an end (although it now looks as if the play was actually staged at the Blackfriars, not the Globe). The on-stage Prospero and the off-stage Shakespeare unite in the common recognition that it's time for the illusion of power and the power of illusion to be renounced. Both are preparing themselves for a humbler, less exciting - and final - phase of life. This may bring other satisfactions and blessings but there'll still be an underlying sense of loss.

As Act 5 begins and 6.00 p.m. shows on his invisible watch – Ariel brings his prisoners before Prospero for trial, conviction and punishment. That's been the plan all along. But then Ariel makes a surprising suggestion. 'If you now beheld them,' he says to his master,

         …your affections'
Would become tender. (5.1.18-19)

'Tender? What's he talking about?' Prospero wonders. 'Ariel is no more capable of compassion than he is of malice. Does he really want me to go easy on these bounders, after all the time and trouble we've had to bring them to book? He can't be serious!'

'Dost thou think so, spirit?' (5.1.19) he asks, and finds that Ariel's prepared to push the 'tender' idea a bit further. 'Mine would, sir, were I human.' (5.1.20)

'And mine shall', Prospero replies. Ariel may not be human, as he is, but he understands, better than **he** does, what being human means.

Hast thou, which art but air, a touch, a feeling
Of their afflictions, and shall not myself
(One of their kind, that relish all as sharply,
Passion as they) be kindlier moved than thou art?
Though with their high wrongs I am struck to th' quick,
Yet with my nobler reason 'gainst my fury
Do I take part. The rarer action is
In virtue than in vengeance. They being penitent,
The sole drift of my purpose doth extend
Not a frown further. Go, release them, Ariel.
My charms I'll break; their senses I'll restore;
And they shall be themselves. (5.1.21-32)

Ariel's all about tricks and deceptions. He's morally empty, so where has this 'tenderness' idea sprung from? His formidable performance as a harpy in Act 3, Scene 3, when he calls upon the 'three men of sin' (3.3.53) to repent, was just that, of course, a **performance.** Its effectiveness depended on his having the right words to say, not on his actually meaning them, and the 'right words' were simply those that would scare the sinners out of their wits and make them fearful of retribution. He had to make them believe it, not to believe it himself. You can't expect sincerity to stick on a 'tricksy' spirit (see 5.1.226) like Ariel, a being of no moral substance, any more than you can expect virtue to stick on the conscience-free Caliban. But he can give a very convincing impression of 'just-like-us' humanity, ethical dimension and all. Dressed as a harpy and speaking as a 'minister of Fate' (3.3.61) he tells 'the three men of sin' that the evil deeds which they expected to get away with are remembered all too well by Fate and Destiny and that they are now at the point of getting it in the neck from the 'avenging powers'. But then he ties an unexpected 'unless' clause to the tail of his snakily uncoiling pronouncement of doom – a promise of reprieve if they repent and reform their lives.

Thee of thy son, Alonso,
They *(i.e. the avenging powers)* have bereft, and do pronounce by me
Ling'ring perdition, worse than any death
Can be at once, shall step by step attend
You and your ways, whose wraths to guard you from –
Which here, in this most desolate isle, else falls
Upon your heads – nothing but heart's sorrow
And a clear life ensuing. (3.3.75-82)

Serious stuff! But we must never forget that Ariel's 'only acting', and performing his master's script.

Sincerity's beside the point. This speech anticipates what Ariel's 'up to' as, later on, he nudges his master in the direction of forgiveness. He wants to exert moral pressure on his master as well as on the three men of sin. And he has good reason. Ariel may not 'care', but his lucidity is unclouded by anger – unlike Prospero's - and he understands from intelligent observation what the effects of 'tenderness' can be in human affairs. Yes, you may say, but why should a morally weightless and emotionally alien pagan spirit be bothered? Well, there's an answer to that. He's a free spirit held in captivity, pining moment-to-moment for his release, and now he's seen his chance. Prospero isn't going to let him go until all this silly business about treacherous courtiers and drunken rebels is sorted out. And 'tenderness' is the quickest and surest way to do it. The sooner he can get the old man down off his high horse and pardoning everybody in sight the sooner he'll be off the hook himself.

Ariel's 'as if' human empathy has let an important cat out of the bag. It has revealed why, in the end, the power of words, like the power of magic, can't in the end be trusted. As an existential interloper in the field of human discourse he doesn't 'mean what he says' in the ordinary sense; his words are no more than contrivances calculated to affect the listeners. Nevertheless, although his invitation to 'the three men of sin' to repent and reform is trickery, if they 'buy' it, their repentance and reform will be valid. Words not meant by the speaker aren't altogether 'weightless' after all. There's something odd – even spooky - about it, but that's how it is.

Ariel's 'insincerity' can be seen as a kind of key to the play itself. Spell-binding eloquence, impersonation, music and costume, etc, lend credibility to the 'baseless fabric of a dream'. Deceptive? Certainly. Salutary? Possibly, sometimes. Dramatic pretences and magical 'tricks' both have a delusive power that enthrals for a while but which ends, and needs to end, in disbelief. A play will never pass a truth test, at least if we insist on 'truth' being a more cut-and-dried affair than it can ever be in a play. Nevertheless, we can hold on to this idea, perhaps: that although the words come out of 'nothing' other than the play-wright's imagination, and are ownerless except in relation to the actors that say them, the audience, no less than the three men of sin, can be altered by them. Magic and drama share a dazzling 'dodginess' upon which Shakespeare himself as well as Prospero are getting ready to turn their backs. Here's the old (47!) playwright ventriloquising the retired magus in a renunciation of his amazing powers to raise visions, cast charms, bewilder us, control events and contrive happy endings. To underline his point – and it's an inspired touch - Shakespeare has Prospero tell the audience in the Epilogue that now only **they** can make everything work out well. It's a sort of handover of power and it makes a lot of sense. What the characters said and did on stage has come and gone; all that matters now is whether what they heard and saw has made them kinder people. If so, here's an opportunity to show it. If they really welcome the happy end let them muster a bit of Gonzalo-like faith and good will, put their hands together and cheer the restored Duke of Milan on his way home! As if we didn't already understand that the play was all about how mercy (usually) comes to sinners the final lines underline the point by adding Prospero, and implicitly Shakespeare, to the list of those who need to plead for 'indulgence'.

..........................Now I want
Spirits to enforce, art to enchant;
And my ending is despair
Unless I be relieved by prayer,
Which pierces so that it assaults
Mercy itself, and frees all faults.
As you from crimes would pardoned be,
Let your indulgence set me free. (Epilogue: 15-20)

Prospero feels a strong pang of regret, which we largely share, as he prepares to give up magic. Life will be less fun. It'll be sad to see the end of those highly entertaining showbiz spectaculars – shock-and-awe tempests, Ovidian transmorphisms, apparitions and invisibilities, echo-voices, entrancing music, etc, – that he, with more than a little help from his stage manager Ariel, has been entertaining us with. The show will soon be over, costumes doffed, and where will the great showman be then, poor thing? His farewell to all that has the poignancy of a farewell to the beauty of life itself.

Ye elves of hills, brooks, standing lakes and groves,
And ye that on the sands with printless foot
Do chase the ebbing Neptune, and do fly him
When he comes back; you demi-puppets that
By moonshine do the green sour ringlets make,
Whereof the ewe not bites; and you whose pastime
Is to make midnight mushrooms, that rejoice
To hear the solemn curfew, by whose aid –
Weak masters though you be – I have bedimmed
The noontide sun, called forth the mutinous winds,
And twixt the green sea and the azured vault
Set roaring war; to the dread-rattling thunder
Have I given fire and rifted Jove's stout oak
With his own bolt: the strong-based promontory
Have I made shake, and by the spurs plucked up
The pine and cedar….But this rough magic
I here abjure; and when I have required
Some heavenly music (which even now I do)
To work mine end upon their senses that
This airy charm is for, I'll break my staff,
Bury it certain fathoms in the earth,
And deeper than did ever plummet sound
I'll drown my book. (5.1.33-57)

Yes, it must all go - but not **quite** yet. Right up to the very end Prospero has a remaining trace of his old control-freak tetchiness, which we spot in his 'weak masters though you be' line. (5.1.40) You're 'wonderful creatures, spirits,' he's saying, 'and where would I be (correction: where **will** I be) without you? But likewise where will you be without me? Listen up one last time, Ariel. The play's not over yet. You're still under orders.'

The danger is that now we know that everything's going to turn out all right the play will become a shoo-in, devoid of spectacle, underlining spiritual values perhaps but lacking new spectacle and further psychological surprises. Worry not! The play still has a lot more up its sleeve. That trace of tetchiness alerts us again to Prospero's continuing inner turmoil as he hones in on the elusive goal of reconciliation. It's still far from plain sailing. He's destroyed the courtiers' resistance and he's bent on forgiving them but he still can't recall past wrongs without the old fury bubbling up inside him. Even in the middle of his 'release them' speech to Ariel he can't refrain from saying: 'With their high wrongs I'm struck to the quick,' (5.1.25) reminding us how deeply hurt he was by the treason in Milan and suggesting that the boil of his anger remains un-lanced. Even if, by the end of the play, he gets his enemies to accept his forgiveness will he also manage to subdue the part of himself that doesn't really want to forgive them?

He sets the usual condition. He will forgive them if they repent.

> They being penitent
> The sole drift of my purpose doth extend
> Not a frown further. (5.1.28-30)

But what will he do if, after all his exhortation and chastisement, they still refuse to repent? He just hopes it won't come to that.

Unfortunately, though, in the case of his own flesh and blood, brother Antonio, it does come to that.

Like Duke Vincenzio in 'Measure for Measure' Prospero has a tendency to equate suffering with contrition. He's prepared to make a lot of people suffer, in the belief that it'll 'break their spirit'. That's been the assumption behind his treatment of Caliban and he doesn't see why it shouldn't work with the offending courtiers, including his brother Antonio. It doesn't seem to cross his mind that punishment inflicted by an irascible magician isn't at all the same as voluntary admission of guilt. Prospero and Duke Vincenzio suppose (as ruling elites readily do) that if people won't repent off their own bat – and they often don't – they have ways to bring them to it. They have 'powers', don't they?

The courtiers stand 'spell-stopped' (5.1.61) in the circle of spiritual pain in front of Prospero's cave. The stage direction (usually taken as authorial) describes them as 'raving', i.e. not just a bit confused but stark staring bonkers. It's as if they've died and gone to Purgatory, the between-here-and-there place. Until the spell lifts – and it's just beginning to lift – they remain unable to speak or to take anything in. Gonzalo's the one exception. He too is very muddled and tearful but he's the only one who can be spoken to, even if he's not in much of a state to reply. Seeing him, Prospero addresses him as 'Holy Gonzalo'. (5.1.62)

Holy Gonzalo! He's already home and dry - as he was always going to be. But what about the others? Prospero, his own face streaked with sympathetic tears for this good old man, is nevertheless keeping his punitive reflexes in good working order as he turns on the others. To Sebastian and says:

Thou art pinched for't now, Sebastian. (5.1.74)

So he gets the Caliban treatment.

But then he turns to Antonio.

> Flesh and blood,
> You, brother mine, that entertained ambition,
> Expelled remorse and nature, whom with Sebastian
> (Whose inward pinches therefore are most strong)
> Would here have killed your king, I do forgive thee,
> Unnatural though thou art. (5.1.74-79)

Antonio is spared 'pinching', perhaps because he's a tougher nut to crack. The moment has come for Prospero to play his trump card. He drops the repentance condition and forgives him anyway. His 'I do forgive thee' is clear enough, but it comes after a painful, comma-stretching pause (after the word 'king' in 5.1.78) which Antonio, perhaps still semi-conscious, doesn't seem to register. His silence makes Prospero revert immediately to the note of wounded denunciation – 'unnatural though thou art'.

As a reconciliation scene this leaves much to be desired.

Like the other courtiers, Antonio's understanding is 'beginning to swell' (5.1.79-80) but

> Not one of them
> That yet looks on me or would know me. (5.1.82-83)

As we noted before, Shakespeare has his characters say things only to have them say them again, in a revised version, a little later. It's a sort of 'double take' technique that he uses when he's making an important point that he doesn't want us to miss. The first utterance primes our ears for the second. One example is Ariel's recommendation of repentance at the end of his speech to the three men of sin; it anticipates the recommendation of mercy that he gives his master a bit later. Another example is Prospero's eloquent announcement of his abdication from magic in Act Four, well in advance of his actually getting round to doing anything about it. Now here's another example. In his urgency to get his pardon off his chest Prospero can't wait for Antonio and the other courtiers to get their wits back before announcing it. Fifty-odd lines later he'll have to say it all over again. The obvious thing would be for Prospero's first speech to Antonio and Sebastian, when they can't take it in, to be an angry offer of forgiveness, which, as we've seen, is exactly what happens; but then have him make a second gentler offer of forgiveness, more in keeping with the play's concluding note of reconciliation, in the 'repeat' speech, when they're *compos mentis* again. But that might be a bit too obvious, even sentimental. Prospero's going to have to earn his dramatic keep right up to the end. Between the first forgiveness speech and the second he has a quick change into his Duke garb, pardons the readily repentant Alonso, is gentle with 'holy' Gonzalo and offers a genial official invitation to all and sundry to call on him in his cell. Only then does his voice dip into a 'private' aside to Sebastian and Antonio. He hisses:

But you, my brace of lords, were I so minded,
I here could pluck his highness' frown upon you
And justify you traitors! (5.1.126-128)

Here he pauses for effect. What do they have to say to that? Aren't they going to fall on their knees to beg for mercy? They don't, so he continues:

At this time

379

I will tell no tales. (5.1.128-129)

'At this time'? The brace of lords must be wondering what that's supposed to mean. Are they forgiven or is their treacherous plot, which Alonso knows nothing about, to be held over their heads on condition of good future behaviour?

Sebastian, perhaps still not recognising this as Prospero's characteristically abrasive version of absolution, replies with: 'The devil speaks in him.' (5.1.129) Prospero silences him with an abrupt 'No!' In other words, 'I'm not a devil, but I am still angry.'

Prospero can say this 'No!' a different way each night of the run if he so wishes, just as Sebastian's free to give his silent reaction to it in at least as many ways. Shakespeare leaves the moment wide open to interpretation.

Not having had much luck with Sebastian Prospero turns to Antonio.

For you, most wicked sir, whom to call brother
Would even infect my mouth, I do forgive
Thy rankest fault – all of them: and require
My dukedom of thee, which perforce I know
Thou must restore. (5.1.130-134)

He's administering justice, but he can't stem the rage that still wells up inside him. He **does** forgive, though, even if Antonio shows no sign of wanting to be forgiven. In fact, he's given only one more line to say in the play, a typically flippant one about Caliban, which gives no answer to the question we all have on our minds.

To sum up then.

The tempest looked set to claim many lives, but no-one has died.

The Master and the Boatswain are back on duty. Ariel has just whisked them out of the ship as they rub the sleep out of their eyes. They'll get everyone back to Italy in a sound ship.

Prospero's banishment has been reversed. He returns to Milan as the right and unchallenged Duke.

Young Miranda and Ferdinand, representing dynastic security and continuity, will succeed to power. Their kingdom in Naples will be hugely enlarged by the addition of Milan.

For the time being Alonso will continue as King of Naples, a sadder, wiser and better man.

Sebastian, resigned or not, will reoccupy his secondary status at the court in Naples.

'Holy' Gonzalo, that *rara avis,* a courtier devoid of ambition, rises to new heights of respect and esteem.

Stephano and Trinculo are re-assigned to their humble positions in life. Their revolutionary aspirations were only ever drunken delusions. Their day will never come.

Caliban can't be fitted so easily into the restored order of things, unless….but let's not go into all that again.

And Ariel is free.

But Antonio still preys on our minds. A high-born aristocrat, he can't match Caliban for natural wickedness although he's a highly qualified Machiavellian. For twelve years he's been filling Big Bruv's place in Milan, and he clearly knows his way around in the world of politics. A directorial 'others/brothers' concept could no doubt bring out other physical, vocal and sartorial similarities between the two brothers. But these would be stitched-on, rather than essential insights, which we don't need.

This 'wicked sir' is Prospero's hardest challenge. He rants at him roundly, right up to the end: 'infect my mouth', 'rankest fault', 'I require my dukedom of thee', etc, but Antonio's silence leaves us seriously wondering what his choice would be - if he had the choice - between Big Bruv's forgiveness and keeping his ill-gotten dukedom of Milan.

There are no guaranteed right answers to these questions.

Antonio can be 'lost in the crowd' as other business moves our attention on. Or he can stand there for the last ten minutes, glowering ominously and party-pooping the official mood of reconciliation. Or he can stay inscrutable until the last minute before finally signalling his acceptance of Prospero's clemency. Or Big Bruv can take the matter into his own hands, clasping him in a bear-hug that he has no chance of escaping physically or emotionally, and leading him off into the cell with his arm round his shoulders. You could object that this would be 'out of character' for both brothers, but there would be this to be said for it: that forgiveness and reconciliation **are** 'character-changers'.

Lightning Source UK Ltd.
Milton Keynes UK
UKOW03f0134200416

272605UK00005B/123/P